George Orwell

NINETEEN EIGHTY FOUR

George Orwell

NINETEEN EIGHTY FOUR

[Edited with Introduction, Author's Information, Complete Text, Summary and Analysis and Study Questions]

Misha Kandhari
M.A., M. Phil. English,
Delhi University

ANMOL PUBLICATIONS PVT. LTD.
NEW DELHI - 110 002 (INDIA)

ANMOL PUBLICATIONS PVT. LTD.
H.O.: 4374/4B, Ansari Road, Darya Ganj,
New Delhi-110 002 (India)
Ph.: 23278000, 23261597
B.O.: No. 1015, Ist Main Road, BSK IIIrd Stage
IIIrd Phase, IIIrd Block
Bangalore - 560 085 (India)
Visit us at: www.anmolpublications.com

Nineteen Eighty Four

First Published, 2009

PRINTED IN INDIA

Printed at Balaji Offset Press, Delhi.

Contents

	Preface	*ix*
1.	**Introduction**	**1**
2.	**Biography George Orwell**	**12**
3.	**Context of 1984**	**20**
4.	**Character List**	**23**
5.	**Plot Overview**	**32**
6.	**Short Summary**	**35**
7.	**Background**	**43**
8.	**Major Themes**	**95**
9.	**Complete Summary with Analysis**	**102**
10.	**Text**	**150**
11.	**Glossary of Terms**	**294**
12.	**Important Quesions**	**298**
	Q. Analyse the of Major Characters of the novel.	298
	Q. Discuss the major Themes, Motifs & Symbols in the novel.	300
	Q. Explain the given lines "Who controls the past controls the future. Who controls the present controls the past."	307
	Q. Explain the given lines "In the end the Party would announce that two and two made five, and you would have to believe it. It was inevitable that they should make that claim sooner or later: the logic of their position demanded it. Not merely	

the validity of experience, but the very existence of external reality was tacitly denied by their philosophy." 308

Q. Explain the given lines "And when memory failed and written records were falsified-when that happened, the claim of the Party to have improved the conditions of human life had got to be accepted, because there did not exist and never again could exist, any standard against which it could be tested."
Or

Q. Explain the given lines "And perhaps you might pretend, afterwards, that it was only a trick and that you just said it to make them stop and didn't really mean it. But that isn't true. At the time when it happens you do mean it. You think there's no other way of saving yourself and you're quite ready to save yourself that way. You want it to happen to the other person. You don't give a damn what they suffer. All you care about 0is yourself." 309

Q. 1984 is full of images and ideas that do not directly affect the plot, but nevertheless attain thematic importance. What are some of these symbols and motifs, and how does Orwell use them? 310

Q. Discuss the idea of doublethink. How important is doublethink to the Party's control of Oceania? How important is it to Winston's brainwashing? 311

Q. Describe Julia's character as it relates to Winston. How is she different from him? How is she similar to him? How does Julia's age make her attitude toward the Party very different from Winston's?

Or

Q. Discuss George Orwell 's 1984 as a novel where no personal freedom exists. 312

Q. Discuss Satire in 1984 319

Bibliography **321**

Preface

George Orwell is the pen name of Eric Arthur Blair: essayist, novelist, literary critic, advocate and fighter for political change, and man of contradictions. Blair was born on June 25, 1903, in the Bengal region of Eastern India, which was a British territory.

At the age of seventeen Orwell had his first experiences as an "amateur tramp" in Plymouth, where he was stranded accidentally without much money. A few of the popular works of George Orwell are DOWN AND OUT IN PARIS AND LONDON, 1933-Puilla paljailla Pariisissa ja Lontoossa, BURMESE DAYS, 1934, CLERGYMAN'S DAUGHTER, 1935, KEEP THE ASPIDISTRA FLYING, 1936 - Eläköön tuonenkielo!-film A Merry War (1997), dir. by Robert Bierman, starring Helena Bonham Carter, Richard E. Grant, Jim Carter, Harriet Walter, THE ROAD TO WIGAN PIER, 1937 - Tie Wiganin aallonmurtajalle etc.

Chapter 1

Introduction

George Orwell, who had "encapsulate the thesis at the heart of his novel" in 1944, wrote most of Nineteen Eighty-Four on the island of Jura, Scotland during 1947-1948 while critically ill with tuberculosis. He sent the final typescript to his friends, Secker and Warburg, on 4 December 1948, who published the book on 8 June 1949.

Nineteen Eighty-Four has been translated to sixty-two languages. The novel's title, its terms, and its language, and its author's surname are bywords for personal privacy lost to national state security. The adjective "Orwellian" denotes totalitarian action and organization; the phrase: Big Brother is Watching You connotes pervasive, invasive surveillance.

Although the novel has been banned or challenged in some countries, it is, along with Brave New World by Aldous Huxley, and Fahrenheit 451 by Ray Bradbury, among the most famous literary representations of dystopia. In 2005, Time magazine listed it among the hundred best English-language novels published since 1923.The dystopian novel We by Yevgeny Zamyatin is largely considered to have been a primary influence for Nineteen Eighty-Four.

Background

Nineteen Eighty-Four introduces Oceania, one of the world's three intercontinental totalitarian super-states. The story occurs in London, the "chief city of Airstrip One",itself a province of Oceania that "had been called England or Britain". Posters of "Big Brother", the Party leader, with the caption big brother is watching you, dominate the city landscapes; two-way television dominates the private and public spaces of the populace. Oceania's people are in three classes:

- The Inner Party,
- The Outer Party,
- The Proles.

This government, the Party, controls them via the Ministry of Truth, where Winston Smith, the protagonist, works; he is a member of the Outer Party. His job in Minitrue is the continual rewriting and altering of history so that the government is always right and correct: destroying evidence, amending newspaper articles, deleting the existence of people identified as unpersons.

The story begins on April 4, 1984: "It was a bright cold day in April, and the clocks were striking thirteen." The date is questionable, because it is what Winston Smith perceives. In the story's course, he concludes it as irrelevant, because the State can arbitrarily alter it; the year 1984 and its world are transmutable.

The novel does not render the world's full history to 1984. Indeed, since the novel's only description of world history is contained in a book within a book given to Winston by a Party member, it is possible that what we read is itself meant to be a deception, and the history of the world of 1984 is somewhat different. Winston's recollections, and what he reads in The Theory and Practice of Oligarchical Collectivism, by Emmanuel Goldstein, reveal that after the Second World War, the United Kingdom fell to civil war, becoming part of Oceania. Simultaneously, the Soviet Union encompassed mainland Europe, forming Eurasia; the third super state, Eastasia, comprises the east Asian countries around China and Japan.

There was an atomic war, fought mainly in Europe, western Russia, and North America. It is unclear what occurred first: the civil war wherein the Party assumed power or the United States' annexation of the British Empire or the war during which Colchester was bombed.

During the Second World War, George Orwell repeatedly said that British democracy, as it existed before 1939, would not survive the war; the question being: Would it end via

Fascist coup d'état or via Socialist revolution ? During the war, Orwell admitted events proved him wrong: "What really matters is that I fell into the trap of assuming that 'the war and the revolution are inseparable' ".

Story

Ministry of Truth bureaucrat Winston Smith is the protagonist; although unitary, the story is three-fold. The first describes the world of 1984 as he perceives it; the second is his illicit romance with Julia and his intellectual rebellion from The Party; the third is his capture and imprisonment, interrogation, torture, and re-education in the Ministry of Love.

Oceania is a totalitarian state of omnipresent, two-way television surveillance; informants are everywhere; and Winston's romance with Julia is betrayed as a political transgression. Their imprisonment at the Ministry of Love (the most feared of the four ministries) features torture, brainwashing, and re-education in Room 101 (via the prisoner's worst fear). Those degradations re-educate them to love only Big Brother and The Party.

Afterwards, disgusted by his love affair with Julia, Winston Smith surrenders his mind, body, and soul to Big Brother; like-wise Julia. On release, each admits having betrayed the other to survive, something they had vowed not to do; each is apathetic toward the other's betrayal.

The thematic likenesses between Nineteen Eighty-Four and Animal Farm are: the betrayed revolution; the person's subordination to the Party collective; the rigorously enforced class distinctions among Party members, i.e. the Inner Party, the Outer Party, the Proletariat; the Cult of Personality; concentration camps; Thought Police; compulsory, regimented, daily exercise; the youth leagues.

As in the Nazi and Stalinist regimes, propaganda is pervasive; Smith's job is rewriting historical documents to match the contemporaneous party line, the orthodoxy of which changes daily. He re-writes and re-prints newspaper articles (society's official records) to delete from the collective memory all people rendered unpersons by Party order.

Plot

A pyramid diagram of Oceania's social classes; Big Brother atop, The Party in middle, the Proles at bottom.

The intellectual Winston Smith is a member of the Outer Party, lives in the ruins of London (the "chief city of Airstrip One", a province of Oceania), who grew up in the post-World War II United Kingdom, during the revolution and the civil war. As his parents disappeared in the civil war, the English Socialism Movement ("Ingsoc" in Newspeak), put him in an orphanage for training and employment in the Outer Party.

His squalid existence consists of living in a one-room apartment, eating a subsistence diet of black bread and synthetic meals washed down with Victory-brand gin. He is discontented, and keeps an illegal journal of dissenting, negative thoughts and opinions about The Party. If detected, it, and his eccentric behaviour, would result in torture and death by the Thought Police.

In his journal he explains thoughtcrime: Thoughtcrime does not entail death. Thoughtcrime IS death. The Thought Police have two-way telescreens (in the living quarters of every Party member and in every public area), hidden microphones, and anonymous informers to spy potential thought-criminals who might endanger The Party. Children are indoctrinated to informing; to spy and report suspected thought-criminals-especially their parents.

Winston Smith is a bureaucrat in the Records Department of the Ministry of Truth, revising historical records to match The Party's contemporaneous, official version of the past. The revisionism is required so that the past reflect the shifts of the day in the Party's orthodoxy. Smith's job is perpetual; he re-writes the official record, re-touches official photographs, deleting people officially rendered as unpersons. The original or older document is dropped into a "memory hole" chute leading to an incinerator.

Although he likes his work, especially the intellectual challenge of revising a complete historical record, he also is fascinated by the true past, and eagerly tries to learn more about that forbidden truth. One day, in the office, a woman surreptitiously hands him a note. She is "Julia", a dark-haired mechanic who repairs the Ministry of Truth's novel-writing machines. Before that day, he had felt deep loathing for her, based on his assumptions that she was a brainwashed, fanatically devoted member of the Party; particularly annoying to him is her red sash of renouncement of and scorn for sexual intercourse. His preconceptions vanish on reading her hand-printed note: "I love you".

After that, they begin a clandestine romantic relationship, first meeting in the countryside and at a ruined belfry, then regularly in a rented room atop an antiques shop in the city's proletarian neighbourhood. The shop owner chats him up with facts about the pre-revolutionary past, sells him period artifacts, and rents him the room to meet Julia. The lovers believe their hiding place paradisiacal (the shop keeper having told them it has no telescreen) and think themselves alone and safe. As their romance deepens, Winston's views change, and questions Ingsoc. Unknown to him, the Thought Police have been spying on him and Julia. Later, when approached by Inner Party member O'Brien, Winston believes that he's come into contact with The Brotherhood, opponents of the Party. O'Brien gives him a copy of "the book", The Theory and Practice of Oligarchical Collectivism, a searing criticism of Ingsoc said to be written by the dissident Emmanuel Goldstein, the leader of the Brotherhood; it explains the perpetual war and exposes the truth behind the Party's slogan, "War is Peace; Freedom is Slavery; Ignorance is Strength."

The Thought Police capture Winston and Julia in their sanctuary bedroom and they are separately interrogated at the Ministry of Love, where the regime's opponents are tortured and killed, but sometimes released (to be executed at a later date); Charrington, the shop keeper who rented them the room reveals himself an officer of the Thought Police. In the Ministry of Love torture chamber, O'Brien tells Smith that he will be cured of his hatred for the Party. During a session, he explains to Winston that torture's purpose is to alter his way of thinking, not to extract a fake confession, adding that once cured-accepting reality as the Party describes-he then will be executed; electroshock torture will achieve that, continuing until O'Brien decides Winston is cured. One night, a dreaming Winston suddenly wakes, yelling: "Julia! Julia! Julia, my love! Julia!" O'Brien rushes in and questions him, and then sends him to Room 101, the most feared room in the Ministry of Love. This is where a person's greatest fear is forced upon him or her for the final re-education step: acceptance. Winston, who has a primal fear of rats, is shown a wire cage filled with starving rats and told that it will be fitted over his head like a mask, so that when the cage door is opened, the rats will bore into his face until it is stripped to the bone. Just as the cage brushes his cheek, he shouts frantically: "Do it to Julia!" The torture ends, Winston is returned to society, brainwashed to accept Party doctrine.

After his release, Winston and Julia fortuitously meet in a park. With distaste, they remember the "bad" feelings they once shared; they acknowledge having betrayed each other; they are apathetic. Torture and re-education were successful; Winston happily reconciled to his impending execution, and accepting the Party line about the past and the present. In his mind, he celebrates the false fact of a news bulletin reporting Oceania's recent, decisive victory over Eurasia. Winston imagines himself back at the Ministry of Love. He imagines the scene he created during his imprisonment of walking down the white hallway and being shot by the guard. He finally accepts that he loves Big Brother.

Origin of Title

The novel's original title was The Last Man in Europe, but publisher Frederic Warburg suggested changing it to a marketable title. Orwell's reasons for the title are unknown; he might be alluding to the centenary of the socialist Fabian Society founded in 1884, or to Jack London's novel The Iron Heel (wherein a political movement's acme in power is 1984), or to G. K. Chesterton's The Napoleon of Notting Hill, set in 1984, or to the poem "End of the Century, 1984", by Eileen O'Shaughnessy. According to the introduction of the Penguin Modern Classics edition, Orwell originally meant 1980 as the

George Orwell

NINETEEN EIGHTY FOUR

story's time, but as the writing became prolonged, he re-titled it 1982, then 1984. The full title of the first edition was Nineteen Eighty-Four. A novel. He also might have titled the book 1984 because he began writing it in 1948, so he switched that year's digits 4 and 8.

Orwell's Influences

In the essay Why I Write, Orwell explains that all the serious work he wrote since the Spanish Civil War in 1936 was "written, directly or indirectly, against totalitarianism and for democratic socialism."Therefore, Nineteen Eighty-Four is an anti-totalitarian cautionary tale about the betrayal of a revolution by its defenders. He already had stated distrust of totalitarianism and betrayed revolutions in Homage to Catalonia and Animal Farm. Coming Up For Air, at points, celebrates the personal and political freedoms lost in Nineteen Eighty-Four.

Much of Oceanic society is based upon Stalin's Soviet Union. The "Two Minutes' Hate" was the ritual demonisation of State enemies and rivals; Big Brother resembles Joseph Stalin; the Party's archenemy, Emmanuel Goldstein, resembles Leon Trotsky (both are Jewish, both have the same physiognomy, and Trotsky's real surname was 'Bronstein'). Another suggested inspiration for Goldstein is Emma Goldman, the famous Anarchist figure. Doctored photography is a propaganda technique and the creation of unpersons in the story, analogous to Stalin's enemies being made nonpersons and being erased from official photographic records; the police treatment of several characters recalls the Moscow Trials of the Great Purge.

Biographer Michael Shelden notes these influences: the Edwardian world of his childhood in Henley-for the golden country; being bullied at St. Cyprian's-empathy with victims; his policeman's life in the Indian Burma Police-the techniques of violence; and suffering censorship in the BBC-capriciously-wielded authority.

Specific literary influences include Darkness at Noon and The Yogi and the Commissar by Arthur Koestler, The Iron Heel

(1908) by Jack London; Brave New World (1932) by Aldous Huxley; We (1921) by Yevgeny Zamyatin, which Orwell read in French and reviewed in 1946; and The Managerial Revolution (1940) by James Burnham, predicting permanent war among three totalitarian superstates, broadly equivalent to those in Nineteen Eighty-Four. Orwell told Jacintha Buddicom that he would write a novel stylistically like A Modern Utopia by H. G. Wells.

World War II acts as the grounding for Orwell's more fantastic elements. Most of the novel contains direct parallels, and occasional outright pastiche, of the rhetoric and politics surrounding the end of the war and the changing alliances of the nascent Cold War. The overseas service of the BBC, controlled by the Ministry of Information, was the model for the Ministry of Truth. The Ministry of Love's ultimate weapon against dissidents, Room 101, is named after a conference room at BBC Broadcasting House where Orwell used to sit through tedious meetings. The Senate House, where the Ministry of Information was housed, is the architectural inspiration for the Ministry of Truth. Nineteen Eighty-Four's world reflects the socio-political life of the UK and the USA, i.e. the poverty of Britain in 1948, when the economy was poor, the Empire dissolving, while newspapers reported imperial triumphs, and wartime ally Soviet Russia was becoming a peacetime foe.

Oceania is a metamorphosed future British Empire that geographically includes the United States, and whose currency is the dollar. As its name suggests, it is a naval power, with much militarism focused on venerating sailors serving aboard floating fortresses greater than Dreadnoughts. Moreover, most of the fighting by Oceania's troops is in defending India (the "Jewel in the Crown" of the British Empire).

The term "English Socialism" also has many precedents in Orwell's wartime writings. In The Lion and the Unicorn of 1940, Orwell stated that "the war and the revolution are inseparable the fact that we are at war has turned Socialism from a textbook word into a realizable policy". The reason for that, according to Orwell, was that the outmoded British class system constituted a major hindrance to the war effort, and only a Socialist society would be able to defeat Hitler. Since the middle classes were in process of realizing this, too, they would support the revolution, and only the most outright reactionary elements in British society would oppose it-which would limit the amount of force the revolutionaries would need in order to gain power and keep it.

Thus, an "English Socialism" would come about which "...will never lose touch with the tradition of compromise and the belief in a law that is above the State. It will shoot traitors, but it will give them a solemn trial beforehand and occasionally it will acquit them. It will crush any open revolt promptly and cruelly, but it will interfere very little with the spoken and written word".

Orwell's words in this and other writings at the time leave no doubt that in 1940 he regarded "English Socialism" as highly desirable and was actively trying to bring about its victory. Yet in the nightmare world he envisioned eight years later, the same term-contracted to "Ingsoc"-is the monstrous ideology of a totally oppressive regime, far from the relative moderate revolution which Orwell foresaw in 1940. When the vision of "The Lion and the Unicorn" is compared with that of "Nineteen Eighty-Four" it is evident that Orwell saw the regime presided over by Big Brother not only as a betrayal and perversion of Socialist ideals in general, but also as a perversion of Orwell's own specifically and dearly cherished vision and hope of Socialism-"English Socialism".

Major Characters

Winston Smith-The novel's protagonist

Julia-Winston's lover

Big Brother-The dictator of Oceania in the year 1984; he is based upon Joseph Stalin.

O'Brien-A government agent who deceives Winston and Julia into believing that he is a member of the resistance, convinces them to "join," and later uses it against them to incarcerate and torture them.

Emmanuel Goldstein-A former top member and now opposer of the ruling Party; he is based upon Leon Trotsky, a dissident member of the Soviet Communist Party who was forced to flee the Soviet Union to save himself from Stalin's persecutions.

Minor Characters

Aaronson-Old party leader

Ampleforth-Winston's colleague

Mr. Charrington-Ostensibly the owner of a junk store in the prole district; actually a member of the dreaded Thought Police.

Jones-Old party leader

Katharine-Winston's wife. It is unknown whether or not she is alive at the time of the novel because of the fact that she and Winston separated several years earlier.

Martin-O'Brien's servant

Parsons-Winston's naive neighbour

Rutherford-Old party leader

Syme-Winston's intelligent coworker; works with the language Newspeak, and is later vaporized (Made so as to seem he never existed). Syme's disappearance is an allusion to the Stalin Purges.

Ministries of Oceania

Oceania's four ministries are housed in huge pyramidal structures, each roughly 930 feet high and visible throughout London, displaying the three slogans of the party on their façades.

Ministry of Peace

Conducts Oceania's perpetual war.

Ministry of Plenty

Responsible for rationing and controlling food and goods, along with all production of all domestic goods. The Ministry of Plenty declares false claims to have increased the standard of living every time by a considerable amount, where in actual fact the ministry counteracts its own claims.

Ministry of Truth: The propaganda arm of Oceania's regime, controlling information: news, entertainment, education, and the fine arts. Winston Smith works for the

Records Department of Minitrue, "rectifying" historical records and newspaper articles to make them conform to Big Brother's most recent pronouncements, thus making everything that the Party says true.

Ministry of Love: The agency is responsible for the identification, monitoring, arrest and torture of dissidents, real or imagined. Based on Winston's experience there at the hands of O'Brien, the basic procedure is to pair the subject with his or her worst fear for an extended period, eventually breaking down the person's mental faculties and ending with a sincere embrace of the Party by the brainwashed subject. The Ministry of Love differs from the other ministry buildings in that it has no windows in it at all.

The ministries' names are an example of doublethink-"The Ministry of Peace concerns itself with war, the Ministry of Truth with lies, the Ministry of Love with torture and the Ministry of Plenty with starvation." (Part II, Chapter IX-chapter I of Goldstein's book)

Double Think

This word has two mutually contradictory meanings. Applied to an opponent, it means the habit of impudently claiming that black is white, in contradiction of the plain facts. Applied to a Party member, it means a loyal willingness to say that black is white when Party discipline demands this. But it means also the ability to believe that black is white, and more, to know that black is white, and to forget that one has ever believed the contrary. This demands a continuous alteration of the past, made possible by the system of thought which really embraces all the rest, and which is known as doublethink. Doublethink is basically the power of holding two contradictory beliefs in one's mind simultaneously, and accepting both of them.

Chapter 2

Biography George Orwell

George Orwell is the pen name of Eric Arthur Blair: essayist, novelist, literary critic, advocate and fighter for political change, and man of contradictions. Blair was born on June 25, 1903, in the Bengal region of Eastern India, which was a British territory. He was the son of Richard Walmesley Blair, a civil servant, and Ida Mabel Blair. Their only son was the middle child. He moved to England with his mother and sisters at the age of one. He displayed academic talent from a young age, so his mother took pains to ensure his attendance at a well-known boarding school called St. Cyprian's. His family was neither poor nor wealthy, and Blair attended St. Cyprian's on a scholarship.

Blair excelled academically there but faced many hardships in its puritanical, cutthroat environment. In the autobiographical essay "Such, Such Were the Joys," Blair/ Orwell describes the social challenges he endured as a scholarship student among England's wealthy elite. (These challenges would inform his satires of social stratification in his literary works, including Animal Farm.) In the essay, he describes his child self with much sympathy and feeling for the child's perspective. Such experiments in empathy prepared him to create Animal Farm's brilliantly naive narrator.

Blair's academic prowess continued in secondary school at Eton, a renowned secondary school (more recently famous for Prince William's attendance there). Blair graduated from Eton in 1921. Despite his intelligence, he could not afford to attend college. In 1922, he joined the Indian Imperial Police in Burma. He had spent the first year of his life in a British colony, and this time, he got a thorough experience of British colonial life and despised what he saw. His experiences made him a champion of the poor and downtrodden, a role in which he would continue for the rest of his life. Moreover, he could not stand the fact that his job put him directly in the position of privileged oppressor. He resigned from the Indian Imperial Police five years later while on leave in England.

Blair/Orwell thus became devoted to the problems of class and government power long before he wrote Animal Farm. As Louis Menand writes, "He turned his life into an experiment in classlessness, and the intensity of his commitment to that experiment was the main reason that his friends and colleagues found him a perverse and sometimes exasperating man." To complete his rejection of elitism, Blair lived after the fashion of the poorest Englanders. This included refusing to wear warm clothing in winter or to display table manners. It is questionable whether his destitute lifestyle contributed to his frequent illnesses, but such choices indubitably influenced his written works. Blair tried his luck in Paris briefly but found he could not make a living there as a writer. He returned to England in 1929, where he published essays and continued his fascination with and incorporation into the dregs of society. He began to slip into poverty in earnest, so he took a job as a teacher at Frays College. He also secured himself a literary agent. Blair/ Orwell published Down and Out in Paris in 1932. Before the book's publication, Blair assumed the pen name by which he would become famous. Accounts of why the writer chose the pen name "George Orwell" vary. Some say the name is deeply symbolic while others state that it was merely one of a list of names from which he allowed his publishers to choose.

From 1934 on, Orwell thrust himself fully into the writer's arena. He quit his teaching job and moved to Hempstead, an epicenter for young writers at the time, where he worked in a used-book store. He published his first fictional work, Burmese Days, in 1934, and followed with A Clergyman's Daughter in 1935. Orwell's presence in Hempstead and his interest in the lower class did not go unnoticed. In 1936, the Left Book Club commissioned him to write an account of the destitute state of Northern England. Orwell threw himself into the project, conducting firsthand research in his quest for authenticity. In his travels, he met and married Eileen O'Shaughnessy. The controversial account was published in 1936 under the name The Road to Wigan Pier. He published Aspidistra Flying in the same year. Around the time The Road to Wigan Pier was published, Orwell took his offensive against elitism and tyranny a step further, volunteering to fight in the Spanish Civil War on the side of the Republicans.

He joined POUM, a Trotskyist socialist party that emphasized the need for a working-class uprising and opposed the Spanish Communist Party's belief in collaborating with the middle class (Orwell was a revolutionary socialist). Orwell's experiences in the war, including being shot almost fatally, cemented his hatred of totalitarianism in its many guises. This included Stalinism, against which he held a lifetime grudge. Ironically, Orwell's neck injury very nearly-and literally-robbed the outspoken writer of his voice. However, he did recover, and while doing so Orwell completed a novel, Coming Up for Air. Orwell described his social observations of Spain in Homage to Catalonia.

In 1940, Orwell and his wife moved to central London, where he worked as a reviewer. When World War II began, he rose to fight for the cause of freedom again, this time for England. He joined the Home Guard and worked for the BBC to compose and disseminate wartime propaganda. Orwell knew of what he spoke when he skewered propaganda in Animal Farm and 1984. Orwell based his satires not just on hearsay and research but also on personal experience; writing propaganda is said to have made him feel corrupt.

He was also a war correspondent. During wartime, Orwell and his wife adopted a son, but his wife died shortly afterwards. Also during this time, Orwell completed Animal Farm, which was published in England in 1945. It was at this point, just when Orwell's personal life was in shambles, that his legend took flight. The book met with immediate and far-reaching public success, especially since it was so topical. Orwell continued to write for periodicals while completing his second renowned novel, 1984. He remarried, in 1949, to Sonia Brownell. Orwell, who was prone to illness, had his career and his life cut short when he died of tuberculosis on January 21, 1950. His friend, David Astor, arranged for Orwell's burial in a small county churchyard. Orwell is buried under his birth name. He left a strong literary and political legacy, being one of those artists who influenced not only the literary universe, but also the real world in which he lived. As he wrote in "Politics and the English Language": "In our age there is no such thing as 'keeping out of politics.' All issues are political issues, and politics itself is a mass of lies, evasions, folly, hatred and schizophrenia." This statement also illustrates the pessimism for which Orwell was known. Like some other disillusioned people of his generation, Orwell believed that totalitarian governments would inevitably take over the West.

Life of George Orwell

Eric Blair was born in 1903 in Motihari, Bengal, in the then British colony of India, where his father, Richard, worked for the Opium Department of the Civil Service. His mother, Ida, brought him to England at the age of one. He did not see his father again until 1907, when Richard visited England for three months before leaving again until 1912. Eric had an older sister named Marjorie and a younger sister named Avril. With his characteristic humour, he would later describe his family's background as "lower-upper-middle class."

Education

At the age of five, Blair was sent to a small Anglican parish school in Henley, which his sister had attended before him. He never wrote of his recollections of it, but he must have impressed the teachers very favourably for two years later he was recommended to the headmaster of one of the most successful preparatory schools in England at the time: St Cyprian's School, in Eastbourne, Sussex. Young Eric attended St Cyprian's on a scholarship that allowed his parents to pay only half of the usual fees. Many years later, he would recall his time at St Cyprian's with biting resentment in the essay "Such, Such

Were the Joys," but he did well enough to earn scholarships to both Wellington and Eton colleges. After a term at Wellington, Eric moved to Eton, where he was a King's Scholar from 1917 to 1921. Later in life he wrote that he had been "relatively happy" at Eton, which allowed its students considerable independence, but also that he ceased doing serious work after arriving there. Reports of his academic performance at Eton vary: some claim he was a poor student, others deny this. It is clear that he was disliked by some of his teachers, who resented what they perceived as disrespect for their authority. In any event, during his time at the school Eric made lifetime friendships with a number of future British intellectuals.

Burma and Afterwards

After finishing his studies at Eton, having no prospect of gaining a university scholarship and his family's means being insufficient to pay his tuition, Eric joined the Indian Imperial Police in Burma. He resigned and returned to England in 1928 having grown to hate imperialism (as shown by his first novel Burmese Days, published in 1934, and by such essays as 'A Hanging', and 'Shooting an Elephant'). He adopted his pen name in 1933, while writing for the New Adelphi. He chose a pen name that stressed his deep, lifelong affection for the English tradition and countryside: George is the patron saint of England (and George V was monarch at the time), while the River Orwell in Suffolk was one of his most beloved English sites.

Orwell lived for several years in poverty, sometimes homeless, sometimes doing itinerant work, as he recalled in the book Down and Out in Paris and London. He eventually found work as a schoolteacher until ill health forced him to give this up to work part-time as an assistant in a secondhand bookshop in Hampstead, an experience later recounted in the short novel Keep the Aspidistra Flying.

Spanish Civil War

Soon after the outbreak of the Spanish Civil War, Orwell volunteered to fight for the Republicans against Franco's

Nationalist uprising. As a sympathiser of the Independent Labour Party (of which he became a member in 1938), he joined the militia of its sister party in Spain, the non-Stalinist far-left POUM (Workers' Party of Marxist Unification), in which he fought as an infantryman. In Homage to Catalonia he described his admiration for the apparent absence of a class structure in the revolutionary areas of Spain he visited. He also depicted what he saw as the betrayal of that workers' revolution in Spain by the Spanish Communist Party, abetted by the Soviet Union and its secret police, after its militia attacked the anarchists and the POUM in Barcelona in May 1937. Orwell was shot in the neck on May 20, 1937, an experience he described in his short essay "Wounded by a Fascist Sniper", as well as in Homage to Catalonia. He and his wife Eileen left Spain after narrowly missing being arrested as "Trotskyites" when the communists moved to suppress the POUM in June 1937.

World War and After

Orwell began supporting himself by writing book reviews for the New English Weekly until 1940. During World War II he was a member of the Home Guard and in 1941 began work for the BBC Eastern Service, mostly working on programmes to gain Indian and East Asian support for Britain's war efforts. He was well aware that he was shaping propaganda, and wrote that he felt like "an orange that's been trodden on by a very dirty boot." Despite the good pay, he resigned in 1943 to become literary editor of Tribune, the left-wing weekly then edited by Aneurin Bevan and Jon Kimche. Orwell contributed a regular column entitled 'As I Please.'

In 1944 Orwell finished his anti-Stalinist allegory Animal Farm, which was published the following year with great critical and popular success. The royalties from Animal Farm provided Orwell with a comfortable income for the first time in his adult life. From 1945 Orwell was the Observer's war correspondent and later contributed regularly to the Manchester Evening News. He was a close friend of the Observer's editor/owner, David Astor and his ideas had a strong influence on Astor's editorial policies. In 1949 his best-known work, the dystopian Nineteen Eighty-Four, was published. He wrote the novel during his stay on the island of Jura, off the coast of Scotland.

Between 1936 and 1945 Orwell was married to Eileen O'Shaughnessy, with whom he adopted a son, Richard Horatio Blair. She died in 1945 during an operation. In the autumn of 1949, shortly before his death, he married Sonia Brownell.

In 1949 Orwell was approached by a friend, Celia Kirwan, who had just started working for a Foreign Office unit, the Information Research Department, which had been set up by the Labour government to publish pro-democratic and anti-communist propaganda. He gave her a list of 37 writers and artists he considered to be unsuitable as IRD authors because of their pro-communist leanings. The list, not published until 2003, consists mainly of journalists (among them the editor of the New Statesman, Kingsley Martin) but also includes the actors Michael Redgrave and Charlie Chaplin. Orwell's motives for handing over the list are unclear, but the most likely explanantion is the simplest: that he was helping out a friend in a cause-anti-Stalinism-that both supported. There is no indication that Orwell ever abandoned the democratic socialism that he consistently promoted in his later writings-or that he believed the writers he named should be suppressed. Orwell's list was also accurate: the people on it had all at one time or another made pro-Soviet or pro-communist public pronouncements.

Orwell died at the age of 46 from tuberculosis which he had probably contracted during the period described in Down and Out in Paris and London. He was in and out of hospitals for the last three years of his life. Having requested burial in accordance with the Anglican rite, he was interred in All Saints' Churchyard, Sutton Courtenay, Oxfordshire with the simple epitaph: Here lies Eric Arthur Blair, born June 25th 1903, died January 21st 1950.

Orwell's Work

During most of his career Orwell was best known for his

journalism, both in the British press and in books of reportage such as Homage to Catalonia (describing his experiences during the Spanish Civil War), Down and Out in Paris and London (describing a period of poverty in these cities), and The Road to Wigan Pier (which described the living conditions of poor miners in northern England).

According to Newsweek, Orwell "was the finest journalist of his day and the foremost architect of the English essay since Hazlitt." Contemporary readers are more often introduced to Orwell as a novelist, particularly through his enormously successful titles Animal Farm and Nineteen Eighty-Four. The former is considered an allegory of the corruption of the socialist ideals of the Russian Revolution by Stalinism, and the latter is Orwell's prophetic vision of the results of totalitarianism. Orwell denied that Animal Farm was a reference to Stalinism. Orwell had returned from Catalonia a staunch anti-Stalinist and anti-Communist, but he remained to the end a man of the left and, in his own words, a 'democratic socialist'.

Orwell is also known for his insights about the political implications of the use of language. In the essay "Politics and the English Language", he decries the effects of cliche, bureaucratic euphemism, and academic jargon on literary styles, and ultimately on thought itself. Orwell's concern over the power of language to shape reality is also reflected in his invention of Newspeak, the official language of the imaginary country of Oceania in his novel Nineteen Eighty-Four. Newspeak is a variant of English in which vocabulary is strictly limited by government fiat.

The goal is to make it increasingly difficult to express ideas that contradict the official line-with the final aim of making it impossible even to conceive such ideas. (cf. Sapir-Whorf Hypothesis). A number of words and phrases that Orwell coined in Nineteen Eighty-Four have entered the standard vocabularly, such as "memory hole," "Big Brother," "Room 101," "doublethink," "thought police," and "newspeak."

Chapter 3

Context of 1984

About 1984

In 1984, George Orwell presents his vision of dystopia, a world consisting of three massive totalitarian states constantly at war with each other and using technological advancements to keep their respective Party members and masses under careful observation and control. Written in 1948 and published in 1949, this novel is often touted as one of the greatest novels written in the English language. In writing the work, Orwell was influenced and inspired by totalitarian regimes of the time, including Hitler's Nazi Germany and Stalin's Soviet Union. Both regimes glorified their respective leaders as demi-gods and saviors, required the destruction of all individuality in order to promote the Party's needs over the individual's, demanded absolute loyalty from their citizens, and resorted to violence whenever disloyalty was suspected. Moreover, both regimes consistently demonized their enemies, just as the Party and Big Brother do in 1984, through the Two Minutes Hate, Hate Week, and daily mass propaganda. Other parallels include the Thought Police as a reinvention of the Gestapo, NKVD (People's Comissariat for Internal Affairs), which orchestrated large scale purges and terror, and the Spies and Youth League as a reinvention of the Hitler Youth and the Little Octoberists, which indoctrinated young people to the Party and encouraged them to report disloyalty observed in their elders, even among family members.

The similarities between 1984's Oceania and Stalin's regime are particularly striking. Like Stalin, the Oceanian government embraces characteristics of both fascist and communist authoritarianism: the former glorifies the wisdom of the leader, and the latter, the infallibility of the Party. We can see both trends in 1984, where Big Brother (albeit apparently a fictitious entity) is worshipped as a wise and loving leader, and the Party is practically structured around its own supposed infallibility. In addition, many of the particulars of the Oceanian system, such as the Three-Year Plans and the forced labour camps, appear to be thinly veiled allusions to aspects of Stalin's rule. It is even often suggested that Oceania's Big Brother, with his dark hair and heavy mustache, is inspired by the larger-than-life images of Josef Stalin's visage so commonly seen in the Soviet Union.

Orwell's time working with the Indian Imperial Police in Burma introduced him to the shameful activities of the British in the Far East, and appears to have encouraged his exploration of the lives of the urban poor. After returning to Europe, Orwell continued to focus on this subject and began to develop a vague distrust of machine-age capitalist society that later blossomed into a firm adherence to Socialism, bolstered by his time working with the revolutionary Marxist POUM (Partido Obrero de Unificacion Marxista, or Worker's Party of Marxist Unification), the dissident faction of the Spanish Communist party. However, when the Stalin-backed Communists turned on their far-left anarchist allies and labeled POUM pro-fascist, Orwell fled to avoid prison, or worse, death. This experience taught Orwell the danger of abandoning true Socialist revolutionary ideals, and he developed both a fixation on totalitarianism and an abhorrence for Stalinist Communism, both of which are clearly expressed in 1984. World War II's introduction of totalitarianism through fascist and communist regimes solidified Orwell's hatred of the ideology.

During the war, Orwell was equally unimpressed by his experience in Britain. From 1940-1943, Orwell was employed by the BBC, under the control of the British Ministry of Information, which served as inspiration for Winston's position at the Ministry of Truth, and perhaps for Newspeak. In this capacity, Orwell witnessed the propagation of stories glorifying Britain's triumphs while the British Empire was simultaneously steadily declining. This type of disconnect between reality and the information disseminated to the public clearly makes its way into the novel.

It is unclear to what extent Orwell believed 1984 to be an accurate prediction of the future, but many critics agree that he wrote the book as a warning to modern society of the damage that can come from embracing totalitarian regimes. The novel mourns the loss of personal identity while demonstrating how to effectively rid a person of their independence, particularly through extensive sexual repression and the prohibition of individual thought. Many of the concepts and themes presented in 1984 have steadily made their way into the common vernacular. For instance, the phrase "Big Brother" is often used to refer to the advancement and expansion of technology used to observe and record behaviour, such as video cameras placed on city streets and government monitoring of phone and Internet communication. The adjective "Orwellian" is also commonly used to describe such real-world developments reminiscent of 1984.

Orwell wrote 1984 while seriously ill with tuberculosis, and afterward commented that had he not been so ill, the book might not have been so bleak. To his consternation, after its publication, 1984 was used as propaganda itself, especially by Western forces in post-World War II Germany. Much later, there were many attempts to censor the novel, particularly on the grounds that it contains pro-Communist material and sexual references. The book has also been adapted to both television shows and movies, and has served as inspiration for a variety of other artistic endeavors, such as David Bowie's Diamond Dogs album, which includes a song titled 1984.

Chapter 4

Character List

Winston Smith

The novel's protagonist. Winston is a quiet 39-year-old man living in Oceania in the year 1984. A Party member, Winston works at the Ministry of Truth correcting "errors" in past publications. Winston is also an amateur intellectual who nurses a secret hatred of the Party. To protect himself from discovery, Winston goes through the motions of outward orthodoxy, but relishes his internal world of dreams, memories and speculation about the past. Winston is married but separated, and has no children. Upon meeting Julia, he finds an outlet for his heretical opinions and for the love he yearns to share with another human being. His physical and mental health improves, and Winston starts to believe more powerfully in an established covert movement against the Party. Unfortunately, the affair is short-lived, and the couple is arrested. Winston is taken to the Ministry of Love and subjected to extensive torture and humiliation, which force him into submission. As a result of this experience, Winston loses all rebellious thoughts, gains unadulterated love for Big Brother and the Party, and eradicates his love for Julia. In short, Winston loses his humanity. Upon his release, he is a shell of a man, yet also an ideal, loyal, and devoted Party member. A minor member of the ruling Party in near-future London, Winston Smith is a thin, frail, contemplative, intellectual, and fatalistic thirty-nine-year-old. Winston hates the totalitarian control and enforced repression that are characteristic of his government. He harbors revolutionary dreams.

Orwell's primary goal in 1984 is to demonstrate the terrifying possibilities of totalitarianism. The reader experiences the nightmarish world that Orwell envisions through the eyes of the protagonist, Winston. His personal tendency to resist the stifling of his individuality, and his intellectual ability to reason about his resistance, enables the reader to observe and understand the harsh oppression that the Party, Big Brother, and the Thought Police institute. Whereas Julia is untroubled and somewhat selfish, interested in rebelling only for the pleasures to be gained, Winston is extremely pensive and curious, desperate to understand how and why the Party exercises such absolute power in Oceania. Winston's long reflections give Orwell a chance to explore the novel's important themes, including language as mind control, psychological and physical intimidation and manipulation, and the importance of knowledge of the past.

Apart from his thoughtful nature, Winston's main attributes are his rebelliousness and his fatalism. Winston hates the Party passionately and wants to test the limits of its power; he commits innumerable crimes throughout the novel, ranging from writing "down with big brother" in his diary, to having an illegal love affair with Julia, to getting himself secretly indoctrinated into the anti-Party Brotherhood. The effort Winston puts into his attempt to achieve freedom and independence ultimately underscores the Party's devastating power. By the end of the novel, Winston's rebellion is revealed as playing into O'Brien's campaign of physical and psychological torture, transforming Winston into a loyal subject of Big Brother.

One reason for Winston's rebellion, and eventual downfall, is his sense of fatalism-his intense (though entirely justified) paranoia about the Party and his overriding belief that the Party will eventually catch and punish him. As soon as he writes "down with big brother" in his diary, Winston is positive that the Thought Police will quickly capture him for committing a thoughtcrime. Thinking that he is helpless to evade his doom, Winston allows himself to take unnecessary risks, such as trusting O'Brien and renting the room above Mr.

Charrington's shop. Deep down, he knows that these risks will increase his chances of being caught by the Party; he even admits this to O'Brien while in prison. But because he believes that he will be caught no matter what he does, he convinces himself that he must continue to rebel. Winston lives in a world in which legitimate optimism is an impossibility; lacking any real hope, he gives himself false hope, fully aware that he is doing so.

Julia

A 26-year-old Party member who works in the Fiction Department of the Ministry of Truth. Julia also secretly despises the Party, but accepts its rule over her and therefore outwardly appears to be zealously devoted to the Party's causes. Julia declares her love for Winston, thus beginning their affair and setting them down the path towards their eventual imprisonment. Unlike Winston, Julia sees life simply, and is interested only in her survival and personal rebellion against the Party-not in long-term plans for the resurgence of democracy. Julia is arrested along with Winston and tortured in the Ministry of Love. When they meet again after their respective releases, Julia is spiritless, physically broken, and even nurses a vague dislike for Winston. Just like Winston, Julia leaves the Ministry of Love as a mere shell of a human being. Winston's lover, a beautiful dark-haired girl working in the Fiction Department at the Ministry of Truth. Julia enjoys sex, and claims to have had affairs with many Party members. Julia is pragmatic and optimistic. Her rebellion against the Party is small and personal, for her own enjoyment, in contrast to Winston's ideological motivation.

Julia is Winston's lover and the only other person who Winston can be sure hates the Party and wishes to rebel against it as he does. Whereas Winston is restless, fatalistic, and concerned about large-scale social issues, Julia is sensual, pragmatic, and generally content to live in the moment and make the best of her life. Winston longs to join the Brotherhood and read Emmanuel Goldstein's abstract manifesto; Julia is more concerned with enjoying sex and making practical plans to avoid getting caught by the Party. Winston essentially sees their affair as temporary; his fatalistic attitude makes him unable to imagine his relationship with Julia lasting very long. Julia, on the other hand, is well adapted to her chosen forms of small-scale rebellion. She claims to have had affairs with various Party members, and has no intention of terminating her pleasure seeking, or of being caught (her involvement with Winston is what leads to her capture). Julia is a striking contrast with Winston: apart from their mutual sexual desire and hatred of the Party, most of their traits are dissimilar, if not contradictory.

O'Brien

A prominent Inner Party member with whom Winston feels a strange bond. Winston feels that even if O'Brien is an enemy, it wouldn't matter because he knows O'Brien will understand him without explanation. O'Brien is a large, graceful, and clearly intelligent man who leads Winston to believe he is part of an underground movement against the Party, but in fact helps turn Winston in for thoughtcrime and tortures him in the Ministry of Love.

O'Brien is full of strange contradictions. He can be fatherly-and even tender-even while fanatically expressing his devotion to the Party by torturing Winston. A mysterious, powerful, and sophisticated member of the Inner Party whom Winston believes is also a member of the Brotherhood, the legendary group of anti-Party rebels.

One of the most fascinating aspects of 1984 is the manner in which Orwell shrouds an explicit portrayal of a totalitarian world in an enigmatic aura. While Orwell gives the reader a close look into the personal life of Winston Smith, the reader's only glimpses of Party life are those that Winston himself catches. As a result, many of the Party's inner workings remain unexplained, as do its origins, and the identities and motivations of its leaders.

This sense of mystery is centralized in the character of O'Brien, a powerful member of the Inner Party who tricks Winston into believing that he is a member of the revolutionary group called the Brotherhood. O'Brien inducts Winston into the Brotherhood. Later, though, he appears at Winston's jail cell to abuse and brainwash him in the name of the Party. During the process of this punishment, and perhaps as an act of psychological torture, O'Brien admits that he pretended to be connected to the Brotherhood merely to trap Winston in an act of open disloyalty to the Party.

This revelation raises more questions about O'Brien than it answers. Rather than developing as a character throughout the novel, O'Brien actually seems to un-develop: by the end of the book, the reader knows far less about him than they previously had thought. When Winston asks O'Brien if he too has been captured by the Party, O'Brien replies, "They got me long ago." This reply could signify that O'Brien himself was once rebellious, only to be tortured into passive acceptance of the Party. One can also argue that O'Brien pretends to sympathize with Winston merely to gain his trust. Similarly, one cannot be sure whether the Brotherhood actually exists, or if it is simply a Party invention used to trap the disloyal and give the rest of the populace a common enemy. The novel does not answer these questions, but rather leaves O'Brien as a shadowy, symbolic enigma on the fringes of the even more obscure Inner Party.

Big Brother

The symbol of Oceania and the Party, Big Brother is Oceania's supreme leader, and is omnipresent through telescreen projections, coins, and even large posters warning, "BIG BROTHER IS WATCHING YOU." Big Brother is theoretically one of the original founders of the Party and the Revolution, but Winston assumes he does not exist, will never age, and will never die. He is the mouthpiece of the Party, and the symbol all Party members worship.

Though he never appears in the novel, and though he may not actually exist, Big Brother, the perceived ruler of Oceania, is an extremely important figure. Everywhere Winston looks he sees posters of Big Brother's face bearing the message "BIG BROTHER IS WATCHING YOU." Big Brother's image is stamped on coins and broadcast on the unavoidable telescreens; it haunts Winston's life and fills him with hatred and fascination.

Mrs. Parsons

The wife of Tom Parsons and neighbour of Winston's. A tired, aged woman with "dust in the creases of her face," Mrs. Parsons is the mother of two horrific children belonging to the Spies and Youth League and who are bound to eventually denounce her and her husband to the Thought Police. At the beginning of the novel, Mrs. Parsons knocks on Winston's door when he is writing in his diary to ask for his help unclogging the kitchen sink. Winston obliges.

Tom Parsons

Husband to Mrs. Parsons, and Winston's neighbour and coworker. Tom is a heavy, sweaty, simple man whom Winston despises for his unquestioning acceptance of everything the Party tells him. Parsons is active in his community groups, and appears to truly believe Party claims and doctrine. However, his daughter eventually denounces him to the Thought Police, claiming he was saying "Down with Big Brother" in his sleep. Winston sees Tom while imprisoned in the Ministry of Love, and Tom is ironically proud of his seven-year-old daughter for having done her duty. A fat, obnoxious, and dull Party member who lives near Winston and works at the Ministry of Truth. He has a dull wife and a group of suspicious, ill-mannered children who are members of the Junior Spies.

Tillotson

A coworker of Winston's, Tillotson sits across from him in the Records Department and is extremely secretive about his work.

Ampleforth

A coworker of Winston's, and a poet who works in the Records Department rewriting politically or ideologically objectionable Oldspeak poems. By the end of the novel, Ampleforth is in prison along with Winston, for, he believes having left the word "God" in one of his poems.

Syme

A "friend" of Winston's and a philologist working on the Eleventh Edition of the Newspeak Dictionary. Although Winston dislikes Syme, he enjoys having somewhat interesting conversations with him. Winston notices that Syme, although a devoted Party member, is too smart and too vocal for his own good. He predicts Syme will be vaporized, and is proven correct when he suddenly disappears.

An intelligent, outgoing man who works with Winston at the Ministry of Truth. Syme specializes in language. As the novel opens, he is working on a new edition of the Newspeak dictionary. Winston believes Syme is too intelligent to stay in the Party's favour.

Katharine

Winston's wife, who never appears directly in the book but is discussed at some length. Winston describes her as "unthinkful" and claims she was absurdly devoted to the Party, to the point where she referred to sleeping with Winston to produce offspring as her "duty to the Party." The two never had children, and eventually separated. In a conversation with Julia, Winston reveals he was once tempted to murder Katharine when they were separated from others on a nature walk. However, he did not, and he assumes Katharine still lives, although he has not seen her in years.

Mr. Charrington

The owner of the antique shop where Winston first buys his diary, pen, and later on a glass paperweight. Winston rents the room above the shop from Mr. Charrington for his love affair with Julia. Mr. Charrington appears to be a kind old man interested in history and the past, but later reveals himself to be a member of the Thought Police. Mr. Charrington leads Winston and Julia into his trap, and observes their action from the hidden telescreen in the room above the shop. As he is being arrested, Winston notices that Mr. Charrington looks entirely different, and has clearly been working under disguise for quite some time. An old man who runs a secondhand store in the prole district. Kindly and encouraging, Mr. Charrington seems to share Winston's interest in the past. He also seems to support Winston's rebellion against the Party and his relationship with Julia, since he rents Winston a room without a telescreen in which to carry out his affair. But Mr. Charrington is not as he seems. He is a member of the Thought Police. Martin: O'Brien's servant, Martin is a small, dark-haired man who Winston believes might be Chinese. He leads Winston and Julia into O'Brien's apartment and sits in on their meeting, but does not speak.

Comrade Withers

A former prominent Inner Party member who received the Order of Conspicuous Merit, Second Class. The subject of a "correction" Winston must make at the Ministry of Truth after Withers is vaporized.

Comrade Ogilvy: A man Winston invents to replace Comrade Withers when "correcting" the news story surrounding the honors Withers, an unperson, received from the Party.

Jones, Aaronson and Rutherford

Three Inner Party members wrongly arrested in 1965 and forced to incriminate themselves of various crimes, including treason and murder. They are eventually killed. Winston finds a clipping proving their innocence and destroys the document, but never forgets holding the proof that Party "fact" was fiction.

Wilsher

A coworker of Winston's who delays his first conversation with Julia by inviting Winston to sit with him in the canteen.

Prole Washer Woman

A large, brawny, stocky prole woman who is constantly

hanging laundry and singing below the window in Mr. Charrington's apartment.

Starving Man

A man briefly placed in Winston's holding cell who is clearly being starved to death. When told to go to Room 101 he tells them to take the man who offered him food instead-anything but 101.

Bumstead

A prisoner in the Ministry of Love who offers the starving man a piece of old bread. He is immediately punished with a violent attack that breaks his jaw and causes heavy bleeding

Emmanuel Goldstein

Another figure who exerts an influence on the novel without ever appearing in it. According to the Party, Goldstein is the legendary leader of the Brotherhood. He seems to have been a Party leader who fell out of favour with the regime. In any case, the Party describes him as the most dangerous and treacherous man in Oceania.

Chapter 5

Plot Overview

Plot Overview

Winston Smith is a low-ranking member of the ruling Party in London, in the nation of Oceania. Everywhere Winston goes, even his own home, the Party watches him through telescreens; everywhere he looks he sees the face of the Party's seemingly omniscient leader, a figure known only as Big Brother. The Party controls everything in Oceania, even the people's history and language. Currently, the Party is forcing the implementation of an invented language called Newspeak, which attempts to prevent political rebellion by eliminating all words related to it. Even thinking rebellious thoughts is illegal. Such thoughtcrime is, in fact, the worst of all crimes.

As the novel opens, Winston feels frustrated by the oppression and rigid control of the Party, which prohibits free thought, sex, and any expression of individuality. Winston dislikes the party and has illegally purchased a diary in which to write his criminal thoughts. He has also become fixated on a powerful Party member named O'Brien, whom Winston believes is a secret member of the Brotherhood-the mysterious, legendary group that works to overthrow the Party.

Winston works in the Ministry of Truth, where he alters historical records to fit the needs of the Party. He notices a coworker, a beautiful dark-haired girl, staring at him, and worries that she is an informant who will turn him in for his thoughtcrime. He is troubled by the Party's control of history: the Party claims that Oceania has always been allied with

Eastasia in a war against Eurasia, but Winston seems to recall a time when this was not true. The Party also claims that Emmanuel Goldstein, the alleged leader of the Brotherhood, is the most dangerous man alive, but this does not seem plausible to Winston. Winston spends his evenings wandering through the poorest neighborhoods in London, where the proletarians, or proles, live squalid lives, relatively free of Party monitoring.

One day, Winston receives a note from the dark-haired girl that reads "I love you." She tells him her name, Julia, and they begin a covert affair, always on the lookout for signs of Party monitoring. Eventually they rent a room above the secondhand store in the prole district where Winston bought the diary. This relationship lasts for some time. Winston is sure that they will be caught and punished sooner or later (the fatalistic Winston knows that he has been doomed since he wrote his first diary entry), while Julia is more pragmatic and optimistic. As Winston's affair with Julia progresses, his hatred for the Party grows more and more intense. At last, he receives the message that he has been waiting for: O'Brien wants to see him.

Winston and Julia travel to O'Brien's luxurious apartment. As a member of the powerful Inner Party (Winston belongs to the Outer Party), O'Brien leads a life of luxury that Winston can only imagine. O'Brien confirms to Winston and Julia that, like them, he hates the Party, and says that he works against it as a member of the Brotherhood. He indoctrinates Winston and Julia into the Brotherhood, and gives Winston a copy of Emmanuel Goldstein's book, the manifesto of the Brotherhood. Winston reads the book-an amalgam of several forms of class-based twentieth-century social theory-to Julia in the room above the store. Suddenly, soldiers barge in and seize them. Mr. Charrington, the proprietor of the store, is revealed as having been a member of the Thought Police all along.

Torn away from Julia and taken to a place called the Ministry of Love, Winston finds that O'Brien, too, is a Party spy who simply pretended to be a member of the Brotherhood in order to trap Winston into committing an open act of rebellion against the Party. O'Brien spends months torturing and brainwashing Winston, who struggles to resist. At last, O'Brien sends him to the dreaded Room 101, the final destination for anyone who opposes the Party. Here, O'Brien tells Winston that he will be forced to confront his worst fear. Throughout the novel, Winston has had recurring nightmares about rats; O'Brien now straps a cage full of rats onto Winston's head and prepares to allow the rats to eat his face. Winston snaps, pleading with O'Brien to do it to Julia, not to him.

Giving up Julia is what O'Brien wanted from Winston all along. His spirit broken, Winston is released to the outside world. He meets Julia, but no longer feels anything for her. He has accepted the Party entirely and has learned to love Big Brother.

Chapter 6

Short Summary

The novel's protagonist, Winston Smith, is a citizen of Oceania, one of the world's three superstates (along with Eurasia and Eastasia). It is the year 1984, and Winston lives in Airstrip One, which used to be known as Great Britain. Winston is a member of the Party, which rules Oceania under the principles of Ingsoc. Oceania is an oligarchy, under hierarchical rule. The Party consists of Inner Party members, who are the ruling elite, and regular Party members, who are citizens of Oceania. Outside of the Party are the proles, non-Party members and simple people who live in poverty and are free from Party regulations. The Party's leader is Big Brother, and there are massive images of his kind visage, complete with dark hair and a substantial mustache, displayed throughout London, some accompanied by the words "Big Brother is Watching You." The Party's three slogans are: "War is Peace," "Freedom is Slavery," and "Ignorance is Strength."

Winston lost his parents and little sister during the Revolutionary period that destroyed capitalism and instituted Ingsoc in Oceania. He was placed in a Party orphanage and integrated into the Party system. Now he works in the Records Department of the Ministry of Truth, which handles all Party publications and propaganda, altering previously published Party publications to ensure that the Party's version of the Past is never questioned. Such alterations often remove a person from history, or make previously flawed predictions accurate. The other three ministries are the Ministry of Love, which handles all Party prisoners, the Ministry of Peace, which handles war, and the Ministry of Plenty, which manages the production of Party goods, including Victory cigarettes, Victory gin, and Victory coffee, all of which are of extremely poor quality.

Winston has never quite accepted the principles of Ingsoc and the Party. He believes in an unalterable past, and finds Party politics reprehensible. Winston wishes for privacy, intimacy, freedom and love, but cannot express any of this in the open for fear of death. Such thoughts constitute "throughtcrimes," which are highly punishable offenses resulting in arrest, imprisonment, torture, and often death.

When the book opens, Winston is at home during his lunch break. He has returned to his apartment in the Victory Mansions, a dilapidated Party housing building, to write in a diary, a relic of the past he obtained from an old junk shop. Winston's apartment is meager, and like every other Party member's home, contains a telescreen. The telescreen transmits Party information and propaganda, and also allows the Thought Police to watch and listen to Party members at all times. In Oceania, there is no such thing as privacy. Winston is fortunate to have a small nook in his apartment out of the view of the telescreen, and it is in this nook that he begins to write in his diary, despite his overwhelming fear of being caught. Undoubtedly, Winston will eventually be caught, imprisoned, and tortured by the Thought Police. For now, however, he chooses to forge ahead with his rebellion.

Winston writes of various memories, all related to the Party and his life. Many include violent imagery, which is quite common in the age of Oceania, and reveal anti-Party feelings. Winston clearly does not subscribe to Party doctrine. Winston is briefly interrupted at one point by a knock on his door. At first he panics, thinking he has already been caught, but it is only his neighbour, Mrs. Parsons, who needs help unclogging her sink. Winston obliges, and interacts briefly with Mrs. Parsons' two hellish children who are members of the Spies and Youth League, and clearly powerfully indoctrinated in the ways of the Party. Winston predicts that eventually these children will turn their loyal, simple, innocent parents into the Thought Police. Such tragedies, it seems, are quite common.

Winston returns to his diary, and in one of his reveries reflecting on the past and his memories and dreams, finds himself writing "DOWN WITH BIG BROTHER" in large letters over and over on the page. Eventually, time runs out and Winston must return to work, which he enjoys. Once Winston found a newspaper clipping among his daily assignments that proved the innocence of three men: Jones, Aaronson, and Rutherford. In examining the clipping, he knew it meant the Party was wrong, and that he had real evidence of an accurate version of the past. Rather than risk discovery, however, he destroyed the clipping, placing it in a memory hole that sucked it into the building's internal furnaces.

At the Ministry of Truth Winston is surrounded by loyal Party members, and is always on guard to prevent his true feelings from being perceived by others. At work, Winston sits through the daily Two Minutes Hate, which rails against Oceania's enemy, Eurasia, and the supposed leader of the opposition movement, Emmanuel Goldstein. The propaganda is powerful, and the people around him begin shouting at the screen. Of course, Winston must join in to avoid suspicion.

Finding himself increasingly curious about the past, Winston wanders the streets, among the proles. He believes that if there is hope for a successful rebellion, it lies in the proles. Winston meets an old man in a prole pub and questions him about life before the Revolution. To his frustration, the man focuses on his own personal memories rather than on the generalities and conceptual differences Winston is interested in. Winston returns to the junk shop where he bought his diary and purchases a glass paperweight with a piece of coral inside. The proprietor, a kind old man named Mr. Charrington, shows him a room above the shop and Winston thinks about what it might be like to rent it out and live among old things, free from the constant presence of the telescreen.

At work and on his walk, Winston sees a dark-haired girl who is seemingly a violently loyal Party member and apparently has taken notice of him. He fears she is a member of the Thought Police. One day, at the Ministry of Truth, the girl slips him a note after falling down in the hallway, requiring

Winston's assistance. The note says "I love you." Winston is astounded, but extremely excited by the possibility of a love affair. The affair must be secret, as the Party is entirely against any sort of sexual pleasure. In fact, sexual repression is a tenet of Ingsoc. The Party must approve every marriage, and it is unacceptable for a man and a woman to express any physical attraction for one another. All energy must be devoted to the Party. Winston was once in such a marriage. His wife Katharine was a frigid, mindless woman who was extremely loyal to the Party, but thought sex was a vile activity. However, she regularly scheduled times for her and Winston to make love, calling it her "duty to the Party." She had been taught from childhood that she must bear children.

With a great deal of effort to remain undetected, the girl finally tells Winston where and how they can meet. On a Sunday afternoon, he travels into the country, as per Julia's instructions, to meet her in a secluded clearing in a wooded area. Finally, they can speak. Winston learns that her name is Julia, they discuss their beliefs regarding the Party, and they begin their love affair. At one point, Winston notices that the secluded spot she has led them to exactly matches a place he constantly sees in his dreams that he has termed the Golden Country.

Winston and Julia, who has a knack for finding abandoned locales and for obtaining black market goods such as real coffee, bread and sugar, continue to meet in secret. They are limited to interacting only in public places and having only the most minimal conversations, but the two discover a mutual hatred of the Party and eventually fall in love. Winston believes that it is possible to overthrow the Party, while Julia is satisfied simply living a double life. On the surface, she is loyal to the extreme, a member of the Junior Anti-Sex League, a volunteer in many Party activities, and a vocal participant in loyalty-testing events such as the Two Minutes Hate. On the inside, she thinks of it all as a game. She hates the Party and all it stands for, but knows she can do nothing to change it. Eventually Winston rents the room above Mr. Charrington's flat. Winston and Julia meet often in the room, which is simply furnished, with an old twelve-hour clock (the Party uses twenty-four hour time), and a picture of an old London church, St. Clement's Dane. Mr. Charrington taught him the first lines of an old poem about the church, "Oranges and lemons say the bells of St. Clement's," and Julia knows a few more lines that her grandfather taught her when she was very small. Outside their window, a middle-aged prole woman is constantly hanging her wash and singing simple prole songs, many of which have been created by machines in the Ministry of Truth specifically for the proles.

Another Party member suddenly takes on an important role in Winston's life. Winston has always noticed O'Brien at the Ministry of Truth. He seems to be an intelligent man, and Winston believes in his heart that O'Brien feels the same way he does about the Party. Once, during the Two Minutes Hate, the two men locked eyes and Winston felt sure of O'Brien's thoughts. In a dream, Winston once heard someone tell him, "We will meet in the place where there is no darkness," and he believes the voice to have been O'Brien's. For Winston, O'Brien represents the possibility of an underground movement. Perhaps the Brotherhood, led my Emmanuel Goldstein, is real.

O'Brien approaches Winston at work under the pretense of discussing the Tenth Edition of the Newspeak Dictionary (Newspeak is the official language of Oceania, and its goal is to reduce and simplify vocabulary). O'Brien gives Winston his home address, supposedly so he can come pick up an advance copy of the new book. Winston takes the slip of paper with amazement. He knows that O'Brien has approached him because he is part of the underground movement. His true path towards rebellion has begun.

After some time, Winston and Julia visit O'Brien, an Inner Party member who has a lush apartment, a servant, and the freedom to turn off his telescreen. Winston renounces the Party and discusses his belief in the Brotherhood. O'Brien welcomes Winston and Julia into the Brotherhood and tells them that they must be willing to do anything to work towards its cause. They agree, but say that they will not do anything that would prevent them from seeing each other ever again. O'Brien tells Winston that he will give him a copy of Goldstein's book, and outlines a complicated version of events that will lead toward the exchange. Winston leaves after a final toast with O'Brien, in which Winston finishes O'Brien's statement, saying that they "will meet in the place with no darkness."

During Hate Week, the Party's enemy becomes Eastasia rather than Eurasia, and Winston must spend a great deal of time at work, sometimes even staying overnight, to "correct" all Party publications previously referring to war with Eurasia. The Party is at war with Eastasia, and has always been at war with Eastasia. In the midst of Hate Week, a man brings Winston a brief case, suggests that he dropped it, and leaves. The book is inside. When he has finally completed the Hate Week corrections, Winston escapes to Mr. Charrington's apartment and begins to read. Julia arrives, and he reads aloud to her about the history of Oceania, capitalism versus totalitarianism, and the main goals of the Party. Most of this information Winston already knows, but he finds it helpful to read it in the detailed, clear words of Emmanuel Goldstein.

Winston and Julia eventually fall asleep. The wake hours later, and go to stand at the window. Winston repeats his oft-stated phrase, "We are the dead." Suddenly, a voice coming from the wall echoes him, "You are the dead." There is a telescreen hidden behind the picture of St. Clement's Dane. They are caught. The Thought Police storm the room. Mr. Charrington walks in, and it becomes clear that he is a member of the Thought Police. He has been disguised as a kind old man, but is far younger than Winston imagined, with different hair and eyes. Winston and Julia are arrested, separated, and brought to the Ministry of Love.

While in a holding cell, Winston sees men from the Ministry of Truth come and go. Each has been arrested for thoughtcrime. Parsons arrives, and it turns out that his daughter turned him in, claiming to have heard him say "Down with Big Brother" in his sleep. Winston's prediction, it appears, was sadly accurate. In his holding cell, Winston sees a great deal of violence, and notices guards constantly referring to "Room 101," a phrase that seems to instill great fear in some of the prisoners. Eventually, O'Brien arrives. It becomes clear that he was never part of the underground movement, but actually works in the Ministry of Love. Winston's entire interaction with O'Brien was a ruse. Winston is removed from the holding cell, and his torture begins.

At first the torture is extremely violent, and he is forced to admit to a litany of crimes he did not commit, including murder and espionage. Eventually, the torture becomes less violent and O'Brien takes over. He begins to break Winston's spirit, telling him that his memory is flawed and that he is insane. Winston's discussions with O'Brien dwell on the nature of the past and reality, and reveal much about the Party's approach to those concepts. The Party, O'Brien explains with a lunatic intensity, seeks absolute power, for power's own sake. This is why it will always be successful, is always right, and will ultimately control the entire world. Winston cannot argue; every time he does, he is faced with obstinate logical fallacies, a completely different system of reasoning that runs counter to all reason. Winston believes in a past that never existed, and is hounded by false memories. To be cured, Winston must overcome his own insanity and win the war against his own mind. Little by little, O'Brien shows Winston, with the use of electric shock machines, beatings and starvation, the way of the Party. He forces Winston to accept that if the Party says so, two plus two equals five.

Winston had once written in his diary that freedom meant being able to say that two plus two is four. His final attempt to argue with O'Brien ends in O'Brien showing Winston himself in the mirror. Winston is beyond horrified to see that he has turned into a sickly, disgusting sack of bones, beaten into a new face. Broken to the core, Winston finally submits to his re-education. He is no longer beaten, is fed at regular intervals, is allowed to sleep (though the lights, of course, never go out), and begins to regain his health. Although seemingly making progress in accepting the reality of the Party, Winston is still holding onto the last remaining kernel of himself and his humanity: his love for Julia. This comes out when, in the midst of a dream, Winston cries aloud, "Julia! Julia! Julia, my love! Julia!" O'Brien's last efforts with Winston are focused on forcing him to betray Julia. He takes Winston to Room 101, containing the worst thing in the world, which is different for everyone. For Winston, "the worst thing in the world" is a rat. Winston is tied to a chair, and O'Brien begins to attach a mask/ cage contraption containing huge, hungry, carnivorous rats to his face. Winston feels a desperate, deep, panicked fear. He cannot take it, and finally screams for O'Brien to put someone else in his place-anyone, even Julia. O'Brien has succeeded.

Winston, a damaged, changed, empty shell of a man, is released into the world. In his new life, he sees Julia once, by chance, but they are no longer in love. Each betrayed the other, and prison changed them powerfully. There is no hope for their relationship. Winston obtains a somewhat trivial, meaningless job that pays surprisingly well. He spends his time at the Chestnut Tree Cafe drinking Victory Gin and playing chess. His life is buried in gin. In the final pages of the novel, we find Winston in his regular seat at the cafe, drinking gin, playing chess, and waiting for a report from the front in Central Africa, where Eurasia (Oceania was always at war with Eurasia) has invaded.

He is excited about the report, because with this invasion, Eurasia might actually be able to break Oceania's line of defence and put the entire nation at risk for takeover. A Eurasian success in Central Africa might mean the end of the Party. Before the report comes, Winston suddenly recalls a very happy day in his childhood spent playing board games with his mother and little sister. He pushes it out of his mind, realizing it is a false memory and resolving to allow fewer of those to creep up on him. Eventually, the report reveals that Oceania has succeeded in repelling the Eurasian advance.

There is jubilation on the telescreen and in the streets. Staring into the eyes of a poster of Big Brother, Winston realizes that he knew this news would come. With tears dripping down his face, Winston realizes he has finally completed the rehabilitation he started in the Ministry of Love. He loves Big Brother.

Chapter 7

Background

Essays By George Orwell

Politics and the English Language (1946)

Most people who bother with the matter at all would admit that the English language is in a bad way, but it is generally assumed that we cannot by conscious action do anything about it. Our civilization is decadent and our language--so the argument runs--must inevitably share in the general collapse. It follows that any struggle against the abuse of language is a sentimental archaism, like preferring candles to electric light or hansom cabs to aeroplanes. Underneath this lies the half-conscious belief that language is a natural growth and not an instrument which we shape for our own purposes.

Now, it is clear that the decline of a language must ultimately have political and economic causes: it is not due simply to the bad influence of this or that individual writer. But an effect can become a cause, reinforcing the original cause and producing the same effect in an intensified form, and so on indefinitely. A man may take to drink because he feels himself to be a failure, and then fail all the more completely because he drinks. It is rather the same thing that is happening to the English language. It becomes ugly and inaccurate because our thoughts are foolish, but the slovenliness of our language makes it easier for us to have foolish thoughts. The point is that the process is reversible. Modern English, especially written English, is full of bad habits which spread by imitation and which can be avoided if one is willing to take the necessary trouble. If one gets rid of these habits one can think more clearly, and to think clearly is a necessary first step toward political regeneration: so that the fight against bad English is not frivolous and is not the exclusive concern of professional writers. I will come back to this presently, and I hope that by that time the meaning of what I have said here will have become clearer. Meanwhile, here are five specimens of the English language as it is now habitually written.

These five passages have not been picked out because they are especially bad--I could have quoted far worse if I had chosen--but because they illustrate various of the mental vices from which we now suffer. They are a little below the average, but are fairly representative examples. I number them so that I can refer back to them when necessary.

Totalitarianism in Europe (1919-1939)

In the years immediately after the First World War, a promising new era of democracy seemed to be unfolding. The autocratic regimes in Russia, Germany and Austria, were all overthrown and replaced by republics. The seven newly-created states in Europe all adopted the republican form of government. Democracy seemed triumphant in the post-war world. Yet within two decades, many democratic countries in Europe were taken over by some kind of dictatorship. Russia became a Communist state. Italy and Germany became Fascist states. Of the powers in Europe, only Britain and France remained staunchly democratic. Actually the First World War brought some negative effects to Europe.(See the results of the First World War)

Before we proceed, perhaps we should have an understanding of the two political terms-democratic state and totalitarian state-which will be used rather frequently by us. Between the two World Wars, Britain and France might be regarded as democratic states. Within these two states, the individuals had freedom of speech and of the press, of petition and of assembly, and freedom from arrest for political opinions. They could form political parties and elect the party or the parties they liked to rule. In short, the individual was an end in himself. The government helped to provide for the fullest development and security of all individuals. Russia (1917-1939), Italy (1922-1939) and Germany (1933-1939) might be regarded as mean totalitarian states. Within these states, the individuals had no right of free speech, free publications and free associations. The individuals had no right to form political parties. There was only one governmental party which imposed its dictatorial rule on the people. This one-party regime was concerned with the 'total' activities of its people-their work, their leisure, their religion, even their private lives. The basic concept of the totalitarian state was best expressed in Mussolini's well-known phrase, "all within the state, nothing outside the state, nothing against the state." In short, the state was the master, the individual the servant.

The Prevention of Literature 1946

About a year ago I attended a meeting of the P.E.N. Club, the occasion being the tercentenary of Milton's Aeropagitica--a pamphlet, it may be remembered, in defence of freedom of the press. Milton's famous phrase about the sin of "killing" a book was printed on the leaflets advertising the meeting which had been circulated beforehand.

There were four speakers on the platform. One of them delivered a speech which did deal with the freedom of the press, but only in relation to India; another said, hesitantly, and in very general terms, that liberty was a good thing; a third delivered an attack on the laws relating to obscenity in literature. The fourth devoted most of his speech to a defence of the Russian purges. Of the speeches from the body of the hall, some reverted to the question of obscenity and the laws that deal with it, others were simply eulogies of Soviet Russia.

Moral liberty--the liberty to discuss sex questions frankly in print--seemed to be generally approved, but political liberty was not mentioned. Out of this concourse of several hundred people, perhaps half of whom were directly connected with the writing trade, there was not a single one who could point out that freedom of the press, if it means anything at all, means the freedom to criticize and oppose. Significantly, no speaker quoted from the pamphlet which was ostensibly being commemorated. Nor was there any mention of the various books which have been "killed" in England and the United States during the war. In its net effect the meeting was a demonstration in favour of censorship.

There was nothing particularly surprising in this. In our age, the idea of intellectual liberty is under attack from two directions. On the one side are its theoretical enemies, the apologists of totalitarianism, and on the other its immediate, practical enemies, monopoly and bureaucracy. Any writer or journalist who wants to retain his integrity finds himself thwarted by the general drift of society rather than by active persecution. The sort of things that are working against him are the concentration of the press in the hands of a few rich men, the grip of monopoly on radio and the films, the unwillingness of the public to spend money on books, making it necessary for nearly every writer to earn part of his living by hackwork, the encroachment of official bodies like the M.O.I. and the British Council, which help the writer to keep alive but also waste his time and dictate his opinions, and the continuous war atmosphere of the past ten years, whose distorting effects no one has been able to escape.

Everything in our age conspires to turn the writer, and every other kind of artist as well, into a minor official, working on themes handed down from above and never telling what seems to him the whole of the truth. But in struggling against this fate he gets no help from his own side; that is, there is no large body of opinion which will assure him that he's in the right. In the past, at any rate throughout the Protestant centuries, the idea of rebellion and the idea of intellectual integrity were mixed up. A heretic--political, moral, religious, or aesthetic--was one who refused to outrage his own conscience. His outlook was summed up in the words of the Revivalist hymn:

Dare to be a Daniel
Dare to stand alone
Dare to have a purpose firm
Dare to make it known

To bring this hymn up to date one would have to add a "Don't" at the beginning of each line. For it is the peculiarity of our age that the rebels against the existing order, at any rate the most numerous and characteristic of them, are also rebelling against the idea of individual integrity. "Daring to stand alone" is ideologically criminal as well as practically dangerous. The independence of the writer and the artist is eaten away by vague economic forces, and at the same time it is undermined by those who should be its defenders. It is with the second process that I am concerned here.

Freedom of thought and of the press are usually attacked by arguments which are not worth bothering about. Anyone who has experience of lecturing and debating knows them off backwards. Here I am not trying to deal with the familiar claim that freedom is an illusion, or with the claim that there is more freedom in totalitarian countries than in democratic ones, but with the much more tenable and dangerous proposition that freedom is undesirable and that intellectual honesty is a form of anti-social selfishness.

Although other aspects of the question are usually in the foreground, the controversy over freedom of speech and of the press is at bottom a controversy of the desirability, or otherwise, of telling lies. What is really at issue is the right to report contemporary events truthfully, or as truthfully as is consistent with the ignorance, bias and self-deception from which every observer necessarily suffers. In saying this I may seem to be saying that straightforward "reportage" is the only branch of literature that matters: but I will try to show later that at every literary level, and probably in every one of the arts, the same issue arises in more or less subtilized forms. Meanwhile, it is necessary to strip away the irrelevancies in which this controversy is usually wrapped up.

The enemies of intellectual liberty always try to present their case as a plea for discipline versus individualism. The issue truth-versus-untruth is as far as possible kept in the background. Although the point of emphasis may vary, the writer who refuses to sell his opinions is always branded as a mere egoist. He is accused, that is, of either wanting to shut himself up in an ivory tower, or of making an exhibitionist display of his own personality, or of resisting the inevitable current of history in an attempt to cling to unjustified privilege. The Catholic and the Communist are alike in assuming that an opponent cannot be both honest and intelligent. Each of them tacitly claims that "the truth" has already been revealed, and that the heretic, if he is not simply a fool, is secretly aware of "the truth" and merely resists it out of selfish motives. In Communist literature the attack on intellectual liberty is usually masked by oratory about "petty-bourgeois individualism," "the illusions of nineteenth-century liberalism," etc., and backed up by words of abuse such as "romantic" and "sentimental," which, since they do not have any agreed meaning, are difficult to answer.

In this way the controversy is maneuvered away from its real issue. One can accept, and most enlightened people would accept, the Communist thesis that pure freedom will only exist in a classless society, and that one is most nearly free when one is working to bring such a society about. But slipped in with this is the quite unfounded claim that the Communist Party is itself aiming at the establishment of the classless society, and that in the U.S.S.R. this aim is actually on the way to being realized. If the first claim is allowed to entail the second, there is almost no assault on common sense and common decency that cannot be justified. But meanwhile, the real point has been dodged. Freedom of the intellect means the freedom to report what one has seen, heard, and felt, and not to be obliged to fabricate imaginary facts and feelings. The familiar tirades against "escapism" and "individualism," "romanticism," and so forth, are merely a forensic device, the aim of which is to make the perversion of history seem respectable. Fifteen years ago, when one defended the freedom of the intellect, one had to defend it against Conservatives, against Catholics, and to some extent--for they were not of great importance in England--against Fascists.

Today one has to defend it against Communists and "fellow-travelers." One ought not to exaggerate the direct influence of the small English Communist Party, but there can be no question about the poisonous effect of the Russian mythos on English intellectual life. Because of it known facts are suppressed and distorted to such an extent as to make it doubtful whether a true history of our times can ever be written. Let me give just one instance out of the hundreds that could be cited. When Germany collapsed, it was found that very large numbers of Soviet Russians--mostly, no doubt, from non-political motives--had changed sides and were fighting for the Germans. Also, a small but not negligible portion of the Russian prisoners and displaced persons refused to go back to the U.S.S.R., and some of them, at least, were repatriated against their will.

These facts, known to many journalists on the spot, went almost unmentioned in the British press, while at the same time Russophile publicists in England continued to justify the purges and deportations of 1936-38 by claiming that the U.S.S.R. "had no quislings." The fog of lies and misinformation that surrounds such subjects as the Ukraine famine, the Spanish civil war, Russian policy in Poland, and so forth, is not due entirely to conscious dishonesty, but any writer or journalist who is fully sympathetic for the U.S.S.R.--sympathetic, that is, in the way the Russians themselves would want him to be--does have to acquiesce in deliberate falsification on important issues. I have before me what must be a very rare pamphlet, written by Maxim Litvinoff in 1918 and outlining the recent events in the Russian Revolution. It makes no mention of Stalin, but gives high praise to Trotsky, and also to Zinoviev, Kamenev, and others.

What could be the attitude of even the most intellectually scrupulous Communist towards such a pamphlet? At best, the obscurantist attitude of saying that it is an undesirable document and better suppressed. And if for some reason it were decided to issue a garbled version of the pamphlet, denigrating Trotsky and inserting references to Stalin, no Communist who remained faithful to his party could protest. Forgeries almost as gross as this have been committed in recent years. But the significant thing is not that they happen, but that, even when they are known about, they provoke no reaction from the left-wing intelligentsia as a whole. The argument that to tell the truth would be "inopportune" or would "play into the hands of" somebody or other is felt to be unanswerable, and few people are bothered by the prospect of the lies which they condone getting out of the newspapers and into the history books.

The organized lying practiced by totalitarian states is not, as is sometimes claimed, a temporary expedient of the same nature as military deception. It is something integral to totalitarianism, something that would still continue even if concentration camps and secret police forces had ceased to be necessary. Among intelligent Communists there is an underground legend to the effect that although the Russian government is obliged now to deal in lying propaganda, frame-up trials, and so forth, it is secretly recording the true facts and will publish them at some future time. We can, I believe, be quite certain that this is not the case, because the mentality implied by such an action is that of a liberal historian who believes that the past cannot be altered and that a correct knowledge of history is valuable as a matter of course. From the totalitarian point of view history is something to be created rather than learned. A totalitarian state is in effect a theocracy, and its ruling caste, in order to keep its position, has to be thought of as infallible.

But since, in practice, no one is infallible, it is frequently necessary to rearrange past events in order to show that this or that mistake was not made, or that this or that imaginary triumph actually happened. Then again, every major change in policy demands a corresponding change of doctrine and a revelation of prominent historical figures. This kind of thing happens everywhere, but is clearly likelier to lead to outright falsification in societies where only one opinion is permissible at any given moment. Totalitarianism demands, in fact, the continuous alteration of the past, and in the long run probably demands a disbelief in the very existence of objective truth. The friends of totalitarianism in this country usually tend to argue that since absolute truth is not attainable, a big lie is no worse than a little lie. It is pointed out that all historical records are biased and inaccurate, or on the other hand, that modern physics has proven that what seems to us the real world is an illusion, so that to believe in the evidence of one's senses is simply vulgar philistinism. A totalitarian society which succeeded in perpetuating itself would probably set up a schizophrenic system of thought, in which the laws of common sense held good in everyday life and in certain exact sciences, but could be disregarded by the politician, the historian, and the sociologist. Already there are countless people who would think it scandalous to falsify a scientific textbook, but would see nothing wrong in falsifying an historical fact. It is at the point where literature and politics cross that totalitarianism exerts its greatest pressure on the intellectual. The exact sciences are not, at this date, menaced to anything like the same extent. This partly accounts for the fact that in all countries it is easier for the scientists than for the writers to line up behind their respective governments.

To keep the matter in perspective, let me repeat what I said at the beginning of this essay: that in England the immediate enemies of truthfulness, and hence of freedom of thought, are the press lords, the film magnates, and the bureaucrats, but that on a long view the weakening of the desire for liberty among the intellectuals themselves is the most serious symptom of all. It may seem that all this time I have been talking about the effects of censorship, not on literature as a whole, but merely on one department of political journalism. Granted that Soviet Russia constitutes a sort of forbidden area in the British press, granted that issues like Poland, the Spanish civil war, the Russo-German pact, and so forth, are debarred from serious discussion, and that if you possess information that conflicts with the prevailing orthodoxy you are expected to either distort it or keep quiet about it--granted all this, why should literature in the wider sense be affected? Is every writer a politician, and is every book necessarily a work of straightforward "reportage"?

Even under the tightest dictatorship, cannot the individual writer remain free inside his own mind and distill or disguise his unorthodox ideas in such a way that the authorities will be too stupid to recognize them? And in any case, if the writer himself is in agreement with the prevailing orthodoxy, why should it have a cramping effect on him? Is not literature, or any of the arts, likeliest to flourish in societies in which there are no major conflicts of opinion and no sharp distinction between the artist and his audience? Does one have to assume that every writer is a rebel, or even that a writer as such is an exceptional person?

Whenever one attempts to defend intellectual liberty against the claims of totalitarianism, one meets with these arguments in one form or another. They are based on a complete misunderstanding of what literature is, and how--one should perhaps say why--it comes into being. They assume that a writer is either a mere entertainer or else a venal hack who can switch from one line of propaganda to another as easily as an organ grinder changing tunes. But after all, how is it that books ever come to be written? Above a quite low level, literature is an attempt to influence the viewpoint of one's contemporaries by recording experience. And so far as freedom of expression is concerned, there is not much difference between a mere journalist and the most "unpolitical" imaginative writer. The journalist is unfree, and is conscious of unfreedom, when he is forced to write lies or suppress what seems to him important news; the imaginative writer is unfree when he has to falsify his subjective feelings, which from his point of view are facts. He may distort and caricature reality in order to make his meaning clearer, but he cannot misrepresent the scenery of his own mind; he cannot say with any conviction that he likes what he dislikes, or believes what he disbelieves. If he is forced to do so, the only result is that his creative faculties will dry up.

Nor can he solve the problem by keeping away from controversial topics. There is no such thing as a genuinely non-political literature, and least of all in an age like our own, when fears, hatreds, and loyalties of a directly political kind are near to the surface of everyone's consciousness. Even a single taboo can have an all-round crippling effect upon the mind, because there is always the danger that any thought which is freely followed up may lead to the forbidden thought. It follows that the atmosphere of totalitarianism is deadly to any kind of prose writer, though a poet, at any rate a lyric poet, might possibly find it breathable. And in any totalitarian society that survives for more than a couple of generations, it is probable that prose literature, of the kind that has existed during the past four hundred years, must actually come to an end.

Literature has sometimes flourished under despotic regimes, but, as has often been pointed out, the despotisms of the past were not totalitarian. Their repressive apparatus was always inefficient, their ruling classes were usually either corrupt or apathetic or half-liberal in outlook, and the prevailing religious doctrines usually worked against perfectionism and the notion of human infallibility. Even so it is broadly true that prose literature has reached its highest levels in periods of democracy and free speculation. What is new in totalitarianism is that its doctrines are not only unchallengeable but also unstable. They have to be accepted on pain of damnation, but on the other hand, they are always liable to be altered on a moment's notice. Consider, for example, the various attitudes, completely incompatible with one another, which an English Communist or "fellow-traveller" has had to adopt toward the war between Britain and Germany. For years before September, 1939, he was expected to be in a continuous stew about "the horrors of Nazism" and to twist everything he wrote into a denunciation of Hitler: after September, 1939, for twenty months, he had to believe that Germany was more sinned against than sinning, and the word "Nazi," at least as far as print went, had to drop right out of his vocabulary. Immediately after hearing the 8 o'clock news bulletin on the morning of June 22, 1941, he had to start believing once again that Nazism was the most hideous evil the world had ever seen.

Now, it is easy for the politician to make such changes: for a writer the case is somewhat different. If he is to switch his allegiance at exactly the right moment, he must either tell lies about his subjective feelings, or else suppress them altogether. In either case he has destroyed his dynamo. Not only will ideas refuse to come to him, but the very words he uses will seem to stiffen under his touch. Political writing in our time consists almost entirely of prefabricated phrases bolted together like the pieces of a child's Meccano set. It is the unavoidable result of self-censorship. To write in plain, vigorous language one has to think fearlessly, and if one thinks fearlessly one cannot be politically orthodox. It might be otherwise in an "age of faith," when the prevailing orthodoxy has long been established and is not taken too seriously. In that case it would be possible, or might be possible, for large areas of one's mind to remain unaffected by what one officially believed. Even so, it is worth noticing that prose literature almost disappeared during the only age of faith that Europe has ever enjoyed. Throughout the whole of the Middle Ages there was almost no imaginative prose literature and very little in the way of historical writing; and the intellectual leaders of society expressed their most serious thoughts in a dead language which barley altered during a thousand years.

Totalitarianism, however, does not so much promise an age of faith as an age of schizophrenia. A society becomes totalitarian when its structure becomes flagrantly artificial: that is, when its ruling class has lost its function but succeeds in clinging to power by force or fraud. Such a society, no matter how long it persists, can never afford to become either tolerant or intellectually stable. It can never permit either the truthful recording of facts or the emotional sincerity that literary creation demands. But to be corrupted by totalitarianism one does not have to live in a totalitarian country. The mere prevalence of certain ideas can spread a kind of poison that makes one subject after another impossible for literary purposes. Wherever there is an enforced orthodoxy--or even two orthodoxies, as often happens--good writing stops. This was well illustrated by the Spanish civil war. To many English intellectuals the war was a deeply moving experience, but not an experience about which they could write sincerely. There were only two things that you were allowed to say, and both of them were palpable lies: as a result, the war produced acres of print but almost nothing worth reading.

It is not certain whether the effects of totalitarianism upon verse need be so deadly as its effects on prose. There is a whole series of converging reasons why it is somewhat easier for a poet than a prose writer to feel at home in an authoritarian society. To begin with, bureaucrats and other "practical" men usually despise the poet too deeply to be much interested in what he is saying. Secondly, what the poet is saying--that is, what his poem "means" if translated into prose--is relatively unimportant, even to himself. The thought contained in a poem is always simple, and is no more the primary purpose of the poem than the anecdote is the primary purpose of the picture. A poem is an arrangement of sounds and associations, as a painting is an arrangement of brushmarks.

For short snatches, indeed, as in the refrain of a song, poetry can even dispense with meaning altogether. It is therefore fairly easy for a poet to keep away from dangerous subjects and avoid uttering heresies; and even when he does utter them, they may escape notice. But above all, good verse, unlike good prose, is not necessarily and individual product. Certain kinds of poems, such as ballads, or, on the other hand, very artificial verse forms, can be composed co-operatively by groups of people. Whether the ancient English and Scottish ballads were originally produced by individuals, or by the people at large, is disputed; but at any rate they are non-individual in the sense that they constantly change in passing from mouth to mouth. Even in print no two versions of a ballad are ever quite the same. Many primitive peoples compose verse communally. Someone begins to improvise, probably accompanying himself on a musical instrument, somebody else chips in with a line or a rhyme when the first singer breaks down, and so the process continues until there exists a whole song or ballad which has no identifiable author.

In prose, this kind of intimate collaboration is quite impossible. Serious prose, in any case, has to be composed in solitude, whereas the excitement of being part of a group is actually an aid to certain kinds of versification. Verse--and perhaps good verse of its own kind, though it would not be the highest kind--might survive under even the most inquisitorial regime. Even in a society where liberty and individuality had been extinguished, there would still be a need either for patriotic songs and heroic ballads celebrating victories, or for elaborate exercises in flattery; and these are the kinds of poems that can be written to order, or composed communally, without necessarily lacking artistic value. Prose is a different matter, since the prose writer cannot narrow the range of his thoughts without killing his inventiveness. But the history of totalitarian societies, or of groups of people who have adopted the totalitarian outlook, suggests that loss of liberty is inimical to all forms of literature.

German literature almost disappeared during the Hitler regime, and the case was not much better in Italy. Russian literature, so far as one can judge by translations, has deteriorated markedly since the early days of the revolution, though some of the verse appears to be better than the prose. Few if any Russian novels that it is possible to take seriously have been translated for about fifteen years. In western Europe and America large sections of the literary intelligentsia have either passed through the Communist Party or have been warmly sympathetic to it, but this whole leftward movement has produced extraordinarily few books worth reading. Orthodox Catholicism, again, seems to have a crushing effect upon certain literary forms, especially the novel. During a period of three hundred years, how many people have been at once good novelists and good Catholics?

The fact is that certain themes cannot be celebrated in words, and tyranny is one of them. No one ever wrote a good book in praise of the Inquisition. Poetry might survive in a totalitarian age, and certain arts or half-arts, such as architecture, might even find tyranny beneficial, but the prose writer would have no choice between silence or death. Prose literature as we know it is the product of rationalism, of the Protestant centuries, of the autonomous individual. And the destruction of intellectual liberty cripples the journalist, the sociological writer, the historian, the novelist, the critic, and the poet, in that order. In the future it is possible that a new kind of literature, not involving individual feeling or truthful observation, may arise, but no such thing is at present imaginable. It seems much likelier that if the liberal culture that we have lived in since the Renaissance comes to an end, the literary art will perish with it.

Of course, print will continue to be used, and it is interesting to speculate what kinds of reading matter would survive in a rigidly totalitarian society. Newspapers will presumably continue until television technique reaches a higher level, but apart from newspapers it is doubtful even now whether the great mass of people in the industrialized countries feel the need for any kind of literature. They are unwilling, at any rate, to spend anywhere near as much on reading matter as they spend on several other recreations. Probably novels and stories will be completely superseded by film and radio productions. Or perhaps some kind of low grade sensational fiction will survive, produced by a sort of conveyor-belt process that reduces human initiative to the minimum.

It would probably not be beyond human ingenuity to write books by machinery. But a sort of mechanizing process can already be seen at work in the film and radio, in publicity and propaganda, and in the lower reaches of journalism. The Disney films, for instance, are produced by what is essentially a factory process, the work being done partly mechanically and partly by teams of artists who have to subordinate their individual style. Radio features are commonly written by tired hacks to whom the subject and the manner of treatment are dictated beforehand: even so, what they write is merely a kind of raw material to be chopped into shape by producers and censors. So also with the innumerable books and pamphlets commissioned by government departments. Even more machine-like is the production of short stories, serials, and poems for the very cheap magazines.

Papers such as the Writer abound with advertisements of literary schools, all of them offering you ready-made plots at a few shillings a time. Some, together with the plot, supply the opening and closing sentences of each chapter. Others furnish you with a sort of algebraical formula by the use of which you can construct plots for yourself. Others have packs of cards marked with characters and situations, which have only to be shuffled and dealt in order to produce ingenious stories automatically. It is probably in some such way that the literature of a totalitarian society would be produced, if literature were still felt to be necessary. Imagination--even consciousness, so far as possible--would be eliminated from the process of writing. Books would be planned in their broad lines by bureaucrats, and would pass through so many hands that when finished they would be no more an individual product than a Ford car at the end of the assembly line. It goes without saying that anything so produced would be rubbish; but anything that was not rubbish would endanger the structure of the state. As for the surviving literature of the past, it would have to be suppressed or at least elaborately rewritten.

Meanwhile, totalitarianism has not fully triumphed anywhere. Our own society is still, broadly speaking, liberal. To exercise your right of free speech you have to fight against economic pressure and against strong sections of public opinion, but not, as yet, against a secret police force. You can say or print almost anything so long as you are willing to do it in a hole-and-corner way. But what is sinister, as I said at the beginning of this essay, is that the conscious enemies of liberty are those to whom liberty ought to mean most. The big public do not care about the matter one way or the other. They are not in favour of persecuting the heretic, and they will not exert themselves to defend him. They are at once too sane and too stupid to acquire the totalitarian outlook. The direct, conscious attack on intellectual decency comes from the intellectuals themselves.

It is possible that the Russophile intelligentsia, if they had not succumbed to that particular myth, would have succumbed to another of much the same kind. But at any rate the Russian myth is there, and the corruption it causes stinks. When one sees highly educated men looking on indifferently at oppression and persecution, one wonders which to despise more, their cynicism or their shortsightedness. Many scientists, for example, are the uncritical admirers of the U.S.S.R. They appear to think that the destruction of liberty is of no importance so long as their own line of work is for the moment unaffected. The U.S.S.R. is a large, rapidly developing country which has an acute need of scientific workers and, consequently, treats them generously.

Provided that they steer clear of dangerous subjects such as psychology, scientists are privileged persons. Writers, on the other hand, are viciously persecuted. It is true that literary prostitutes like Ilya Ehrenburg or Alexei Tolstoy are paid huge sums of money, but the only thing which is of any value to the writer as such--his freedom of expression--is taken away from him. Some, at least, of the English scientists who speak so enthusiastically of the opportunities to be enjoyed by scientists in Russia are capable of understanding this. But their reflection appears to be: "Writers are persecuted in Russia. So what? I am not a writer." They do not see that any attack on intellectual liberty, and on the concept of objective truth, threatens in the long run every department of thought.

For the moment the totalitarian state tolerates the scientist because it needs him. Even in Nazi Germany, scientists, other than Jews, were relatively well treated and the German scientific community, as a whole, offered no resistance to Hitler. At this stage of history, even the most autocratic ruler is forced to take account of physical reality, partly because of the lingering-on of liberal habits of thought, partly because of the need to prepare for war. So long as physical reality cannot altogether be ignored, so long as two and two have to make four when you are, for example, drawing the blueprint of an aeroplane, the scientist has his function, and can even be allowed a measure of liberty. His awakening will come later, when the totalitarian state is firmly established. Meanwhile, if he wants to safeguard the integrity of science, it is his job to develop some kind of solidarity with his literary colleagues and not disregard it as a matter of indifference when writers are silenced or driven to suicide, and newspapers systematically falsified.

But however it may be with the physical sciences, or with

music, painting and architecture, it is--as I have tried to show--certain that literature is doomed if liberty of thought perishes. Not only is it doomed in any country which retains a totalitarian structure; but any writer who adopts the totalitarian outlook, who finds excuses for persecution and the falsification of reality, thereby destroys himself as a writer. There is no way out of this. No tirades against "individualism" and the "ivory tower," no pious platitudes to the effect that "true individuality is only attained through identification with the community," can get over the fact that a bought mind is a spoiled mind. Unless spontaneity enters at some point or another, literary creation is impossible, and language itself becomes something totally different from what it is now, we may learn to separate literary creation from intellectual honesty. At present we know only that the imagination, like certain wild animals, will not breed in captivity. Any writer or journalist who denies that fact--and nearly all the current praise of the Soviet Union contains or implies such a denial--is, in effect, demanding his own destruction.

Why I Write (1947)

From a very early age, perhaps the age of five or six, I knew that when I grew up I should be a writer. Between the ages of about seventeen and twenty-four I tried to abandon this idea, but I did so with the consciousness that I was outraging my true nature and that sooner or later I should have to settle down and write books.

I was the middle child of three, but there was a gap of five years on either side, and I barely saw my father before I was eight. For this and other reasons I was somewhat lonely, and I soon developed disagreeable mannerisms which made me unpopular throughout my schooldays. I had the lonely child's habit of making up stories and holding conversations with imaginary persons, and I think from the very start my literary ambitions were mixed up with the feeling of being isolated and undervalued. I knew that I had a facility with words and a power of facing unpleasant facts, and I felt that this created a sort of private world in which I could get my own back for my failure in everyday life. Nevertheless the volume of serious--i.e. seriously intended--writing which I produced all through my childhood and boyhood would not amount to half a dozen pages. I wrote my first poem at the age of four or five, my mother taking it down to dictation. I cannot remember anything about it except that it was about a tiger and the tiger had "chair-like teeth"--a good enough phrase, but I fancy the poem was a plagiarism of Blake's "Tiger, Tiger." At eleven, when the war or 1914-18 broke out, I wrote a patriotic poem which was printed in the local newspaper, as was another, two years later, on the death of Kitchener. From time to time, when I was a bit older, I wrote bad and usually unfinished "nature poems" in the Georgian style. I also attempted a short story which was a ghastly failure. That was the total of the would-be serious work that I actually set down on paper during all those years.

However, throughout this time I did in a sense engage in literary activities. To begin with there was the made-to-order stuff which I produced quickly, easily and without much pleasure to myself. Apart from school work, I wrote vers d'occasion, semi-comic poems which I could turn out at what now seems to me astonishing speed--at fourteen I wrote a whole rhyming play, in imitation of Aristophanes, in about a week--and helped to edit a school magazines, both printed and in manuscript. These magazines were the most pitiful burlesque stuff that you could imagine, and I took far less trouble with them than I now would with the cheapest journalism.

But side by side with all this, for fifteen years or more, I was carrying out a literary exercise of a quite different kind: this was the making up of a continuous "story" about myself, a sort of diary existing only in the mind. I believe this is a common habit of children and adolescents. As a very small child I used to imagine that I was, say, Robin Hood, and picture myself as the hero of thrilling adventures, but quite soon my "story" ceased to be narcissistic in a crude way and became more and more a mere description of what I was doing and the things I saw. For minutes at a time this kind of thing would be running through my head: "He pushed the door open and entered the room. A yellow beam of sunlight, filtering through the muslin curtains, slanted on to the table, where a match-box, half-open, lay beside the inkpot. With his right hand in his pocket he moved across to the window. Down in the street a tortoiseshell cat was chasing a dead leaf," etc. etc. This habit continued until I was about twenty-five, right through my non-literary years. Although I had to search, and did search, for the right words, I seemed to be making this descriptive effort almost against my will, under a kind of compulsion from outside. The "story" must, I suppose, have reflected the styles of the various writers I admired at different ages, but so far as I remember it always had the same meticulous descriptive quality. When I was about sixteen I suddenly discovered the joy of mere words, i.e. the sounds and associations of words. The lines from Paradise Lost--

So hee with difficulty and labour hard
Moved on: with difficulty and labour hee.

Which do not now seem to me so very wonderful, sent shivers down my backbone; and the spelling "hee" for "he" was an added pleasure. As for the need to describe things, I knew all about it already. So it is clear what kind of books I wanted to write, in so far as I could be said to want to write books at that time. I wanted to write enormous naturalistic novels with unhappy endings, full of detailed descriptions and arresting similes, and also full of purple passages in which words were used partly for the sake of their own sound. And in fact my first completed novel, Burmese Days, which I wrote when I was thirty but projected much earlier, is rather that kind of book. I give all this background information because I do not think one can assess a writer's motives without knowing something of his early development.

His subject matter will be determined by the age he lives in--at least this is true in tumultuous, revolutionary ages like our own--but before he ever begins to write he will have acquired an emotional attitude from which he will never completely escape. It is his job, no doubt, to discipline his temperament and avoid getting stuck at some immature stage, in some perverse mood; but if he escapes from his early influences altogether, he will have killed his impulse to write. Putting aside the need to earn a living, I think there are four great motives for writing, at any rate for writing prose. They exist in different degrees in every writer, and in any one writer the proportions will vary from time to time, according to the atmosphere in which he is living. They are:

Sheer egoism. Desire to seem clever, to be talked about, to be remembered after death, to get your own back on the grown-ups who snubbed you in childhood, etc., etc. It is humbug to pretend this is not a motive, and a strong one. Writers share this characteristic with scientists, artists, politicians, lawyers, soldiers, successful businessmen--in short, with the whole top crust of humanity. The great mass of human beings are not acutely selfish. After the age of about thirty they almost abandon the sense of being individuals at all--and live chiefly for others, or are simply smothered under drudgery. But there is also the minority of gifted, willful people who are determined to live their own lives to the end, and writers belong in this class. Serious writers, I should say, are on the whole more vain and self-centered than journalists, though less interested in money.

Aesthetic enthusiasm. Perception of beauty in the external world, or, on the other hand, in words and their right arrangement. Pleasure in the impact of one sound on another, in the firmness of good prose or the rhythm of a good story. Desire to share an experience which one feels is valuable and ought not to be missed. The aesthetic motive is very feeble in a lot of writers, but even a pamphleteer or writer of textbooks will have pet words and phrases which appeal to him for non-utilitarian reasons; or he may feel strongly about typography, width of margins, etc. Above the level of a railway guide, no book is quite free from aesthetic considerations.

Historical impulse. Desire to see things as they are, to find out true facts and store them up for the use of posterity. Political purpose--using the word "political" in the widest possible sense. Desire to push the world in a certain direction, to alter other peoples' idea of the kind of society that they should strive after. Once again, no book is genuinely free from political bias. The opinion that art should have nothing to do with politics is itself a political attitude.

It can be seen how these various impulses must war against one another, and how they must fluctuate from person to person and from time to time. By nature--taking your "nature" to be the state you have attained when you are first adult--I am a person in whom the first three motives would outweigh the fourth. In a peaceful age I might have written ornate or merely descriptive books, and might have remained almost unaware of my political loyalties. As it is I have been forced into becoming a sort of pamphleteer. First I spent five years in an unsuitable profession (the Indian Imperial Police, in Burma), and then I underwent poverty and the sense of failure. This increased my natural hatred of authority and made me for the first time fully aware of the existence of the working classes, and the job in Burma had given me some understanding of the nature of imperialism: but these experiences were not enough to give me an accurate political orientation. Then came Hitler, the Spanish Civil War, etc. By the end of 1935 I had still failed to reach a firm decision. I remember a little poem that I wrote at that date, expressing my dilemma:

A happy vicar I might have been
Two hundred years ago
To preach upon eternal doom
And watch my walnuts grow;
But born, alas, in an evil time,
I missed that pleasant haven,
For the hair has grown on my upper lip
And the clergy are all clean-shaven.
And later still the times were good,
We were so easy to please,
We rocked our troubled thoughts to sleep
On the bosoms of the trees.
All ignorant we dared to own
The joys we now dissemble;
The greenfinch on the apple bough

Could make my enemies tremble.
But girl's bellies and apricots,
Roach in a shaded stream,
Horses, ducks in flight at dawn,
All these are a dream.
It is forbidden to dream again;
We maim our joys or hide them:
Horses are made of chromium steel
And little fat men shall ride them.
I am the worm who never turned,
The eunuch without a harem;
Between the priest and the commissar
I walk like Eugene Aram;
And the commissar is telling my fortune
While the radio plays,
But the priest has promised an Austin Seven,
For Duggie always pays.
I dreamt I dwelt in marble halls,
And woke to find it true;
I wasn't born for an age like this;
Was Smith? Was Jones? Were you?

The Spanish war and other events in 1936-37 turned the scale and thereafter I knew where I stood. Every line of serious work that I have written since 1936 has been written, directly or indirectly, against totalitarianism and for democratic socialism, as I understand it. It seems to me nonsense, in a period like our own, to think that one can avoid writing of such subjects. Everyone writes of them in one guise or another. It is simply a question of which side one takes and what approach one follows. And the more one is conscious of one's political bias, the more chance one has of acting politically without sacrificing one's aesthetic and intellectual integrity.

What I have most wanted to do throughout the past ten years is to make political writing into an art. My starting point is always a feeling of partisanship, a sense of injustice. When I sit down to write a book, I do not say to myself, "I am going to produce a work of art." I write it because there is some lie that I want to expose, some fact to which I want to draw attention, and my initial concern is to get a hearing. But I could not do the work of writing a book, or even a long magazine article, if it were not also an aesthetic experience. Anyone who cares to examine my work will see that even when it is downright propaganda it contains much that a full-time politician would consider irrelevant. I am not able, and do not want, completely to abandon the world view that I acquired in childhood. So long as I remain alive and well I shall continue to feel strongly about prose style, to love the surface of the earth, and to take a pleasure in solid objects and scraps of useless information. It is no use trying to suppress that side of myself. The job is to reconcile my ingrained likes and dislikes with the essentially public, non-individual activities that this age forces on all of us.

It is not easy. It raises problems of construction and of language, and it raises in a new way the problem of truthfulness. Let me give just one example of the cruder kind of difficulty that arises. My book about the Spanish civil war, Homage to Catalonia, is of course a frankly political book, but in the main it is written with a certain detachment and regard for form. I did try very hard in it to tell the whole truth without violating my literary instincts. But among other things it contains a long chapter, full of newspaper quotations and the like, defending the Trotskyists who were accused of plotting with Franco. Clearly such a chapter, which after a year or two would lose its interest for any ordinary reader, must ruin the book. A critic whom I respect read me a lecture about it. "Why did you put in all that stuff?" he said. "You've turned what might have been a good book into journalism." What he said was true, but I could not have done otherwise. I happened to know, what very few people in England had been allowed to know, that innocent men were being falsely accused. If I had not been angry about that I should never have written the book.

In one form or another this problem comes up again. The problem of language is subtler and would take too long to discuss. I will only say that of late years I have tried to write less picturesquely and more exactly. In any case I find that by the time you have perfected any style of writing, you have always outgrown it. Animal Farm was the first book in which I tried, with full consciousness of what I was doing, to fuse political purpose and artistic purpose into one whole. I have not written a novel for seven years, but I hope to write another fairly soon. It is bound to be a failure, every book is a failure, but I do know with some clarity what kind of book I want to write. Looking back through the last page or two, I see that I have made it appear as though my motives in writing were wholly public-spirited.

I don't want to leave that as the final impression. All writers are vain, selfish, and lazy, and at the very bottom of their motives there lies a mystery. Writing a book is a horrible, exhausting struggle, like a long bout of some painful illness. One would never undertake such a thing if one were not driven on by some demon whom one can neither resist nor understand. For all one knows that demon is simply the same instinct that makes a baby squall for attention. And yet it is also true that one can write nothing readable unless one constantly struggles to efface one's own personality. Good prose is like a windowpane. I cannot say with certainty which of my motives are the strongest, but I know which of them deserve to be followed. And looking back through my work, I see that it is invariably where I lacked a political purpose that I wrote lifeless books and was betrayed into purple passages, sentences without meaning, decorative adjectives and humbug generally.

Some Other Essays

The Reflection of George Orwell

By Crystal Epps
August 23, 2000

"On each landing, opposite the lift shaft, the poster with the enormous face gazed from the wall. It was one of those pictures which are so contrived that the eyes follow you about when you move. BIG BROTHER IS WATCHING YOU, the caption beneath it ran." (Orwell 4 "Nineteen").

George Orwell's Nineteen Eighty-Four presents a negative utopian picture, a society ruled by rigid totalitarianism. The government which Orwell creates in his novel is ruled by an entity known as Big Brother and consists of four branches. The Ministry of Truth, overseeing the distribution of propaganda and other printed materials, the Ministry of Peace, the Ministry of Plenty, handling economic affairs, and the Ministry of Love, the law enforcement division, make up the government. The main character, Winston Smith, does not completely accept the ideology that is fed to him by the government, through the concept of Big Brother. When one examines George Orwell's life, it can be clearly seen that he personifies his political perceptions, social and aesthetic characteristics, and self-examination of his own writing, through Winston Smith, in Nineteen Eighty-Four.

Orwell's political perceptions, especially his skepticism of mass media, are given life through Winston Smith. Spending time working for the British Broadcasting Company, Orwell experienced many distorted truths and propaganda. This led to an intense distrust of those in power and their influence on the information distributed to and recieved by the general public. Orwell explains how history is altered by whomever is in power. In Orwell's essay "Revising History" he examines the credibility of history and finds that it is based on the person or group in control. Orwell hated totalitarianism, primarily because of its attacks on unbiased truth and so saw it as the enemy. If a person or organization in power finds a fact damaging or out of sync with his cause, he can simply change it by the manner in which it is reported. Orwell states, "A certain degree of truthfulness was possible so long as it was admitted that a fact may be true even if you don't like it.". He is supporting his ideas with an obvious example familiar to most. World War II, Orwell points out, had two very distinct slants depending on whether you subscribe to the Nazi account or that of their enemies.

Another telling example he spoke of was the broadcasted outcome of the Spanish Civil War being decided by the winning power's preferences. Simply put, Orwell boldly claims that "History is written by the winners," (Orwell, "Revising" 1). So Orwell's own distrust is obvious in his creation of the Ministry of Truth. It is here where his main character, Winston, is employed forming propaganda and changing past facts to coincide with whatever lies Big Brother is feeding the general public. According to Woodcock, Orwell definitely based the Ministry of Truth and Winston's work on his experiences at the BBC. Winston's role in Big Brother's government was a projected charicteristic of Orwell's political opinions.

Furter exemplifying the attribution of Orwell's characteristics through Winston Smith, is the manifestation of Orwell's political views in Winston's own writings. Although Orwell wrote publicly, and Winston wrote in a private diary, they both passionately wrote for their own cause. Orwell was against totalitarianism and used Winston to reflect that when he wrote against the "evils of Igsoc". Igsoc is the doctirne by which the government of Oceania, under which Winston lived, was operated. In Nineteen Eighty-Four, Winston Smith writes in his diary: "For whom, it suddenly occurred to him to wonder was he writing this diary? For the future, for the unborn..." "For the first time the magnitude of what he had undertaken came home to him. How could you communicate with the future? It was of its nature impossible. Either the future would resemble the present in which case it would not listen to him, or it would be different from it, and his predicament would be meaningless". Although both Winston and Orwell recognize their objective is hopeless, they still cling to the hope that maybe through their words and descriptions, (as opposed to logical arguments) that they might, even for a moment alter another's thinking.

Orwell writes in his essay, "Why I Write" that "Every line of serious work that I have written since 1936 has been written directly or indirectly against totalitarianism and for democratic socialism, as I understand it". Serving as England's "moral conscience," he sought to boldly reveal the truth, even to those who denied its existence. Winston, much like Orwell, seemed to be sole possesor of any sort of a sense of morality as he struggled against immense odds to reveal the inequity and unjust nature of the government. Winston and Orwell both had overcome the problem of communication to others; in order to be understood, the person receiving the message must have similar a "world-view". Winston writes in his diary, "Until they become conscious they will never rebel, and until after they have rebelled they cannot become conscious" (Orwell, "Nineteen" 61) Winston, trying to overcome the oppression by Big Brother and Orwell is writing to those oppressed by Communism and cannot be reached by Western publications and are oblivious to his work.

He recognizes that one "Can only preach to the converted".Writing not to create some wonderful, entertaining work, instead, Orwell,s motive was to reveal lies, expose them to the public, and make his views known. In "Why I Write" Orwell explains one of his primary reasons for writing as a "political purpose", a desire to alter other's political direction, to change the world. Orwell sought to have a purpose in life, much like Winston. A monotonous lifestyle was not enough for Winston, who felt the need to somehow be influential. As a result he became obsessed with politics and his rebellion against totaitariansim. Everything Winston does has political motives, even sex. Orwell's political motives behind his writing, and his goal to expose the truth to the public was demonstrated repeatedly through Winston Smith's character.

Yet another example of a revelation of Orwell's character through Winstons is the similarly displayed attitudes towards authority figures and upper level government officials. According to Grigson, Nineteen Eighty-Four is not so much about a Utopia as it is "power and corruption at high levels". Woodcock explains that Orwell was, in his novel, expressing his concerns about men in power who would sacrifice everything for a mere crumb of power. O'Brien, an inner party member and Winston's boss, brags of the Party's "eternal power" much like Hitler boasted of the" millennial Reich", a leader viewed warily by Orwell. Winston is unsure of his relationship with O'Brien, whether he is freind or foe, and his opinions of him fluctuate throughout the book. However, despite his hate of dictators, Orwell felt a certain, unexplainable, sympathy for Hitler, much like Winston, who at the end of Nineteen Eighty-Four realizes that he loves Big Brother. Again, Orwell has created Winston to hold his own perceptions of governmental leaders, thus holding the image of Orwell's political beliefs.

In addition, Orwell displays his understanding of social economic classes through Winston. In Nineteen Eighty-Four, Winston often takes long walks among the Prole section, finding comfort in their masses. Visiting the Chestnut Tree Cafe, Winston takes advantage of the absence of a telescreen which is normally present everywhere, monitoring every move, to speak to an old man about the past. Winston loves the objects of the Proles, and when he finds a glass ornament with a piece of coral inside an antique shop, he buys it even though it is illegal to posess such objects. Renting a small apartment above the shop, he and Julia, his secret and illegal lover, go there often, as there is no telescreen. He enjoys just simply lounging, listening to the sounds of the lowest class. Like his main character, Orwell too found great comfort in the lower class. After serving 5 years in the Indian Imperial Police in Burma, Orwell realized that the oppression of the Burmese by the British was wrong and he could participate no more.

He left the comforts of middle class society in which one man places himself above another to live amongst the lowest classes of society. Orwell looked upon the lower class as "victims of injustice", and preferred them to his peers, the middle class, who ate unappreciatively off the plate that was prepared by the lower class. Both Orwell and Winston loved to move about the poverty stricken lower classes. Feeling empathy and compassion towards them, Winston and Orwell were inspired, as they placed their trust for the future in the working class. Winston Smith's identification and preference toward the lower class was a direct result of Orwell's own social nature as a part of his personality.

Furthermore, Orwell continued to project his individuality in Winston in some very basic and ordinary manners. Winston has a relatively decent job as an Outer Party member in the Ministry of Truth. However, due to rations resulting from ceaseless wars, Winston is accustomed to scrimping and making the most of whatever he could buy. This stems from Orwell's life as a writer where, during the writing of a book, he practiced frugality until income was received for a publishing. Winston, as an Outer Party member, is not part of the elite Inner Party but neither is he in the lowest class, known as the Proles. Orwell was also middle class. Orwell was said to lack close friends with whom he could discuss deep issues and share his problems. Winston also lacked someone with whom to share his deepest feelings. Although Winston had Julia, she did not care to discuss any kind of politics, instead their relationship was much more superficial. Both being unattractive, Orwell often complained of being ugly and had a lot of health problems, just like Winston who is described as being small and frail with a course face. Sharing Orwell's negative attitude, Winston describes much in the novel as "looking like vomit". Winston can be obviously seen as a direct personification of George Orwell.

Examining yet again his motives behind writing, Orwell used Winston Smith to explain a basic need he felt simply to record history. In Orwell's essay, "Why I Write", he describes writing as a "historical impulse--a desire to see things as they are, find out true facts and store them for use of posterity". In this passage from Nineteen Eighty-Four, Winston Smith is writing in a diary he bought: "For whom, it suddenly occurred to him to wonder was he writing this diary? For the future, for the unborn". Duda explains how, in this passage, Winston is trying to deal with his intellectual rebellion by writing his thoughts in a diary, which is illegal and makes death inevitable. He recognizes that it will probably not have an effect, only quicken his death, but he still clings to the notion that some day it might be found and used to prove the nature of his present state. Winston is writing simply to record a piece of history, that it might be used by the future, another example of Orwell's influence on Winston's character, specifically his motivation for writing.

Orwell expressed many of his fears and self-doubts as a writer through the character Winston Smith. In describing

Winston's writing, he is examining his own purposes in writing. For Orwell, writing is a means of bringing others to the thought. His basis of success is reliant on his effectiveness of reaching others. Orwell felt that his works without "political purpose" resulted in "lifeless books" and "sentences without meaning". Feeling lonely and unappreciated as a child, Orwell knew that he was skilled with words, and felt that it somehow made up for some of his other weaknesses and failures. However, he was still very critical of himself, saying in reference to a book he was preparing to write: 'It is bound to be a failure, every book is a failure". Smith's uncertainty of the worthwhileness of his writings is a direct reflection of Orwell's own wonderment of worth as a writer.

In the novel Nineteen Eighty-Four, Winston Smith is a direct personification of the author, George Orwell. This was seen through Orwell's political perceptions, such as his skepticism about mass media, his politically motivated writings, and his view of governmental figures. The characterization was also displayed in Orwell's attraction to a certain social, economic class, and his basic aesthetic similarities. Orwell's feelings about writing were also exhibited through Winston Smith; his fears of failure and his basic yearning to be remembered. Nineteen Eighty-Four will forever be remembered for its prophetic warnings of a totalitarian society in which individuality is stripped away. In a desperate attempt to pierce through invincible, omnipitant, omni-present Big Brother, Winston Smith fought to preserve his identity, an identity which was a true reflection of George Orwell.

Notes on Nationalism May, 1945

Somewhere or other Byron makes use of the French word longeur, and remarks in passing that though in England we happen not to have the word, we have the thing in considerable profusion. In the same way, there is a habit of mind which is now so widespread that it affects our thinking on nearly every subject, but which has not yet been given a name. As the nearest existing equivalent I have chosen the word "nationalism", but it will be seen in a moment that I am not using it in quite the ordinary sense, if only because the emotion I am speaking about does not always attach itself to what is called a nation--that is, a single race or a geographical area. It can attach itself to a church or a class, or it may work in a merely negative sense, against something or other and without the need for any positive object of loyalty.

By "nationalism" I mean first of all the habit of assuming that human beings can be classified like insects and that whole blocks of millions or tens of millions of people can be confidently labelled "good" or "bad." But secondly--and this is much more important--I mean the habit of identifying oneself with a single nation or other unit, placing it beyond good and evil and recognizing no other duty than that of advancing its interests. Nationalism is not to be confused with patriotism. Both words are normally used in so vague a way that any definition is liable to be challenged, but one must draw a distinction between them, since two different and even opposing ideas are involved. By "patriotism" I mean devotion to a particular place and a particular way of life, which one believes to be the best in the world but has no wish to force on other people. Patriotism is of its nature defensive, both militarily and culturally. Nationalism, on the other hand, is inseperable from the desire for power. The abiding purpose of every nationalist is to secure more power and more prestige, not for himself but for the nation or other unit in which he has chosen to sink his own individuality.

So long as it is applied merely to the more notorious and identifiable nationalist movements in Germany, Japan, and other countries, all this is obvious enough. Confronted with a phenomenon like Nazism, which we can observe from the outside, nearly all of us would say much the same things about it. But here I must repeat what I said above, that I am only using the word "nationalism" for lack of a better. Nationalism, in the extended sense in which I am using the word, includes such movments and tendencies as Communism, political Catholocism, Zionism, Antisemitism, Trotskyism and Pacifism. It does not necessarily mean loyalty to a government or a country, still less to one's own country, and it is not even strictly necessary that the units in which it deals should actually exist. To name a few obvious examples, Jewry, Islam, Christendom, the Proletariat and the White Race are all of them objects of passionate nationalistic feeling: but their existence can be seriously questioned, and there is no definition of any one of them that would be universally accepted.

It is also worth emphasizing once again that nationalist feeling can be purely negative. There are, for example, Trotskyists who have become simply enemies of the USSR without developing a corresponding loyalty to any other unit. When one grasps the implications of this, the nature of what I mean by nationalism becomes a good deal clearer. A nationalist is one who thinks solely, or mainly, in terms of competitive prestige. He may be a positive or a negative nationalist--that is, he may use his mental energy either in boosting or in denigrating--but at any rate his thoughts always turn on victories, defeats, triumphs and humiliations. He sees history, especially contemporary history, as the endless rise and decline of great power units, and every event that happens seems to him a demonstration that his own side is on the upgrade and some hated rival is on the downgrade. But finally, it is important not to confuse nationalism with mere worship of success. The nationalist does not go on the principle of simply ganging up with the strongest side. On the contrary, having picked his side, he persuades himself that it is the strongest, and is able to stick to his belief even when the facts are overwhelmingly against him. Nationalism is power-hunger tempered by self-deception. Every nationalist is capable of the most flagrant dishonesty, but he is also--since he is conscious of serving something bigger than himself--unshakeably certain of being in the right.

Now that I have given this lengthy definition, I think it will be admitted that the habit of mind I am talking about is widespread among the English intelligentsia, and more widespread there than among the mass of the people. For those who feel deeply about contemporary politics, certain topics have become so infected by considerations of prestige that a genuinely rational approach to them is almost impossible. Out of the hundreds of examples that one might choose, take this question: Which of the three great allies, the USSR, Britain and the USA, has contributed most to the defeat of Germany? In theory, it should be possible to give a reasoned and perhaps even a conclusive answer to this question. In practice, however, the necessary calculations cannot be made, because anyone likely to bother his head about such a question would inevitably see it in terms of competitive prestige.

He would therefore start by deciding in favour of Russia, Britain or America as the case might be, and only after this would begin searching for arguments that seemd to support his case. And there are whole strings of kindred questions to which you can only get an honest answer from someone who is indifferent to the whole subject involved, and whose opinion on it is probably worthless in any case. Hence, partly, the remarkable failure in our time of political and military prediction. It is curious to reflect that out of al the "experts" of all the schools, there was not a single one who was able to foresee so likely an event as the Russo-German Pact of 1939. And when news of the Pact broke, the most wildly divergent explanations were of it were given, and predictions were made which were falsified almost immediately, being based in nearly every case not on a study of probabilities but on a desire to make the USSR seem good or bad, strong or weak.

Political or military commentators, like astrologers, can survive almost any mistake, because their more devoted followers do not look to them for an appraisal of the facts but for the stimulation of nationalistic loyalties. And aesthetic judgements, especially literary judgements, are often corrupted in the same way as political ones. It would be difficult for an Indian Nationalist to enjoy reading Kipling or for a Conservative to see merit in Mayakovsky, and there is always a temptation to claim that any book whose tendency one disagrees with must be a bad book from a literary point of view. People of strongly nationalistic outlook often perform this sleight of hand without being conscious of dishonesty.

In England, if one simply considers the number of people involved, it is probable that the dominant form of nationalism is old-fashioned British jingoism. It is certain that this is still widespread, and much more so than most observers would have believed a dozen years ago. However, in this essay I am concerned chiefly with the reactions of the intelligentsia, among whom jingoism and even patriotism of the old kind are almost dead, though they now seem to be reviving among a minority. Among the intelligentsia, it hardly needs saying that the dominant form of nationalism is Communism--using this word in a very loose sense, to include not merely Communist Party members, but "fellow travellers" and russophiles generally. A Communist, for my purpose here, is one who looks upon the USSR as his Fatherland and feels it his duty t justify Russian policy and advance Russian interests at all costs. Obviously such people abound in England today, and their direct and indirect influence is very great. But many other forms of nationalism also flourish, and it is by noticing the points of resemblance between different and even seemingly opposed currents of thought that one can best get the matter into perspective.

Ten or twenty years ago, the form of nationalism most closely corresponding to Communism today was political Catholicism. Its most outstanding exponent--though he was perhaps an extreme case rather than a typical one--was G.K. Chesterton. Chesterton was a writer of considerable talent who whose to suppress both his sensibilities and his intellectual honesty in the cause of Roman Catholic propaganda. During the last twenty years or so of his life, his entire output was in reality an endless repetition of the same thing, under its laboured cleverness as simple and boring as "Great is Diana of the Ephesians."

Every book that he wrote, every scrap of dialogue, had to demonstrate beyond the possibility of mistake the superiority of the Catholic over the Protestan or the pagan. But Chesterton was not content to think of this superiority as merely intellectual or spiritual: it had to be translated into terms of national prestige and military power, which entailed an ignorant idealisation of the Latin countries, especially France. Chesterton had not lived long in France, and his picture of it-

--as a land of Catholic peasants incessantly singing the Marseillaise over glasses of red wine--had about as much relation to reality as Chu Chin Chow has to everyday life in Baghdad. And with this went not only an enormous overstimation of French military power (both before and after 1914-18 he maintained that France, by itself, was stronger than Germany), but a silly and vulgar glorification of the actual process of war. Chesterton's battle poems, such as "Lepanto" or "The Ballad of Saint Barbara", make "The Charge of the Light Brigade" read like a pacifist tract: they are perhaps the most tawdry bits of bombast to be found in our language.

The interesting thing is that had the romantic rubbish which he habitually wrote about France and the French army been written by somebody else about Britain and the British army, he would have been the first to jeer. In home politics he was a Little Englander, a true hater of jingoism and imperialism, and according to his lights a true friend of democracy. Yet when he looked outwards into the international field, he could forsake his principles without even noticing he was doing so. Thus, his almost mystical belief in the virtues of democracy did not prevent him from admiring Mussolini. Mussolini had destroyed the representative government and the freedom of the press for which Chesterton had struggled so hard at home, but Mussolini was an Italian and had made Italy strong, and that settled the matter. Nor did Chesterton ever find a word to say about imperialsm and the conquest of coloured races when they were practised by Italians or Frenchmen. His hold on reality, his literary taste, and even to some extent his moral sense, were dislocated as soon as his nationalistic loyalties were involved.

Obviously there are considerable resemblances between political Catholicism, as exemplified by Chesterton, and Communism. So there are between either of these and for instance Scottish nationalism, Zionism, Antisemitism or Trotskyism. It would be an oversimplification to say that all forms of nationalism are the same, even in their mental atmosphere, but there are certain rules that hold good in all cases. The following are the principal characteristics of nationalist thought: OBSESSION. As nearly as possible, no nationalist ever thinks, talks, or writes about anything except the superiority of his own power unit. It is difficult if not impossible for any nationalist to conceal his allegiance. The smallest slur upon his own unit, or any implied praise of a rival organization, fills him with uneasiness which he can relieve only by making some sharp retort.

If the chosen unit is an actual country, such as Ireland or India, he will generally claim superiority for it not only in military power and political virtue, but in art, literature, sport, structure of the language, the physical beauty of the inhabitants, and perhaps even in climate, scenery and cooking. He will show great sensitiveness about such things as the correct display of flags, relative size of headlines and the order in which different countries are named. Nomenclature plays a very important part in nationalist thought. Countries which have won their independence or gone through a nationalist revolution usually change their names, and any country or other unit round which strong feelings revolve is likely to have several names, each of them carrying a different implication. The two sides of the Spanish Civil War had between them nine or ten names expressing different degrees of love and hatred. Some of these names (e.g. "Patriots" for Franco-supporters, or "Loyalists" for Government-supporters) were frankly question-begging, and there was no single one of the which the two rival factions could have agreed to use.

INSTABILITY The intensity with which they are held does not prevent nationalist loyalties from being transferable. To begin with, as I have pointed out already, they can be and often are fastened up on some foreign country. One quite commonly finds that great national leaders, or the founders of nationalist movements, do not even belong to the country they have glorified. Sometimes they are outright foreigners, or more often they come from peripheral areas where nationality is doubtful. Examples are Stalin, Hitler, Napoleon, de Valera, Disraeli, Poincare, Beaverbrook. The Pan-German movement was in part the creation of an Englishman, Houston Chamberlain. For the past fifty or a hundred years, transferred nationalism has been a common phenomenon among literary intellectuals. With Lafcadio Hearne the transference was to Japan, with Carlyle and many others of his time to Germany, and in our own age it is usually to Russia. But the peculiarly interesting fact is that re-transference is also possible. A country or other unit which has been worshipped for years may suddenly become detestable, ans some other object of affection may take its place with almost no interval. In the first version of H.G. Wells's Outline of History, and others of his writings about that time, one finds the United States praised almost as extravagantly as Russia is praised by Communists today: yet within a few years this uncritical admiration had turned into hostility. The bgoted Communist who changes in a space of weeks, or even days, into an equally bigoted Trotskyist is a common spectacle. In continental Europe Fascist movements were largely recruited from among Communists, and the opposite process may well happen within the next few years. What remains constant in the nationalist is his state of mind: the object of his feelings is changeable, and may be imaginary.

But for an intellectual, transference has an important function which I have already mentioned shortly in connection with Chesterton. It makes it possible for him to be much more nationalistic--more vulgar, more silly, more malignant, more dishonest--that he could ever be on behalf of his native country, or any unit of which he had real knowledge. When one sees the slavish or boastful rubbish that is written about Stalin, the Red Army, etc. by fairly intelligent and sensitive people, one realizes that this is only possible because some kind of dislocation has taken place. In societies such as ours, it is unusual for anyone describable as an intellectual to feel a very deep attachment to his own country. Public opinion--that is, the section of public opinion of which he as an intellectual is aware--will not allow him to do so.

Most of the people surrounding him are sceptical and disaffected, and he may adopt the same attitude from imitativeness or sheer cowardice: in that case he will have abandoned the form of nationalism that lies nearest to hand without getting any closer to a genuinely internationalist outlook. He still feels the need for a Fatherland, and it is natural to look for one somewhere abroad. Having found it, he can wallow unrestrainedly in exactly those emotions from which he believes that he has emancipated himself. God, the King, the Empire, the Union Jack--all the overthrown idols can reappear under different names, and because they are not recognized for what they are they can be worshipped with a good conscience. Transferred nationalism, like the use of scapegoats, is a way of attaining salvation without altering one's conduct.

INDIFFERENCE TO REALITY. All nationalists have the power of not seeing resemblances between similar sets of facts. A British Tory will defend self-determination in Europe and oppose it in India with no feeling of inconsistency. Actions are held to be good or bad, not on their own merits, but according to who does them, and there is almost no kind of outrage--torture, the use of hostages, forced labour, mass deportations, imprisonment without trial, forgery, assassination, the bombing of civilians--which does not change its moral colour when it is committed by "our" side. The Liberal News Chronicle published, as an example of shocking barbarity, photographs of Russians hanged by the Germans, and then a year or two later published with warm approval almost exactly similar photographs of Germans hanged by the Russians. It is the same with historical events. History is thought of largely in nationalist terms, and such things as the Inquisition, the tortures of the Star Chamber, the exploits of the English buccaneers (Sir Francis Drake, for instance, who was given to sinking Spanish prisoners alive), the Reign of Terror, the heroes of the Mutiny blowing hundreds of Indians from the guns, or Cromwell's soldiers slashing Irishwomen's faces with razors, become morally neutral or even meritorious when it is felt that they were done in the "right" cause.

If one looks back over the past quarter of a century, one finds that there was hardly a single year when atrocity stories were not being reported from some part of the world; and yet in not one single case were these atrocities--in Spain, Russia, China, Hungary, Mexico, Amritsar, Smyrna--believed in and disapproved of by the English intelligentsia as a whole. Whether such deeds were reprehensible, or even whether they happened, was always decided according to political predilection. The nationalist not only does not disapprove of atrocities committed by his own side, but he has a remarkable capacity for not even hearing about them.

For quite six years the English admirers of Hitler contrived not to learn of the existence of Dachau and Buchenwald. And those who are loudest in denouncing the German concentration camps are often quite unaware, or only very dimly aware, that there are also concentration camps in Russia. Huge events like the Ukraine famine of 1933, involving the deaths of millions of people, have actually escaped the attention of the majority of English russophiles. Many English people have heard almost nothing about the extermination of German and Polish Jews during the present war. Their own antisemitism has caused this vast crime to bounce off their consciousness. In nationalist thought there are facts which are both true and untrue, known and unknown. A known fact may be so unbearable that it is habitually pushed aside and not allowed to enter into logical processes, or on the other hand it may enter into every calculation and yet never be admitted as a fact, even in one's own mind.

Every nationalist is haunted by the belief that the past can be altered. He spends part of his time in a fantasy world in which things happen as they should--in which, for example, the Spanish Armada was a success or the Russian Revolution was crushed in 1918--and he will transfer fragments of this world to the history books whenever possible. Much of the propagandist writing of our time amounts to plain forgery. Material facts are suppressed, dates altered, quotations removed from their context and doctored so as to change their meaning. Events which it is felt ought not to have happened are left unmentioned and ultimately denied.

In 1927 Chiang Kai Shek boiled hundreds of Communists alive, and yet within ten years he had become one of the heroes of the Left. The re-alignment of world politics had brought him into the anti-Fascist camp, and so it was felt that the boiling of the Communists "didn't count", or perhaps had not happened. The primary aim of progaganda is, of course, to influence contemporary opinion, but those who rewrite history do probably believe with part of their minds that they are actually thrusting facts into the past. When one considers the elaborate forgeries that have been committed in order to show that Trotsky did not play a valuable part in the Russian civil war, it is difficult to feel that the people responsible are merely lying. More probably they feel that their own version was what happened in the sight of God, and that one is justified in rearranging the records accordingly.

Indifference to objective truth is encouraged by the sealing-off of one part of the world from another, which makes it harder and harder to discover what is actually happening. There can often be a genuine doubt about the most enormous events. For example, it is impossible to calculate within millions, perhaps even tens of millions, the number of deaths caused by the present war. The calamities that are constantly being reported--battles, massacres, famines, revolutions--tend to inspire in the average person a feeling of unreality. One has no way of verifying the facts, one is not even fully certain that they have happened, and one is always presented with totally different interpretations from different sources. What were the rights and wrongs of the Warsaw rising of August 1944? Is it true about the German gas ovens in Poland? Who was really to blame for the Bengal famine?

Probably the truth is discoverable, but the facts will be so dishonestly set forth in almost any newspaper that the ordinary reader can be forgiven either for swallowing lies or failing to form an opinion. The general uncertainty as to what is really happening makes it easier to cling to lunatic beliefs. Since nothing is ever quite proved or disproved, the most unmistakable fact can be impudently denied. Moreover, although endlessly brooding on power, victory, defeat, revenge, the nationalist is often somewhat uninterested in what happens in the real world. What he wants is to feel that his own unit is getting the better of some other unit, and he can more easily do this by scoring off an adversary than by examining the facts to see whether they support him. All nationalist controversy is at the debating-society level. It is always entirely inconclusive, since each contestant invariably believes himself to have won the victory. Some nationalists are not far from schizophrenia, living quite happily amid dreams of power and conquest which have no connection with the physical world.

I have examined as best as I can the mental habits which are common to all forms of nationalism. The next thing is to classify those forms, but obviously this cannot be done comprehensively. Nationalism is an enormous subject. The world is tormented by innumerable delusions and hatreds which cut across one another in an extremely complex way, and some of the most sinister of them have not yet impinged on the European consciousness. In this essay I am concerned with nationalism as it occurs among the English intelligentsia. In them, much more than in ordinary English people, it is unmixed with patriotism and therefore can be studied pure. Below are listed the varieties of nationalism now flourishing among English intellectuals, with such comments as seem to be needed. It is convenient to use three headings, Positive, Transferred, and Negative, though some varieties will fit into more than one category.

Positive Nationalism

- *NEO-TORYISM*: Exemplified by such people as Lord Elton, A.P. Herbert, G.M. Young, Professor Pickthorn, by the literature of the Tory Reform Committee, and by such magazines as the New English Review and the Nineteenth Century and After. The real motive force of neo-Toryism, giving it its nationalistic character and differentiating it from ordinary Conservatism, is the desire not to recognize that British power and influence have declined. Even those who are realistic enough to see that Britain's military position is not what it was, tend to claim that "English ideas" (usually left undefined) must dominate the world. All neo-Tories are anti-Russian, but sometimes the main emphasis is anti-American. The significant thing is that this school of thought seems to be gaining ground among youngish intellectuals, sometimes ex-Communists, who have passed throught the usual process of disillusionment and become disillusioned with that. The anglophobe who suddenly becomes violently pro-British is a fairly common figure. Writers who illustrate this tendency are F.A. Voigt, Malcolm Muggeridge, Evelyn Waugh, Hugh Kingsmill, and a psychologically similar development can be observed in T.S. Eliot, Wyndham Lewis, and various of their followers.

- *CELTIC NATIONALISM*: Welsh, Irish and Scottish nationalism have points of difference but are alike in their anti-English orientation. Members of all three movements have opposed the war while continuing to describe themselves as pro-Russian, and the lunatic fringe has even contrived to be simultaneously pro-Russian and pro-Nazi. But Celtic nationalism is not the same thing as anglophobia. Its motive force is a belief in the past and future greatness of the Celtic peoples, and it has a strong tinge of racialism. The Celt is supposed to be spiritually superior to the Saxon--simpler, more creative, less vulgar, less snobbish, etc.--but the usual power hunger is there under the surface. One symptom of it is the delusion that Eire, Scotland or even Wales could preserve its independence unaided and owes nothing to British protection. Among writers, good examples of this school of thought are Hugh MacDiarmid and Sean O'Casey. No modern Irish writer, even of the stature of Yeats or Joyce, is completely free from traces of nationalism
- *ZIONISM*: This has the unusual characteristics of a nationalist movement, but the American variant of it seems to be more violent and malignant than the British. I classify it under Direct and not Transferred nationalism because it flourishes almost exclusively among the Jews themselves. In England, for several

rather incongrous reasons, the intelligentsia are mostly pro-Jew on the Palestine issue, but they do not feel strongly about it. All English people of goodwill are also pro-Jew in the sense of disapproving of Nazi persecution. But any actual nationalistic loyalty, or belief in the innate superiority of Jews, is hardly to be foung among Gentiles.

TRANSFERRED NATIONALISM

- COMMUNISM
- POLITICAL CATHOLOCISM
- *COLOUR FEELING*: The old-style contemptuous attitude towards "natives" has been much weakened in England, and various pseudo-scientific theories emphasizing the superiority of the white race have been abandoned. Among the intelligentsia, colour feeling only occurs in the transposed form, that is, as a belief in the innate superiority of the coloured races. This is now increasingly common among English intellectuals, probably resulting more often from masochism and sexual frustration than from contact with the Oriental and Negro nationalist movements. Even among those who do not feel strongly on the colour question, snobbery and imitation have a powerful influence. Almost any English intellectual would be scandalized by the claim that the white races are superior to the coloured, whereas the opposite claim would seem to him unexceptionable even if he disagreed with it. Nationalistic attachment to the coloured races is usually mixed up with the belief that their sex lives are superior, and there is a large underground mythology about the sexual prowess of Negroes.
- *CLASS FEELING*: Among upper-class and middle-class intellectuals, only in the transposed form--i.e. as a belief in the superiority of the proletariat. Here again, inside the intelligentsia, the pressure of public opinion is overwhelming. Nationalistic loyalty towards the proletariat, and most vicious theoretical

hatred of the bourgeoise, can and often do co-exist with ordinary snobbishness in everyday life.

PACIFISM: The majority of pacifists either belong to obscure religious sects or are simply humanitarians who object to the taking of life and prefer not to follow their thoughts beyond that point. But there is a minority of intellectual pacifists whose real though unadmitted motive appears to be hatred of western democracy and admiration of totalitarianism. Pacifist propaganda usually boils down to saying that one side is as bad as the other, but if one looks closely at the writings of younger intellectual pacifists, one finds that they do not by any means express impartial disapproval but are directed almost entirely against Britain and the United States. Moreover they do not as a rule condemn violence as such, but only violence used in defence of western countries.

The Russians, unlike the British, are not blamed for defending themselves by warlike means, and indeed all pacifist propaganda of this type avoids mention of Russia or China. It is not claimed, again, that the Indians should abjure violence in their struggle against the British. Pacifist literature abounds with equivocal remarks which, if they mean anything, appear to mean that statesmen of the type of Hitler are preferable to those of the type of Churchill, and that violence is perhaps excusable if it is violent enough. After the fall of France, the French pacifists, faced by a real choice which their English colleagues have not had to make, mostly went over to the Nazis, and in England there appears to have been some small overlap of membership between the Peace Pledge Union and the Blackshirts. Pacifist writers have written in praise of Carlyle, one of the intellectual fathers of Fascism. All in all it is difficult not to feel that pacifism, as it appears among a section of the intelligentsia, is secretly inspired by an admiration for power and successful cruelty. The mistake was made of pinning this emotion to Hitler, but it could easily be retransfered.

NEGATIVE NATIONALISM

- *ANGLOPHOBIA*: Within the intelligentsia, a derisive and mildly hostile attitude towards Britain is more or less compulsory, but it is an unfaked emotion in many cases. During the war it was manifested in the defeatism of the intelligentsia, which persisted long after it had become clear that the Axis powers could not win. Many people were undisguisedly pleased when Singapore fell ore when the British were driven out of Greece, and there was a remarkable unwillingness to believe in good news, e.g. el Alamein, or the number of German planes shot down in the Battle of Britain. English left-wing intellectuals did not, of course, actually want the Germans or Japanese to win the war, but many of them could not help getting a certain kick out of seeing their own country humiliated, and wanted to feel that the final victory would be due to Russia, or perhaps America, and not to Britain. In foreign politics many intellectuals follow the principle that any faction backed by Britain must be in the wrong. As a result, "enlightened" opinion is quite largely a mirror-image of Conservative policy. Anglophobia is always liable to reversal, hence that fairly common spectacle, the pacifist of one war who is a bellicist in the next.
- *ANTISEMITISM:* There is little evidence about this at present, because the Nazi persecutions have made it necessary for any thinking person to side with the Jews against their oppressors. Anyone educated enough to have heard the word "antisemitism" claims as a matter of course to be free of it, and anti-Jewish remarks are carefully eliminated from all classes of literature. Actually antisemitism appears to be widespread, even among intellectuals, and the general conspiracy of silence probably helps exacerbate it. People of Left opinions are not immune

to it, and their attitude is sometimes affected by the fact that Trotskyists and Anarchists tend to be Jews. But antisemitism comes more naturally to people of Conservative tendency, who suspect Jews of weakening national morale and diluting the national culture. Neo-Tories and political Catholics are always liable to succumb to antisemitism, at least intermittently.

- *TROTSKYISM:* This word is used so loosely as to include Anarchists, democratic Socialists and even Liberals. I use it here to mean a doctrinaire Marxist whose main motive is hostility to the Stalin regime. Trotskyism can be better studied in obscure pamphlets or in papers like the Socialist Appeal than in the works of Trotsky himself, who was by no means a man of one idea. Although in some places, for instance in the United States, Trotskyism is able to attract a fairly large number of adherents and develop into an organized movement with a petty fuerher of its own, its inspiration is essentially negative. The Trotskyist is against Stalin just as the Communist is for him, and, like the majority of Communists, he wants not so much to alter the external world as to feel that the battle for prestige is going in his own favour. In each case there is the same obsessive fixation on a single subject, the same inability to form a genuinely rational opinion based on probabilities. The fact that Trotskyists are everywhere a persecuted minority, and that the accusation usually made against them, i.e. of collaborating with the Fascists, is obviously false, creates an impression that Trotskyism is intellectually and morally superior to Communism; but it is doubtful whether there is much difference. The most typical Trotskyists, in any case, are ex-Communists, and no one arrives at Trotskyism except via one of the left-wing movements. No Communist, unless tethered to his party by years of habit, is secure against a sudden lapse into Trotskyism. The opposite process does not seem to happen equally often, though there is no clear reason why it should not.

In the classification I have attempted above, it will seem that I have often exaggerated, oversimplified, made unwarranted assumptions and have left out of account the existence of ordinarily decent motives. This was inevitable, because in this essay I am trying to isolate and identify tendencies which exist in all our minds and pervert our thinking, without necessarily occurring in a pure state or operating continuously. It is important at this point to correct the over-simplified picture which I have been obliged to make. To begin with, one has no right to assume that everyone, or even every intellectual, is infected by nationalism. Secondly, nationalism can be intermittent and limited. An intelligent man may half-succumb to a belief which he knows to be absurd, and he may keep it out of his mind for long periods, only reverting to it in moments of anger or sentimentality, or when he is certain that no important issues are involved. Thirdly, a nationalistic creed may be adopted in good faith from non-nationalistic motives. Fourthly, several kinds of nationalism, even kinds that cancel out, can co-exist in the same person.

All the way through I have said, "the nationalist does this" or "the nationalist does that", using for purposes of illustration the extreme, barely sane type of nationalist who has no neutral areas in his mind and no interest in anything except the struggle for power. Actually such people are fairly common, but they are not worth the powder and shot. In real life Lord Elton, D.N. Pritt, Lady Houston, Ezra Pound, Lord Vanisttart, Father Coughlin and all the rest of their dreary tribe have to be fought against, but their intellectual deficiencies hardly need pointing out. Monomania is not interesting, and the fact that no nationalist of the more bigoted kind can write a book which still seems worth reading after a lapse of years has a certain deodorizing effect. But when one has admitted that nationalism has not triumphed everywhere, that there are still peoples whose judgements are not at the mercy of their desires, the fact does remain that the pressing problems--India, Poland,

Palestine, the Spanish civil war, the Moscow trials, the American Negroes, the Russo-German Pact or what have you--cannot be, or at least never are, discussed upon a reasonable level. The Eltons and Pritts and Coughlins, each of them simply an enormous mouth bellowing the same lie over and over again, are obviously extreme cases, but we deceive ourselves if we do not realise that we can all resemble them in unguarded moments. Let a certain note be struck, let this or that corn be trodden on--and it may be corn whose very existence has been unsuspected hitherto--and the most fair-minded and sweet-tempered person may suddenly be transformed into a vicious partisan, anxious only to "score" over his adversary and indifferent as to how many lies he tells or how many logical errors he commits in doing so.

When Lloyd George, who was an opponent of the Boer War, announced in the House of Commons that the British communiques, if one added them together, claimed the killing of more Boers than the whole Boer nation contained, it is recorded that Arthur Balfour rose to his feet and shouted "Cad!" Very few people are proof against lapses of this type. The Negro snubbed by a white woman, the Englishman who hears England ignorantly criticized by an American, the Catholic apologist reminded of the Spanish Armada, will all react in much the same way. One prod to the nerve of nationalism, and the intellectual decencies can vanish, the past can be altered, and the plainest facts can be denied.

If one harbours anywhere in one's mind a nationalistic loyalty or hatred, certain facts, although in a sense known to be true, are inadmissible. Here are just a few examples. I list below five types of nationalist, and against each I append a fact which it is impossible for that type of nationalist to accept, even in his secret thoughts:

BRITISH TORY: Britian will come out of this war with reduced power and prestige.

COMMUNIST: If she had not been aided by Britain and America, Russia would have been defeated by Germany.

IRISH NATIONALIST: Eire can only remain independent because of British protection.

TROTSKYIST: The Stalin regime is accepted by the Russian masses.

PACIFIST: Those who "abjure" violence can only do so because others are committing violence on their behalf.

All of these facts are grossly obvious if one's emotions do not happen to be involved: but to the kind of person named in each case they are also intolerable, and so they have to be denied, and false theories constructed upon their denial. I come back to the astonishing failure of military prediction in the present war. It is, I think, true to say that the intelligentsia have been more wrong about the progress of the war than the common people, and that they were more swayed by partisan feelings. The average intellectual of the Left believed, for instance, that the war was lost in 1940, that the Germans were bound to overrun Egypt in 1942, that the Japanese would never be driven out of the lands they had conquered, and that the Anglo-American bombing offensive was making no impression on Germany. He could believe these things because his hatred for the British ruling class forbade him to admit that British plans could succeed.

There is no limit to the follies that can be swallowed if one is under the influence of feelings of this kind. I have heard it confidently stated, for instance, that the American troops had been brought to Europe not to fight the Germans but to crush an English revolution. One has to belong to the intelligentsia to believe things like that: no ordinary man could be such a fool. When Hitler invaded Russia, the officials of the MOI issued "as background" a warning that Russia might be expected to collapse in six weeks. On the other hand the Communists regarded every phase of the war as a Russian victory, even when the Russians were driven back almost to the Caspian Sea and had lost several million prisoners. There is no need to multiply instances. The point is that as soon as fear, hatred, jealousy and power worship are involved, the sense of reality becomes unhinged. And, as I have pointed out already, the sense of right and wrong becomes unhinged also. There is no crime, absolutely none, that cannot be condoned when "our" side commits it. Even if one does not deny that the crime has happened, even if one knows that it is exactly the same crime as one has condemned in some other case, even if one admits in an intellectual sense that it is unjustified--still one cannot feel that it is wrong. Loyalty is involved, and so pity ceases to function.

The reason for the rise and spread of nationalism is far too big a question to be raised here. It is enough to say that, in the forms in which it appears among English intellectuals, it is a distorted reflection of the frightful battles actually happening in the external world, and that its worst follies have been made possible by the breakdown of patriotism and religious belief. If one follows up this train of thought, one is in danger of being led into a species of Conservatism, or into political quietism. It can be plausibly argued, for instance--it is even possibly true--that patriotism is an inocculation against nationalism, that monarchy is a guard against dictatorship, and that organized religion is a guard against superstition. Or again, it can be argued that no unbiased outlook is possible, that all creeds and causes involve the same lies, follies, and barbarities; and this is often advanced as a reason for keeping out of politics altogether.

I do not accept this argument, if only because in the modern world no one describable as an intellectual can keep out of politics in the sense of not caring about them. I think one must engage in politics--using the word in a wide sense--and that one must have preferences: that is, one must recognize that some causes are objectively better than others, even if they are advanced by equally bad means. As for the nationalistic loves and hatreds that I have spoken of, they are part of the make-up of most of us, whether we like it or not. Whether it is possible to get rid of them I do not know, but I do believe that it is possible to struggle against them, and that this is essentially a moral effort. It is a question first of all of discovering what one really is, what one's own feelings really are, and then of making allowance for the inevitable bias. If you hate and fear Russia, if you are jealous of the wealth and power of America, if you despise Jews, if you have a sentiment of inferiority towards the British ruling class, you cannot get rid of those feelings simply by taking thought. But you can at least recognize that you have them, and prevent them from contaminating your mental processes. The emotional urges which are inescapable, and are perhaps even necessary to political action, should be able to exist side by side with an acceptance of reality. But this, I repeat, needs a moral effort, and contemporary English literature, so far as it is alive at all to the major issues of our time, shows how few of us are prepared to make it.

Chapter 8

Major Themes

Totalitarianism

In writing 1984, Orwell's main goal was to warn of the serious danger totalitarianism poses to society. He goes to great lengths to demonstrate the terrifying degree of power and control a totalitarian regime can acquire and maintain. In such regimes, notions of personal rights and freedoms and individual thought are pulverized under the all-powerful hand of the government. Orwell was a Socialist and believed strongly in the potential for rebellion to advance society, yet too often he witnessed such rebellions go wrong and develop into totalitarian rule. Specifically, Orwell saw such developments during his time in Spain and in Russia, where he witnessed the rise of communism and the accompanying destruction of civil liberties, honest government, and economic strength.

During a time when much of the Western world was lauding communism as a step towards human progress in the development of equality in government, Orwell clearly and definitively spoke out against the practice. In 1984, Orwell presents a dystopia, or in other words, the perfect totalitarian state. In composing this novel, Orwell gave the world a glimpse of what the embrace of communism might lead to if allowed to proceed unchecked. The Party is unflawed in its universal control over society, as evidenced by its ability to break even an independent thinker such as Winston, and has mastered every aspect of psychological control, largely through utilizing technological developments (allowing for inventions such as the telescreen) to their advantage. In ending the novel with Winston defeated in every sense of the term, Orwell clearly suggests that there is no hope for quelling the expansion or growth of such a perfectly established regime. And, more importantly, Orwell warns that at the time, this outcome was within the realm of possibility as long as the world supported and embraced communism.

Propaganda

A major factor in the Party's rule over Oceania lies in its extremely well organized and effective propaganda machine. The Ministry of Truth, which is ironically where Winston works, is responsible for disseminating all Party publications and information. All figures and facts come from the Ministry of Truth, and all are dictated by the Party. In other words, the Party chooses exactly what to tell the public, regardless of what is accurate. The effectiveness of this propaganda machine, which constantly corrects old material to reflect the Party's current position on any subject ranging from chocolate rations to the loyalty of a specific individual, allows the Party to completely dominate the range of information disseminated to the public. Therefore, as O'Brien notes, the machine determines what constitutes reality.

In addition to the massive amounts of doctored information the Party disseminates to the public, there are also basic forms of propaganda, such as the Two Minutes Hate, Hate Week, posters of Big Brother, and required daily participation in the Physical Jerks. The Party uses literally every waking opportunity to instill its ideals into its citizens, and is strikingly successful in achieving its goal of total loyalty. In 1984 we see the vigour and loyalty such propaganda inspires in the citizens. The citizens of Oceania are filled with hatred for the country's stated enemies, but this hatred is easily re-directed if the enemy happens to change. This efficiency is quite disturbing. Orwell's presentation of the power of propaganda significantly supports his warning against totalitarianism. If propaganda rules all information, it is impossible to have any grasp on reality. The world is as the Party defines it.

Love/Sexuality

The Party works to quell all physical sensations of love, and depersonalizes sex to the point where it is referred to as a "duty to the Party" (for the purposes of procreation). Some Party organizations even advocate complete abstinence and procreation only through artificial insemination. Winston suffers the Party's removal of personal fulfillment or enjoyment in relationships in his failed marriage with Katharine. Later, when he finds Julia, Winston relishes the freedom of being able to love someone in a physical and emotional way. So much of Winston's seeming rebellion turns out to be guided and influenced by the Party (Mr. Charrington, O'Brien, the Brotherhood), but his relationship with Julia is not. Winston is only able to rebel against the Party through his affair with Julia, even though this love is destroyed in the end.

Orwell's discussion of love is not only relegated to romantic love. Through Winston's memories of his mother and the contrast between how she cared for him and his sister and the average Party family is striking. Winston's mother deeply loved her children and did all she could to protect them during the aftermath of the Revolution and the Party's rise to power. In Winston's time, the Party has removed such interfamilial loyalty, demanding that all love and loyalty be reserved for Big Brother and the Party. In this way, the bonds between parents and children are broken. Even worse, children commonly report their parents to the Thought Police, placing the Party above the lives of their mother and father. The Party's eventual goal is to destroy the family unit entirely and have all children raised in Party facilities. The Party has no room for love, unless that love is directed with full force at Big Brother and Oceania.

Independence/Identity

Through its effective psychological manipulation tactics, the Party destroys all sense of independence and individuality. Everyone wears the same clothes, eats the same food, and lives in the same grungy apartments. Life is uniform and orderly. No one can stand out, and no one can be unique. To have an independent thought borders on the criminal. For this reason, writing such as Winston does in his diary has been outlawed. People are only permitted to think what the Party tells them to think, which leads to what Syme refers to as "duckspeak." Independent thought can be dangerous, as it might lead to rebellion. This theme comes to a head during Winston's torture, when Winston argues that he is a man, and because he is a man O'Brien cannot tell him what he thinks. O'Brien counters that if Winston is a man, he is the last man on earth. Moreover, O'Brien suggests that this independence is evidence of insanity. O'Brien's view represents the purity of a totalitarian regime, in that independent thought must be destroyed to promote the needs and goals of the Party. Winston and Julia's downfall occurs because they believe they are special. Their arrest and torture, however, breaks this spirit. Once again, through this ultimate loss of individual thought, we witness Orwell's warning against embracing any version of totalitarian rule.

Music: Songs appear throughout the novel, most often when Winston is reflecting on the state of the world. Music appears to inspire Winston and allows him to see beauty and simplicity in an otherwise violent, ugly, and frightening world. He sees a powerful sense of tragedy in "Under the spreading Chestnut Tree," hope for a brighter future in the beautiful thrush song, respect for the true, untouchable past in the "St. Clement's Dane" rhyme, and freedom and hope in the passion with which the prole woman sings while hanging her laundry. Below, listed in chronological order are the musical events that occur in the novel.

Winston describes sitting in the Chestnut Tree Cafe, observing the clearly beaten, defeated, and tragically sad Jones, Aaronson and Rutherford, while the song "Under the spreading Chestnut Tree, I sold you and you sold me" plays over the telescreen. The song seems to reflect the broken spirits of these three men, who were once Inner Party members and now have lost everything.

Mr. Charrington teaches Winston the rhyme that begins "Oranges and lemons say the bells of St. Clement's," which is a vestige of the past. Throughout the novel, Winston holds on to this rhyme and tries to discover its entirety. He succeeds, with the help of Julia, who remembers a few more lines than Mr. Charrington, and O'Brien, who finishes the poem for Winston. Julia and Winston are in the Golden Country, beginning their affair. As they stand next to each other surveying the landscape, a small thrush begins to sing next to them. Winston is taken in by the bird's boundless freedom and wonders what makes him sing so beautifully. To Winston, the bird's song represents all he longs for in life. It is the exact opposite of the Party. Winston hears the prole woman in the yard behind Mr. Charrington's house sing while she works. She belts out the tune without any hesitation, throwing herself into the simple music with a passion Winston reveres.

Winston tells Julia of the poem Mr. Charrington taught him, and she adds two verses. Her grandfather taught her the rhyme when she was young, and Winston is elated to learn the next few lines of the piece. This cooperation reveals a strong bond between Winston and Julia. Winston discusses the Hate Song the Party created solely for the Hate Week celebration. This is the only time we hear of a song created purely for negative means. Winston notes that the Hate Song is not as popular among the proles as some of the more simple tunes the Ministry of Truth has produced for them.

O'Brien completes Mr. Charrington's rhyme, and Winston is immensely satisfied to finally know the complete piece. He feels that gaining the last puzzle piece from O'Brien symbolically represents their bond in rebelling against the Party and pursuing a future steeped in freedom.

Winston again hears the prole woman singing passionately while doing her wash and reflects on the primitivism in song. Winston thinks about the millions of people around the world, just like this woman, who find such pleasure, power and freedom in music and are able to embrace it in their lives. He is arrested immediately after this brief scene, which fulfills the last line of the "St. Clement's Dane" song, "Here comes a chopper to chop off your head!" Winston sits in the Chestnut Tree Cafe, just as Jones, Aaronson and Rutherford once did. He hears the same song he heard when watching those three men, "Under the spreading Chestnut Tree, I sold you and you sold me." Here, the song speaks to the destruction of Winston's independence, and his newly discovered love for Big Brother.

Loyalty

The Party is fueled by loyalty, and thus demands that its citizens support any and all actions it takes in pursuing a greater Oceania. For the Party, loyalty means accepting without question or hesitation. Ironically, when Winston pledges his loyalty to the Brotherhood, he also agrees to accept the goals and requirements of the Brotherhood without question or hesitation. Winston agrees to do anything the Brotherhood requires, even if that means murdering innocents. However, Winston is also loyal to Julia, and refuses to be separated from her forever. This split loyalty is what separates Winston from the other Party members. Party members are loyal to the Party, Big Brother, and Oceania alone. Personal relationships are of no importance. While in the Ministry of Love, O'Brien notes this weakness in Winston's mind and effectively removes it. Through painful physical torture, O'Brien first teaches Winston that the Party's perspective is the accurate perspective. Next, by threatening him with carnivorous rats, O'Brien breaks Winston's loyalty to Julia. In the last scene of the novel, Winston finally comes to love Big Brother, and his transition from split loyalties to a greater single loyalty to the Party is complete.

Poverty vs. Wealth

Oceanian society presents a clear dichotomy in living conditions. The small Inner Party lives luxuriously, with servants and lush, well-furnished apartments. Party members, on the other hand, live in run-down single-room apartments with no amenities and low-quality, tasteless food. The proles live in absolute poverty. The chasm between poverty and wealth in the novel is striking, and is most noticeable during Winston's forays into prole society. The buildings the proles live in are decaying, and the city of London is filled with bombed-out ruins. While the Inner Party comforts itself with luxury, the citizens of Oceania suffer, getting by with the bare minimum in a dying city. Orwell presents this dichotomy to demonstrate how totalitarian societies promote the wealth of the ruling regime while decreasing the quality of life for all other members of society. Such governments often tout their hopes for establishing an equal society when in reality the separation between their living conditions and those of the citizens is vast. Winston looks out on the city of London and sees a dying world. Meanwhile, O'Brien looks out on the city of London and sees a society trapped in a single moment in time, defined and controlled by the Party.

Technology

As previously noted, technology is an extremely important tool that the Party uses to maintain control over its citizens. Without telescreens, the Thought Police would not be nearly as effective, and propaganda would not be so widespread. The constant supervision of the telescreen effectively imprisons citizens of Oceania in their daily lives: they are always under observation. Ironically, other areas of technological development are strikingly stagnant. For example, the printing machines in the Ministry of Truth are still quite basic, and each superstate continues to build the same bombs that were used decades before. Scientific progress has halted, except where it serves the Party's goals (such as in artificial insemination or new methods for psychological manipulation). In the world of Oceania there is no such as thing as progress for the sake of progress; there is only power for the sake of power. When technological developments serve this power, they are encouraged. When they do not, they are stopped.

Language

Newspeak plays an extremely important role in Oceanian society and in the Party's control over its population. As Syme says, Newspeak reduces and limits the number of words in the English language, and removes words used to describe rebellion or independence (with the ultimate goal being to remove citizens' ability to think anti-Party thoughts). Interestingly, the Party works to form a language around itself rather than naturally accepting and assuming the language of the people that make up the country. In this way, language is used as yet another mechanism of mind control.

Chapter 9

Complete Summary with Analysis

Summary and Analysis of Part One I-II

Winston lives in the city of London, in Airstrip One. London is contained in the superstate of Oceania, formerly known as Great Britain. The opening section of the book consists largely of Winston's personal reflections on his existence and the world in which he lives. Oceania is a totalitarian state dominated by the principles of Ingsoc and ruled by an ominous organization known simply as the Party, of which Big Brother is the figurehead. Two other superstates inhabit the world along with Oceania, Eurasia and Eastasia, and the three are constantly involved a series of shifting alliances and battles. Winston is a Party member, and wears the uniform of a Party member: blue overalls.

In the opening pages, we find Winston, having climbed the seven flights to his apartment slowly due to his bothersome varicose ankle ulcer, looking out his apartment window, noting the large and ominous presence of the four Ministry buildings: the Ministry of Truth, which manages news, entertainment, education and fine arts as related to the Party, the Ministry of Peace, which manages war, the Ministry of Love, which manages law and order, and the Ministry of Plenty, which manages economic affairs. In Newspeak, the official language of Oceania, these Ministries are referred to as Minitrue, Minipax, Miniluv, and Miniplenty. Winston sees the Ministry of Truth clearly from his apartment window, and can even make out the three Party slogans carved into the large, pyramid-shaped, glittering white concrete structure: "War is

Peace," "Freedom is Slavery," and "Ignorance is Strength." Winston's apartment contains a telescreen, an oblong metal plaque like a dulled mirror that simultaneously receives and transmits information. The machine constantly spews Party propaganda, but also monitors each Party member, listening to his or her words and observing his or her actions in search of evidence of disloyalty. The telescreens are an important tool of the Thought Police, whose sole responsibility is identifying those disloyal-even with a single word, phrase, or facial expression-to the Party.

Strangely, the telescreen in Winston's apartment is hung at such an angle that there is a small alcove in which Winston cannot be seen. He sits at a desk in this alcove and begins to write in a diary he purchased discreetly from an antique shop. In 1984 Oceania, people do not keep personal documentation. Such behaviour is considered dangerous, as it promotes independence and individual thought. In preparing to write in this diary, Winston knows he is committing thoughtcrime and therefore risking his life. Winston writes, "April 4th, 1984," and then realizes he is not even certain of the year, as it is impossible to tell if the information the Party disseminates is truly accurate anymore.

Winston begins writing about a violent war film with vivid death scenes. He then remembers an event from earlier in the day that inspired him to begin the diary. It occurred at about eleven hundred that morning (time is kept in the twenty-four hour method) during the Two Minutes Hate, a daily propaganda presentation given to groups at their places of work praising Big Brother, Oceania and the Party, and denouncing Emmanuel Goldstein, the figurehead of capitalism and the Party's number one enemy, and Oceania's current enemy of war. While surrounded by fellow Party members caught up in the fervor of denouncing enemies to the Party, literally screaming and throwing things at the screen and praising Big Brother and Oceania, Winston took note of those around him. He observed the dark-haired girl he had often seen in the Ministry who he hated based purely on her apparent worship of the Party, and also a man named O'Brien, an Inner Party member whom he also often saw in the Ministry of Truth. He and O'Brien made eye contact, and immediately Winston felt as though they were both thinking the same things, realizing that O'Brien also found this practice and the Party's propaganda disgusting. O'Brien, he suddenly understood, also yearned for individual freedoms. Bolstered by what he perceived to be nonverbal support of his anti-Party feelings, Winston resolved to begin his diary that day.

While remembering this event, Winston finds he has unknowingly written, DOWN WITH BIG BROTHER over and over in his diary. Winston feels slightly panicked, but then reminds himself that he knows he will be arrested: it is only a matter of time. A knock on the door interrupts his thoughts. Winston assumes that the Thought Police have already found him, but soon discovers that his visitor is Mrs. Parsons from across the hall. Her husband works with Winston at the Ministry of Truth, and Mrs. Parsons has come to ask Winston to help her unclog her sink. Winston obliges, and in doing so meets her son and daughter, who are both members of the Spies and Youth League, and ardent Party supporters, eager to display their loyalty. In fact, they are begging their mother to take them to the hanging of a declared enemy to the Party, an unfortunately common event. Winston predicts that quite soon these children will denounce their innocent parents to the Thought Police and be publicly named "child heroes."

Winston returns to his apartment and begins to reflect on the impossibility of escaping the Party. He begins thinking of O'Brien again, remembering how seven years ago he dreamt he was walking through a dark room, when he suddenly heard O'Brien's voice say, "We shall meet in the place where there is no darkness." Ever since that dream, Winston has increasingly understood O'Brien's shared perception of the Party. Moving on, he ponders the sacred principles of Ingsoc and the mutability of the past, and feels as though he is "wandering in the forests of the sea bottom, lost in a monstrous world where he himself was the monster." Winston feels alone in his internal rebellion and wonders for whom he is writing the diary. The chances of any human other than a member of the Thought

Police ever reading his words is quite small. Before returning to work, Winston writes a few final thoughts in his diary: "From the age of uniformity, from the age of solitude, from the age of Big Brother, from the age of doublethink-greetings!" Finally, with solemn understanding, he notes, "Thoughtcrime does not entail death: thoughtcrime IS death." To be sure he is not discovered, Winston carefully washes the ink off his hands and places the diary in his desk drawer, complete with a noticeable piece of dust on the front cover-a security device that will reveal whether other hands have touched his precious book.

Analysis

In these first chapters of 1984, we meet the main character, Winston Smith, and learn about the totalitarian regime he lives under as a citizen of Airstrip One in Oceania. Winston lives a harsh and limited life: he is watched at every turn, and forced to submit to the Party in almost every aspect of his existence. In Oceania, those who do not submit to the Party suffer the wrath of the Thought Police. Orwell's parallels to totalitarian regimes of the early twentieth century such as Nazi Germany and Stalin's Soviet Union, and the degree of control they maintained over their citizens, are clear. In 1984, the Party maintains control over its citizens through the use of telescreens that transmit constant streams of propaganda while observing citizens, mandatory organized propaganda events such as the Two Minutes Hate and Hate Week, and by instilling the fear of the Thought Police and the retributions of thoughtcrime in all. The Party controls its citizens and maintains its power through the use of extensive psychological manipulation.

Winston views the regularities of his world-the face of Big Brother, the telescreen, the dilapidated apartment complex, and the sad existence of his neighbour and her Party-worshipping children-with sadness and disdain. He has deep reservations about the Party and believes there must be hope for a brighter future, in which personal freedoms are permitted. However, his neighbor's children's powerful allegiance to the Party scares Winston. He sees how young minds can be indoctrinated into the Party through organizations such as the Spies and the Youth League, which encourage children to report anyone they believe to be a thought criminal-even their parents-to the Party. This control and influence over the youngest members of Oceanian society speaks to the massive degree of psychological control the Party holds over its citizens, and again provides a parallel to similar totalitarian organizations of the twentieth century such as the Hitler Youth.

When we meet Winston, these rebellious notions have clearly been festering for quite some time. Now, in writing his diary, he is taking the first physical step towards all-out rebellion. In putting his pen to paper, Winston knows he is committing thoughtcrime. He is now a criminal, and knows that his eventual arrest is inevitable. This fatalistic perspective stays with Winston throughout the novel. As he often says to Julia, "We are the dead." He has no true hope for rebellion in his time, but he cannot submit to the Party. This in-between state forces him to constantly be reminded of his eventual arrest, torture, and death.

Winston is a unique citizen of Oceania. Although he was raised from an early age in the bosom of the Party, Winston harbors a strong sense of individual freedom, while those around him seem to soak in Party propaganda and find no fault with the Party's constant and seemingly obvious revisions of history. Through stressing the significance of Winston's risking his life through the physical act of writing, Orwell demonstrates the great rarity of personal freedom and self-expression in totalitarian regimes and clarifies the massive degree of control the Party holds over its citizens. At the same time, Winston's choice to begin the diary (and his subconsciously writing "DOWN WITH BIG BROTHER") shows us the strength of Winston's anti-Party feelings. Winston feels alone in his act of rebellion and his attitude towards the Party, but holds out hope that O'Brien shares his views. In these chapters we meet O'Brien, a man who becomes a symbol of rebellion in Winston's mind, for the first time. Ultimately, however, it is O'Brien who will guide Winston towards his downfall and will torture him into absolute submission. Winston has vivid dreams that prove to be prophetic. Winston hears O'Brien's voice in a dream, telling him that they will "meet in the place where there is no darkness." They do eventually meet in this dream, but the "place where there is no darkness" is not associated with freedom as Winston had hoped. Rather, it is the interior of the Ministry of Love, where thought criminals such as Winston are tortured, and where the lights are always on. The irony in the naming of each ministry is an obvious notation on the contradictory nature of the Party. Criminals are tortured in the Ministry of Love, war is waged from the Ministry of Peace, misinformation and lies are regularly distributed from the Ministry of Truth, and the Ministry of Plenty oversees and manages the weak economy of Oceania, where most citizens live in poverty. In fact, London is in a serious state of urban decay, which the Party simply ignores, instead stating with a celebratory attitude how wonderful and plentiful the lives of Oceanian citizens are. The Party slogans exhibit similar contradictions: "War is Peace," "Freedom is Slavery," and "Ignorance is Strength." The Party is built and thrives upon such contradictions. Forcing acceptance of such blatant inaccuracies removes the individual's ability to question the Party or think independently.

Summary and Analysis of Part One III-V

Winston dreams of his mother, who disappeared in one of the great purges of the 1950s, when Winston was ten or eleven years old. In his dream his mother is sitting below him with his baby sister in her arms, in some sort of underground room. In this memory, he feels sad because he knows that somehow she has given up her life and that of his sisters for him. He thinks of her death as a tragedy-impossible in current times, because she died loving him and giving herself up to a personal loyalty that current Party rule would never allow.

In his dream, Winston suddenly finds himself in the Golden Country, which he happens upon often in his slumbers. The Golden Country is an "an old rabbit-bitten pasture, with a foot track wandering across it and a molehole here and there...the elm trees were swaying faintly in the breeze, their leaves just stirring in dense masses like women's hair." In this dream, the dark-haired girl from the Ministry whom Winston despises for her Party-fueled fervor approaches him and tears off her clothes in a gesture so "splendid" that its existence alone rebels against the Party. He wakes with the word "Shakespeare" on his lips.

It is time for his morning Physical Jerks, an exercise routine implemented to all Party members through the telescreen, specifically tailored for each age group. Winston falls among the 30s to 40s group. After overcoming his daily morning coughing fit, Winston begins the exercise routine, but lets his mind wander to the history of Oceania. He can't remember a time when Oceania wasn't at war, but he remembers being quite young and rushing to an underground Tube station with his parents and little sister to take shelter during an attack-although he cannot remember the source of the attack. Next, he remembers an era of common London street fighting, and then only an era of permanent war. Winston remembers that only four years ago Oceania was at war with Eastasia, even though it is currently at war with Eurasia and claims this has always been the case. Such was the nature of doublethink-completely accepting the opposite of the known truth and adjusting one's personal memories accordingly. Winston realizes that the past has been not altered, but rather destroyed. Suddenly, a voice from the telescreen interrupts him, yelling out his name and identification number and urging him to "bend lower." Feigning interest and determination, Winston complies, and succeeds in touching his toes for the first time in many years.

At work in the Records Department of the Ministry of Truth, Winston reads his daily assignments, sent to him in the form of small cylindrical paper rolls that spurt out of a pneumatic tube. The messages order him to "rectify" certain articles or news items to ensure the Party is always proven right and good, no matter its original predictions and actual outcomes. For instance, the predictions of the Ministry of Plenty's output of goods need to be "rectified" to reflect recently-published "actual" numbers. Once Winston completes assignments by dictating corrections into the speakwrite at his desk (which translates spoken word into written word), Winston puts all related documentation into a "memory hole," thus sending any evidence of altered data to a large furnace in the centre of the building.

When taking a short break from his work, Winston notices his coworker Tillotson sitting in the cubicle across from him, whispering secretively into his speakwrite and casting suspicious glances about the room. Winston realizes that he barely even knows the people in his department. The little he knows consists of workplace information and basic personal details. For instance, the sandy-haired woman in the cubicle next to him is responsible for tracking down and deleting all mention of any vaporized person, so as to remove their entire existence from the records. Ironically, her husband was vaporized not long ago. Ampleforth, a poet, sits a few cubicles away from Winston and produces "definitive texts," or garbled versions of poems that the Party has deemed ideologically offensive, but for some reason wants to retain. Winston then reflects on all the other departments in the Ministry of Truth, including those areas that create and distribute fiction, film, textbooks, and plays, both at the Party level and at a level specifically produced for the lower class non-Party members, the proletariat, or "proles," including Pornosec, which produces pornography that no Party member is allowed to even look at. Returning to work, Winston admits that his greatest pleasure in life is his work. He is good at it, and although he despises the Party's reinvention of the past, he ironically takes pleasure in finding creative ways to complete particularly challenging assignments. Today, Winston creates a "Comrade Ogilvy" out of thin air to replace the name of a recently named "unperson," Inner Party member Comrade Withers, who once received the honour of the Order of Conspicuous Merit, Second Class. Winston creates an entire life for his fictional Comrade Ogilvy, and is sure his work will be found creative and satisfactory in solving the particularly difficult problem of removing a publicly-lauded Inner Party member from the records. Winston enters the Ministry of Truth canteen and runs into Syme, whom he grudgingly calls his "friend." Syme is a Newspeak specialist working on the Eleventh Edition of the Newspeak Dictionary. The two men speak of the rarity of razor blades, and Winston lies, saying he has none, when he actually has a few saved at home for his personal use. Syme asks Winston why he didn't go to the hanging, suggests he knows that they make Winston uncomfortable, and then goes into grotesque detail about the event, noting how the man's tongue was bright blue and sticking out of his mouth when he died.

Winston and Syme obtain their bland, unrecognizable food, and sit. They begin to discuss the Newspeak dictionary, and Syme goes into great detail about his work, discussing the greatness he sees in the destruction of words and the simplification of language. For instance, why does a language need the word "bad," when "ungood" is sufficient? Syme claims that Oldspeak will be obsolete by the year 2050. Winston begins to say "Except for the proles," but cuts himself off as he realizes it might be unorthodox to make this claim. Despite this, Syme sees Winston's point and argues that he is wrong. In his opinion, Newspeak will take over completely, resulting in a climate without thought. He exclaims, "Orthodoxy means not thinking-not needing to think. Orthodoxy is unconsciousness." Upon hearing this statement, Winston thinks to himself that Syme is too intelligent, and will eventually be vaporized for seeing too clearly and speaking too plainly.

Tom Parsons eventually joins Winston and Syme. Parsons is an overweight, boyish, deeply loyal Party member with a very simple mind. He is quite active in Party activities and collects a subscription fee from Winston for the house by house Hate Week fund, which will be used to purchase flags and patriotic decorations for the event. Parsons apologizes to Winston for his son, who hit him with a toy catapult the other day, and then launches into a story about how his daughter followed a suspicious man during a troop hike and reported him to the authorities, claiming he was a foreigner because he was wearing "a funny kind of shoes." Winston is horrified, but outwardly agrees that she did her duty to the Party. A telescreen announcement lauding the Ministry of Plenty's success in exceeding all production goals interrupts their conversation, and Winston reflects on the lies being told. He knows production did not meet the stated goals, but regardless of actual numbers, production will always be reported as far higher than expected. This supports Party morale and convinces the Party members that they are leading happy lives. The phrase "our new, happy life" is repeated often throughout the broadcast.

In the midst of this announcement, Winston finds himself predicting the fates of those in his life. He believes that he, Mrs. Parsons, Syme, and O'Brien will be vaporized, while Parsons, the dark-haired girl, and other mindless followers of Party doctrine will never be subject to such a fate. Suddenly, he realizes that the dark-haired girl is staring at him. When he returns her gaze, she quickly looks away, and Winston begins to fear that she knows what he has been thinking and will report him for facecrime. Minutes later, Parsons tells another story of his children setting a woman's skirt on fire for having wrapped fish in newspaper containing pictures of Big Brother. A whistle blows, and the men return to work.

Analysis

Winston's prophetic dreams continue in this section. He dreams of the Golden Country, and of a sexual encounter with the dark-haired girl (whom we later learn is Julia). Later in the novel, this event actually takes place. This dark-haired girl is an object of sexual attraction for Winston, but also of hate. He is conflicted in his feelings for her, and represses both for fear of expressing himself too openly.

Throughout this section we clearly see the striking contradictions in the Party's constant revision of the past, which Winston directly contributes to through his position in the Records Department at the Ministry of Truth. Any past documentation challenging a current Party goal, achievement or development must be destroyed or altered to support the Party's current actions. In this way, the "past" is constantly changing, and constantly altered. At one point, Oceania is at war with Eurasia and has always been at war with Eurasia, but later in the novel, Oceania is at war with Eastasia and has always been at war with Eastasia. For the Party, the past is mutable. Winston refuses to accept this, most visibly during the Ministry of Plenty report at the end of Chapter V where Winston listens in awe and disgust to false reports that the Ministry of Plenty has exceeded all production goals.

In detailing Winston's work life, Orwell reveals the inner workings of Party organizations and the fastidious control the Party wields over every detail of information administered to Party members and the masses. To work in the Ministry of Truth, Party members must embrace doublethink. They know they are altering past information, yet as loyal Party members must accept their own personal alterations as the truth. Winston cannot embrace doublethink.

He knows the Party's version of the past is false-he remembers events the Party pretends never happened, and he refuses to ignore this knowledge. Through a detailed account of Winston's work life, we also learn how lonely he is. He has no personal friends, except perhaps for Syme, whom he only grudgingly calls a friend. He observes the people he works among with a great deal of detachment. He knows little about their personal lives, and is generally frustrated by their simpleness. He tends to view them with disdain. This loneliness and separation from fellow mankind will fuel the intensity of Winston's eventual relationship with Julia and his longing for a friendship with O'Brien. In these chapters, we also witness the degree of self-control Winston must wield in order to avoid discovery. In conversations with work colleagues, Winston stops himself from saying what he actually believes, and maintains great control over his facial expressions to avoid expressing discontent when it would be inappropriate to do so. Although Winston has become comfortable with this self-control, he doesn't trust himself completely. Therefore, when he catches the dark-haired girl looking at him during the Ministry of Plenty telescreen report, he is immediately worried that he has revealed himself, and that she will report him for facecrime.

Summary and Analysis of Part One VI-VIII

Winston writes in his diary, revealing the details of a particularly sordid night when he had sex with a prole prostitute with a face thickly painted in makeup (which Party women never wear). Winston struggles with his internal turmoil surrounding this disdainful act, noting to himself that man's nervous system is his worst enemy. There is no way to fight involuntary facial spasms or talking in one's sleep. These are the actions that cannot be stopped, yet can condemn one to death.

Winston remembers his wife Katharine, whom he separated from but never divorced, as per Party practice. Winston describes how the Party works continually to remove all pleasure from sexual acts, seeing eroticism as an enemy. Party marriages must be approved by a committee, and to gain such approval, the man and woman in question must not demonstrate any true physical affection for one another. The goal of a marriage is to produce offspring, not to seek personal pleasure or satisfaction. In fact, certain Party organizations, including the Junior Anti-Sex League (of which the dark-haired girl is a member, as demonstrated by the crimson band around her waist), advocate celibacy and procreation through artsem, Newspeak for artificial insemination, and even suggest that children should be raised in public institutions rather than by parents.

Katharine and Winston separated almost eleven years ago, and Winston rarely thinks of her. He nicknamed her "the human soundtrack" because of her empty mind and willingness to spout Party propaganda. Katharine had always been extremely cold when it came to sex, but insisted that she and Winston must keep trying to have children so she could fulfill her "duty to the Party".

Winston returns to his story of prostitution, revealing that when he turned on the light to look at the nakedness of the woman he was about to have sex with, he realized that she was old. She had no teeth at all, and was at least fifty, but Winston completed the act nevertheless. In writing this admission, Winston struggles, pressing his fingers against his eyes and using every vestige of control to avoid screaming foul words. Some time later, Winston writes, "If there is hope, it lies in the proles." The proles, who comprise eighty-five percent of Oceania's population, are the only ones, he believes, who can overthrow the Party. It is impossible to do so from within. Winston remembers walking down a street and hearing what he thought was a riot-a prole rebellion. In fact, it was women fighting over a limited supply of poorly made frying pans that broke in half during the scuffle. Winston writes, "Until they become conscious they will never rebel, and until after they have rebelled they cannot become conscious." Acknowledging this catch-22, Winston reflects on how the Party has claimed to have liberated the proles from the bondage and slavery of capitalist society, when in actuality the proles still live in squalor, work, produce children, drink beer, and die by age sixty. The Thought Police are always among them, seeking out those deemed too intelligent or too aware of the Party's activities, and removing them from society.

Winston takes a copy of a children's history textbook he obtained from Mrs. Parsons out of his desk drawer and begins to copy a passage describing the ills of capitalist society, including starving children having to work for cruel masters, and capitalist men always wearing long black coats with top hats. Winston then remembers other historical matters he has been taught about the capitalist past, including jus primae noctis, which supposedly was a "law by which every capitalist had the right to sleep with any woman working in one of his factories." Winston notes it is impossible to tell how many of these stories are lies, as nothing can be proved or disproved. Only once in his life has Winston ever held actual proof that Party history is false in his hands.

In the mid-sixties, during a series of great purges removing the original Revolutionary leaders, three men named Jones, Aaronson, and Rutherford were arrested. Under torture, they confessed to a variety of crimes. They were then released and returned to posts within the Party. Winston once saw them at the Chestnut Tree Cafe, and their spirits seemed entirely broken. While he observed them, a song came on over the telescreen: "Under the spreading chestnut tree, I sold you and you sold me..." Shortly afterwards, the three were rearrested and charged with a new string of crimes. Five years later, in 1973, Winston was at work and a newspaper clipping describing the three men at a function in New York on the date that they had confessed to being in Eurasia came into his workstation along with other rolled pieces of paper. Winston held in his hand concrete evidence of their innocence. Ten minutes later, Winston dropped the clipping into the memory hole, destroying it forever. But he never forgot the experience.

Remembering this day, Winston writes "I understand HOW: I do not understand WHY." He wonders if he is alone in this belief that the Party alters history, sometimes for entirely unknown reasons. He wonders if he is a lunatic, and whether it is possible to know that anything is true. Recalling O'Brien's face, he realizes he is sane. With new courage, he writes, "Freedom is the freedom to say that two plus two make four. If that is granted, all else follows."

After work one night, Winston finds himself wandering through the streets of London, among the proles. After being warned, he survives a "steamer" attack, a common occurrence in London, which constantly suffers such attacks. Following the attack, he continues his walk and finds himself near the antique shop where he bought his diary and the stationary shop where he bought his pen and ink. Across the street, he sees a very old man enter a pub and decides to take the risk of following him in and asking him about life before the Revolution. In the pub, the old man keeps asking the bartender for a "pint," and the frustrated bartender keeps explaining to him that there are only liters and half-liters for sale. He does not know what a "pint" is. Winston buys the man a drink and begins to ask him pointed questions about the past and how things have changed since the Revolution. The man acknowledges living before the Revolution, but only refers to life before the Revolution with references to minute details of his life that Winston does not find particularly interesting or satisfying, such as references to top hats, lackeys, and his luck with women. The man simply does not answer Winston as to whether life was better before or after the Revolution. Frustrated, Winston leaves and finds himself in front of the antique shop. He walks in, thinking he can claim that he is looking for razor blades if he is questioned. The owner of the store, Mr. Charrington, is a frail man of about sixty years old with benevolent eyes, thick spectacles, white hair, and bushy eyebrows. Winston notes that he has a "vague air of intellectuality" about him. The man remembers when he was last in the store, buying the rare diary, or, as he calls it, the "young lady's keepsake album." Winston wanders through the shop and finds a paperweight with a piece of coral inside of it. Winston is struck by its beauty and decides to purchase it. Mr. Charrington suggests that Winston take a look at another room, above the shop. The room consists of a strip of carpet, a few pictures, an armchair, a fireplace, an old-fashioned twelve-hour clock, and a large bed. With amazement, Winston realizes that there is no telescreen. The man explains that he never had a need for one, and begins to show Winston a picture on the wall of St. Clement's Dane. He recites part of a nursery rhyme about the old church: "Oranges and lemons, say the bells of St. Clement's...You owe me three farthings, say the bells of St. Martin's" He cannot remember the rest of it, but knows that the rhyme included the names of all the London churches.

Winston eventually extricates himself from Mr. Charrington and leaves the shop. He wanders home, briefly wondering what it might be like to rent the upper room from the old man. While recalling the rhyme Mr. Charrington shared, he suddenly sees the dark-haired girl from the Ministry of Truth on the road in front of him. In a panic, he stands stock still as she quickly walks on. He wanders aimlessly for a few minutes and then stops, wondering if he should turn back, follow the girl, and murder her with the paperweight to prevent himself from being turned in to the Thought Police. He quickly abandons the idea, thinking himself too weak, and heads home. Once back in his apartment, he chides himself for being so fearful and not acting to protect himself. He writes the rhyme down in his diary and begins contemplating what will happen to him when the Thought Police do eventually come to take him away. He will be tortured; his bones will snap; he will bleed and scream in pain. He thinks of O'Brien saying, "We will meet in the place with no darkness." In his train of thought the image of Big Brother merges and then replaces that of O'Brien. He pulls a coin from his pocket to look at the face of Big Brother, and is instead confronted with the Party slogans: "War is Peace," "Freedom is Slavery," and "Ignorance is Strength."

Analysis

Through Winston's painful memory of his experience with an aged prole prostitute, we begin to understand the depths of the Party's sexual repression. The memory pains Winston. Because he was so desperate for a close sexual experience, he continued the encounter even after realizing that the heavily made up woman was toothless and old. The Party represses all sexual acts in an effort to force Party members to channel all of their energy into furthering its own goals and needs. The Party must approve all marriages, and such unions must not appear to be sought because of sexual attraction. Sexual pleasure is an individual act, promoting independent thought and independent experiences. Clearly, sex is required for procreation, but through organizations such as the Junior Anti-Sex League, the Party turns sex into a duty performed purely to continue the Party and propagate the human race rather than an act performed for personal pleasure. Winston's wife Katharine felt this way, and was frigid in the bedroom, much to Winston's frustration and humiliation. As we later learn, the Party even encourages abstinence and advocates procreation only through artificial insemination.

The children's textbook (undoubtedly published in the Ministry of Truth) Winston has obtained is particularly revealing of the Party's revisionist history. The Party demonizes capitalism and capitalists, and Winston does not know what information in the book is true and what is false. Winston's story of the newspaper clipping proving Jones, Aaronson, and Rutherford's innocence further evidences the degree to which he yearns for information about the past.

Although Winston destroyed the clipping, he knows that it existed, and he knows that the Party covered it up. Here, he addresses an important question that will continue to arise throughout the novel, and will only be answered in the Ministry of Love: Why? He understands how the Party revises history, but does not understand why this constant revision is necessary.

When Winston travels out into the prole world, we begin to see how the rest of the Oceanian population lives. The proles are destitute, living in poverty in areas removed from Party business and life. The prole areas are also the only places Winston and the others can go if they wish to find relics of the past. Winston notably visits Mr. Charrington's antique store, purchases a paperweight, and dreams about what it might be like to live in the apartment above the shop, free from the eyes of a telescreen. Winston is in awe of Mr. Charrington's shop, and wishes he could soak in the history of his artifacts. Winston sees great freedom in the prole world, and it is for this reason that be believes that if there is hope, "it lies with the proles." Unfortunately, the proles seem unable to capitalize on their freedoms, and take no interest in Party affairs.

When Winston meets the old man in the bar, we see the stark contrast between his hopes for a prole rebellion and the reality of prole existence. Winston hopes that the old man will reveal ideological differences between life before the Revolution and life under Party control. However, the man focuses only on very personal memories that do not speak to Winston's concerns. Winston becomes frustrated in this conversation because he believes that the proles, who are not subjected to doublethink and the revision of history, hold the true details of history, and therefore the hope for a brighter future.

When visiting Mr. Charrington, Winston sees the picture of St. Clement's Dane for the first time. This picture, and its accompanying rhyme, become symbols of the past for Winston. He holds onto this picture, and to the first few lines of the rhyme that Mr. Charrington remembered, believing that they represent his ideal of incontrovertible truth and rebellion against the Party. The Party cannot control this picture, or this poem. Despite the hope Winston places in this object and this rhyme, both foreshadow his downfall. The rhyme ends with the line, "Here comes a chopper to chop off your head," and much later we will learn that a telescreen is hidden behind the picture. Winston's walk through this prole area of the city further confirms his rebellion, and continues to set him on the path towards eventual arrest and defeat.

Summary and Analysis of Part Two I-III

In the middle of the morning, Winston takes a break from working to go to the bathroom. He notices the dark-haired girl walking towards him. The two are alone in the hallway. The girl falls, and Winston rushes to help her up. While assisting her, she discreetly hands him a small piece of paper. To avoid detection, he waits five minutes at his desk before allowing himself to read it, all the time imagining that perhaps it is a warning or a summons from the Thought Police. Finally he looks at it. It reads, "I love you." Winston is stunned.

At home in bed, Winston is able to think about the paper and work through his feelings. He tries to determine how to get in touch with the girl to arrange a rendezvous. Because she works in the Fiction Department, it would be too obvious if they ran into each other again in the hallway. For the next week, they keep missing each other in the canteen. Finally, he manages to sit an otherwise vacant table, only a few seats away from her. Speaking in near whispers, and not looking at each other, they quickly agree to meet at Victory Square.

In Victory Square, the excitement of a convoy of Eurasian prisoners causes a crowd, and they are able to stand side to side. The girl takes charge of the conversation immediately, outlining a plan to meet in a specific and distant point in the country that Sunday afternoon. Winston agrees. Just before the crowd parts the girls squeezes his hand, and upon touching it Winston feels he has learned every part of it by heart.

On Sunday, Winston travels into the country, following the girl's directions. While he is picking her some wildflowers, she finds him and they head to the secluded spot she has in mind. Before anything happens, Winston tells the girl that he is thirty-nine, and has varicose veins, a wife, and five false teeth. The girl replies that she does not care. They begin talking, and Winston learns that the girl's name is Julia. She has known for some time that he is Winston Smith. Winston reveals that he believed Julia to be part of the Thought Police. Julia finds such a notion quite funny, but appears to take some pleasure in being that believable as a Party devotee.

Julia and Winston stroll through the little enclave. Winston, standing at the edge of their small clearing, suddenly recognizes the scenery: it is the Golden Country from his dreams. A small thrush perched near them begins to sing passionately, and the sound strikes Winston as an example of simple, pure, unstoppable beauty. They head back to the clearing. Just as he saw in his dream, Julia tears off her clothes and they embrace. She reveals that she has done this with many Party members, and Winston explains that the more men she has been with, the more he will love her. He is inspired by her freedom and passionate rebellion, as corruption within the Party gives him hope for the future. After having sex, Winston likens their affair to a political act; a blow against the Party.

When Julia wakes from her short slumber, she immediately becomes businesslike: she dresses herself, and discusses where they should next meet, as it is dangerous to return to the same place more than a couple of times. They are able to meet up again privately once in the month of May, in a ruined church belfry, but otherwise they must be satiated with minor, seemingly accidental and unnoticed encounters in public streets, during which they pretend not to know each other. At the church tower, Winston learns more about Julia's life. She is twenty-six, lives in a hostel with other girls, and works on the novel-writing machine in the Fiction Department. She has no memories of life before the Revolution, and knows barely anyone who does. Throughout her life she has been an ideal Party member, often singled out for leadership roles in youth organizations. She also reveals that she has worked in Pornosec, the pornography section of the Fiction Department, devoted to creating pornographic stories for the proles.

Apparently the Party believes women are better suited for Pornosec, because their morals won't be as tempted by the material as their male counterparts'. She had her first love affair at sixteen, and does not believe in the underground anti-Party Brotherhood movement.

Winston discusses his own life, and talks about his wife, Katharine, calling her "goodthinkful," meaning entirely and completely loyal to the Party, even in her most private thoughts. Winston hated her, and her cold, businesslike approach to their sex life. Julia predicts that Katharine called sex her "duty to the Party," and Winston is surprised to learn that this is a phrase women are taught to use. With this realization, he begins to understand the depths of the Party's sexual Puritanism. Removing sex allows one's energy to be otherwise focused, into violent loyalty to the Party and hatred of its enemies. Moreover, removing the parent instinct removes any loyalty other than that to the Party. Next, Winston reveals that once, while separated from a larger group on a walk in the country, he considered murdering his wife, but did not. Julia states that he should have done it to free himself. Winston agrees.

After a moment, Winston begins to understand that Julia believes it might be possible to continue living a secret life, while Winston knows the Thought Police will find them eventually. Stating his belief, Winston says, "We are the dead." Julia argues that they are not dead yet and begins to describe her next plan for them to meet.

Analysis

In these chapters, Winston takes a significant step in his rebellion against the Party. He begins a love affair, blatantly rejecting the Party's hatred of sexual attraction and enjoyment. In Julia, Winston finally finds a compatriot in his quest against the Party. He is no longer alone. Julia's presence supports Winston's anti-Party thoughts and feelings, but their affair also highlights the differences in their attitudes toward the Party. Julie despises the Party, but accepts it as a permanent ruling government. She has no illusions of bringing the Party down or of a successful rebellion against it. Rather, she enjoys finding her own ways to rebel against the Party, such as efficiently planning her and Winston's encounters. Julia wants to live as long as possible without being caught in her small rebellions, and within the bounds of the Party. In contrast, Winston is sure that he will be arrested and will die. Rather than working to protect his own life, Winston embraces fatalism while holding out hope for a rebellion against the Party and dreams of a Party-free future.

Julia and Winston meet in the square and observe a procession of prisoners of war. Here, we see the brutality of the totalitarian regime. The Party purposely parades these prisoners through a public square to use them as sources of propaganda and to rally the crowd against them. The parade of prisoners suggests that the Party is succeeding in battle and rallies the crowd's support for the Party's war efforts. Here again, the Party is masterfully manipulating the minds of its subjects through carefully planned propaganda efforts. Moreover, these prisoners and others already in Oceania are the only foreigners in the nation. Oceanian citizens never interact with foreigners-yet another method of control that prevents Oceanian citizens from understanding what life would be like outside of Oceania or beyond the reach of the Party. With no basis for comparison, Oceanian citizens have no choice but to be content with their lives.

Winston and Julia's encounter in the Golden Country is an important moment in the novel. Here, Winston sees the vision from his dream-Julia ripping her clothes of in the middle of the Golden Country-transformed into reality. In addition, he is inspired by a thrush's passionate song, which is, in Winston's eyes, a wonderful expression of freedom and beauty. Throughout the novel, Winston finds great inspiration in music. Here, it is through the thrush, and in much of the rest of the novel, it is through the red-armed, large prole woman who sings passionately while doing laundry in her yard.

Winston talks about his wife with Julia, revealing her sexual frigidity, and Julia is not surprised. Again, the Party's puritanical views on sexuality become apparent. Winston is encouraged to learn that Julia has had many affairs, her first at age sixteen. In his eyes, this behaviour is a great act of political rebellion against the Party, and he is eager to take part in it. On a more personal level, Winston is elated to finally be in a sexual relationship where both parties are eager for personal pleasure, and in which the Party plays no role.

Summary and Analysis of Part Two IV-VII

Winston stands in the room above Mr. Charrington's shop, looking around. His paperweight is on the small desk, and the room now contains a small oil stove, a saucepan, and two pots, all supplied by Mr. Charrington. Winston rented the room from Mr. Charrington, clearly for a love affair with Julia. Rather than judging him, Mr. Charrington noted vaguely that privacy was very valuable these days. Winston hears someone singing beneath his window. He looks out and sees a large, stocky prole woman hanging baby diapers, singing, "It was only an 'opless fancy..." Apparently, this is a Party song published for the benefit of the proles, who revel in machine-generated verse.

Winston admits to himself that he has taken a great risk in renting the room, but remembers how hard it had been for he and Julia to meet. Once, she had to cancel a planned reunion because her menstrual cycle was early. At first Winston was furious, but upon recognizing the depth of their bond was calmed by a powerful wave of tenderness towards Julia. His mind wanders to their eventual arrest and what awaits them in the Ministry of Love, but Julia's entrance interrupts his dismal reverie.

Julia has brought with her many black market items, including good bread, real coffee, sugar, makeup, and perfume. When she puts on the makeup and allows Winston to see her, he is pleased. Julia reveals her plan to get a real dress and a pair of silk stockings so that-in Mr. Charrington's apartment, at least-she can be a woman rather than a Party member, and embrace her femininity. Winston and Julia make love on the large bed and sleep for a short time. When they wake, Julia sees a rat poking his head out of a corner of the room. Winston is horrified, revealing that he is more afraid of rats than anything else: "Of all the horrors in the world-a rat!" Winston remembers his recurring nightmare of standing in front of a wall of darkness, knowing that on the other side lies something dreadful.

Julia explores the room, noting the paperweight and the picture on the wall. Winston tells her of Mr. Charrington's poem, and she adds to it: "You owe me three farthings say the bells of St. Martin's/When will you pay me, say the bells of Old Bailey?" Winston is shocked, but Julia reveals that her grandfather, who lived before the war and was vaporized, used to recite it to her. Julia begins to get dressed and clean up, while Winston picks up his paperweight and imagines that his life inside this apartment is like the coral: trapped inside thick, safe, protective crystal, fixed in eternity.

It is some weeks later, and Syme has vanished. Just as Winston predicted, Syme has been vaporized. His name has been deleted from Ministry records, and people begin to behave as though they never knew him. Winston has been working long hours to prepare for Hate Week. The weather has become hot, and the population seems eager for activity: they hang banners, posters and signs, and proudly sing the Hate Song. In the lead-up to Hate Week, Winston has noticed a new, particularly large poster of a Eurasian soldier wielding a machine gun all over the city. Winston and Julia continue to meet in the apartment above Mr. Charrington's shop, dealing with its meager amenities and apparent bug problem in order to revel in their increasing happiness. Winston's ulcer has subsided, his coughing fits have disappeared, and his anger has somewhat abated. He has begun regularly chatting with Mr. Charrington about old times and the things in the shop. The apartment has become a refuge where he feels safe from the Party, able to act as a person rather than a Party member. However, Winston still understands-albeit distantly-that his fate is sealed. Such rebellion will not go unnoticed forever. Their time is precious.

Winston tells Julia of the bond he feels with O'Brien, and she understands why Winston might recognize him as sympathetic to his feelings. Julia believes deeply in the power of such relationships, but also tends to assume that most people are fundamentally against the Party, even though she doubts the existence of the Brotherhood. Although she is rebellious, Julia is somewhat naive in Winston's eyes. She believes that the Party invented the airplane, barely understands who Goldstein was, and cannot remember that Oceania was once at war with Eastasia (rather than Eurasia). The ease with which she accepts the Party's propaganda slightly disturbs Winston.

While walking through a hallway at work, Winston hears a small cough behind him. He turns and sees O'Brien, and feels that finally the day has come when he will receive a message from the Brotherhood. O'Brien begins the conversation by claiming that he knows Winston is interested in Newspeak, even vaguely referring to Syme, who was recently vaporized. O'Brien offers Winston an advance copy of the Tenth Edition of the Newspeak Dictionary and gives Winston his home address so that he can come pick up the copy. Then, as suddenly as he arrived, O'Brien is gone. Winston reflects on the interaction, believing that he is taking yet another step towards complete rebellion, and towards his own grave.

Winston and Julia are in Mr. Charrington's apartment. Winston wakes with eyes full of tears. He tells Julia that he has been dreaming of his mother. He remembers that shortly after his father disappeared, he lived with his mother and his baby sister. Times were difficult, air raids were common, and rations were small. Winston's mother was highly distraught. She performed all her household duties, but rarely spoke, and sometimes held Winston for inexplicably long periods of time. Winston was a selfish young boy who always demanded more food from his mother even though there was barely enough for them to share, and sometimes even stole from his little sister's plate. One day, Winston's mother broke apart the two-ounce chocolate ration, giving three quarters to Winston and one quarter to his little sister. Winston snatched his sister's piece and ran from the house, his mother screaming for him to come back. He never saw her again. When he returned to the apartment several hours later, his mother and sister were gone. After Winston tells his story, Julia responds by saying that she bets he was "a beastly little swine" in those days. Winston tries to explain the point of the story, but Julia falls asleep. He thinks of a violent propaganda movie he saw in which a refugee mother in a small boat tried to protect her son from a bomb by wrapping her arm around him. He finds a similarity between her gesture and his memories of his mother. Both women cared first for their children, and only second for their Party or their country. Such personal loyalty does not exist anymore.

The Party has destroyed it by removing the sex instinct and family bonds. Winston realizes that the proles maintain these loyalties, and discovers a newfound respect for them. He says aloud, "The proles are human beings. We are not human." Julia wakes, and they begin discussing their relationship and what will happen when they are arrested. They agree that the Party will never be able to force them to stop loving each other. Staying human and maintaining their love is the ultimate rebellion against the Party.

Analysis

In these chapters, Winston and Julia settle into their affair. Winston takes another significant step towards his eventual arrest by renting Mr. Charrington's room. Originally he rejects the notion, understanding that to rent the apartment will definitely mean death. However, his love for Julia and their agreed-upon hatred of the Party emboldens him, and he decides to take the risk. When Julia sees the room, she is satisfied. She adds a line to the St. Clement's Dane poem, which thrills Winston. She also suggests cleaning the St. Clement's Dane picture, but never does. If she had, perhaps she and Winston would have discovered the telescreen hiding underneath and avoided arrest.

The paperweight Winston bought from Mr. Charrington earlier on takes on a larger symbolic meaning in these chapters. Just as the painting of St. Clement's Dane and its accompanying rhyme hold special meaning for Winston, so does the paperweight. One day after Julia leaves the apartment,

Winston imagines he and Julia living in a world inside the paperweight, protected by the beautiful glass and removed from any sense of time or place. The paperweight, the apartment, the picture of St. Clement's Dane and its accompanying rhyme all symbolize Winston's hopes for freedom, yet are all false symbols. Each is obtained from Mr. Charrington, who is later revealed to be a member of the Thought Police. Even in what Winston believes is his path towards a greater understanding of the Party, history, reality, and the potential for rebellion, he is being manipulated by the Party. Perhaps the only real thing in his life is Julia. She came to him independently of the Party, and their love is the single act of rebellion that is not defined or controlled by the Party.

The prole woman singing outside the apartment window is another important symbol introduced in these chapters. Winston has already revealed a near-obsession with the proles and a belief that if there is hope, "it lies with the proles." As such, he takes a strong interest in the large, sturdy prole woman who sings simple yet passionate songs while hanging her laundry. In the prole woman, Winston recognizes a zest for life that Party members never enjoy. Listening to her songs and watching her work inspires Winston. She makes him believe that there is hope for humanity outside of the Party, perhaps in the next generation of proles.

In the apartment, Winston reveals his biggest fear: rats. When Julia points out one that is trying to sneak into the room through a hole in the corner, Winston is terrified. He describes a vague nightmare he has always had where a large wall prevents something horrible from reaching him. In the dream he never sees what is behind the wall, but in his mind he knows it is a horde of rats. Here again, Winston's dreams prove quite important to his waking life. Later, in the Ministry of Love, O'Brien will capitalize on this fear to break the last vestiges of Winston's independence and loyalty to Julia. Horrified at the idea of a rat cage being locked onto his face, Winston finally betrays his love.

In this section, Winston learns that his "friend" Syme has been vaporized. Syme is the first character in the novel to be vaporized, and his disappearance drives home the very real threat of arrest and death. Winston is headed down a similar path, but he cannot stop himself. Although death is inevitable, Winston forges on, again embracing his fatalistic outlook.

In this section, Winston finally meets and speaks to O'Brien, who has long been a symbol of the potential for rebellion from within the Party. The meeting is everything Winston had hoped for. O'Brien approaches him and gives him his address, an action Winston immediately recognizes as an invitation to discuss the Brotherhood. He thinks that the moment has finally come: he will join the rebellion, and his life will take on meaning. Tragically, we will later learn that Winston is wrong and that O'Brien is laying a trap.

In waking from a dream in which Winston remembers the last time he ever saw his mother, we begin to understand the suffering Winston endured as a child and the guilt he has carried over his mother and sister's deaths. Winston is deeply pained by the selfish acts of his childhood, and remembers his mother's love for his sister and for himself. Winston begins to understand that before the Party, loyalty to family came before loyalty to the Party. When Winston recognizes this sentiment in a Party propaganda film, he finds hope that somewhere in the world there are people who love each other. Such humanity, which Winston and Julia exhibit in their love, must mean that the potential exists to overthrow the Party. Once again, we see Winston and Julia's love as an act of rebellion in and of itself. They agree that the Party will never be able to destroy their love, and in that way, they are above the power of the Party. Once again, we will later learn that they are wrong in this assumption, and that the Party can indeed break their spirits and their love.

Summary and Analysis of Part Two VIII-X

Winston and Julia, having traveled by different routes, arrive at O'Brien's apartment. Winston is nervous to have even entered the rich, spacious part of town that the Inner Party members live in, which smells of rare foods and tobacco. O'Brien's servant, Martin, is dark-haired, has a diamond-shaped face Winston believes to be Chinese, and wears a crisp white jacket. Martin brings Winston and Julia to O'Brien. O'Brien's flat is luxurious, with thick blue carpeting and clean, cream-colored walls. Before greeting his visitors, O'Brien completes a brief bit of business. Winston suddenly wonders if he is welcome, and whether he should have come. He has no proof that O'Brien is a member of a political conspiracy against the Party. He is acting only on glances, brief conversations, and a feeling in his gut.

O'Brien walks over to his guests, switching off his telescreen on his way. Winston and Julia are astounded. They never knew anyone who had the power to turn off a telescreen. O'Brien explains that Inner Party members have that privilege. The three face each other for a moment, and O'Brien asks, "Shall I say it or will you?" Winston launches into an admission of thoughtcrime, his and Julia's hatred of Big Brother and the Party, and their belief in and eagnerness to join the underground movement. Martin appears with refreshments, which turn out to be wine, something Winston and Julia have never tasted. O'Brien explains that Martin is "one of us" and asks him to sit with them.

O'Brien answers Winston's questions, explaining that Goldstein is real and that the Brotherhood (the anti-Party movement) exists. He then asks Winston and Julia what they are willing to do for the cause. They claim that they are willing to do anything, including murdering innocents and committing suicide, to further the Brotherhood. The only thing that they are unwilling to do is to part and never see each other again. O'Brien sends Martin to the pantry and begins to lecture Winston and Julia, explaining to them that they must obey him no matter what his instructions, and that he must effectively keep them in the dark about the extent of the underground organization so as to keep other members safe from discovery. Once the Thought Police find them, the Brotherhood will abandon Winston and Julia to protect the cause.

Winston and Julia watch O'Brien with a sense of wonder and deep respect, and Winston believes that O'Brien represents hope for mankind. Before sending Julia out, O'Brien calls for a toast. Winston offers, "To the past," and they drink. Julia leaves, and O'Brien and Winston begin to speak of logistics. Winston reveals his "hiding place," Mr. Charrington's shop, and O'Brien tells him he will send him a copy of "the book...Goldstein's book." One day in the near future, Winston will find a misprint on an assignment and will have to ask for a repeat. The next day, he is to leave his briefcase at home. At some point during the day a man will walk up to him saying, "I believe you dropped your briefcase," and give him a briefcase containing the book. Before Winston and O'Brien part, O'Brien again offers a toast, saying "We shall meet again-if we do not meet again..." Winston interrupts hesitantly, stating, "We shall meet in the place of no darkness?" O'Brien agrees. Asked if he has any more questions before he leaves, Winston questions O'Brien about the rhyme Mr. Charrington taught him. O'Brien reveals the rest of the poem, adding, "When I grow rich, say the bells of Shoreditch." The poem is complete. The men shake hands, and Winston leaves.

Winston is walking towards Mr. Charrington's apartment, carrying "the book" and feeling utterly exhausted. He has worked more than ninety hours in five days, along with everyone else in the Party, because of Hate Week. On the sixth day, the enemy changed from Eurasia to Eastasia. Immediately, all the propaganda had to be adjusted to denounce Eastasia rather than Eurasia, Oceania's new ally. Winston recalls that when the event happened, he was watching a speech. The speaker was interrupted and after reading the newsflash, continued on almost seamlessly, denouncing Eastasia rather than Eurasia, which he had been discussing only moments before. The Party worked to "correct" old news stories and propaganda about being at war with Eurasia. In the view of the Party, Oceania had always been at war with Eastasia.

Finally, Winston reaches the apartment, sits on the bed, and opens the book. He reads the title page: "The Theory and Practices of Oligarchical Collectivism by Emmanuel Goldstein." Winston begins to read. The book opens with a discussion of basic class levels. Winston decides to jump ahead and begins reading the third chapter, which discusses how the world was split into three super powers. Russia absorbed Europe, and the United States absorbed Great Britain. A decade later, after a great deal of fighting, Eastasia finally solidified. Eurasia consists of the whole, "northern part of the European and Asiatic land mass, from Portugal to the Bering Strait, Oceania comprises the Americas, the Atlantaic islands including the British Isles, Australasia, and the souther portion of Africa. Eastasia, smaller than the other and with a less definite western frontier, comprises China and the countries to the south of it, the Japanese islands and a large but fluctuating portion of Manchuria, Mongolia, and Tibet."

Goldstein explains that for the past twenty-five years, these superstates have been permanently at war, despite the impossibility of a decisive outcome. Goldstein claims that the goal of modern warfare is to use the products created by society without raising standards of living. When a war is on, massive production is needed, but economic growth is impossible. The superstate populations are kept "bare, hungry, and dilapidated," compared to how they lived before the Revolution.

Goldstein notes the difficulty in maintaining a balance between wealth and power in healthy, growing societies. He explains that it was perceived that the only way to strike an effective balance and make all members of society equals would be to quickly distribute goods to prevent consumer growth: "The essential act of War is destruction." Scientists no longer pursue knowledge alone. Rather, they study facial expressions to determine ways to detect thoughtcrime, or chemistry to develop new weapons. Goldstein even notes that there has been very little development in weaponry. Each country still builds and hoards atomic bombs, which were developed long before the superstates were established.

Oceania is ruled under the ideology of Ingsoc, Eurasia under Neo-Bolshevism, and Eastasia under what can be translated as either "Death-worship" or "Obliteration of the Self." All countries have an Inner Party, a Party, a prole structure, and worship absolute, semi-divine leaders.

Goldstein states, "when war becomes literally continuous, it also ceases to be dangerous...technical progress can cease and the most palpable facts can be denied or disregarded." The people have no way of knowing the true state of the world, and must rely entirely upon the Party. Rather than being a war between nations, the war is waged upon the people to maintain loyalty, unity against a common enemy, and Party domination. Thus, as war maintains order in each individual nation, the meaning of the Party slogan "War is Peace" becomes clear.

Julia arrives, briefly acknowledges the book, and busies herself making coffee. Half an hour later, while lying in bed, Winston tells Julia she must also read the book, and she asks him to read it aloud so that they can both take it in at the same time. He begins again at the first chapter.

Goldstein discusses the pyramidal shape of society, which consists of the High, who wish to remain high, Middle, who wish to change places with the high, and Low, who wish to develop a society based on equality among all men. When the Middle works to overthrow the High, it enlists the Low to achieve its goals, and then pushes the Low back to their place. Thus, the Low are always trod upon, with no hope of true change or progress. This pattern became clear in the nineteenth century, when Socialism began to gain popularity.

The socialist movements among the superstates turned into totalitarian rule, which eventually evolved into Ingsoc, Neo-Bolshevism, and Death-worship, and worked directly towards developing "unfreedom and inequality." The purpose of these systems was to stop progress and "freeze history at a chosen moment." Rather than moving forward, society moved backward, embracing concepts such as "imprisonment without trial, the use of war prisoners as slaves, public executions torture." Goldstein blames the invention of the television for the complete loss of privacy and the drastic increase in domestic spying. The television and propagation of print media allows superstates to develop and maintain complete uniformity in opinion.

Goldstein defines the four dangers to a ruling regime as

being conquered from without, suffering from inefficient government leading to revolt, permitting a strong and independent Middle Group to develop, or losing self-confidence and willingness to govern. The main danger lies in the growth of liberalism. To address this, the government works efficiently to mold consciousness. As such, the infallible, all-powerful Big Brother sits at the apex of Oceanian society, as a representation of the Party to its country and the world, and "a focus point for love, fear, and reverence, emotions which are more easily felt toward an individual than toward an organization." Next lies the Inner Party, numbering approximately six million, less than two percent of the population. The Outer Party follows, filled with workers who allow the Party to maintain society, and finally come the proles, the "dumb masses" and non-Party members consisting of eighty-five percent of the population. Membership in these groups is defined by heredity, and each is monitored closely by the Thought Police to weed out any independent thinkers.

Goldstein goes on to discuss the advent of Newspeak, the total lack of privacy demanded by the Party, and the central notion of the mutability of the past. Goldstein focuses specifically on the Newspeak word "doublethink," which means "the power of holding two contradictory beliefs in one's mind simultaneously, and accepting both of them." Goldstein notes that the Party tends to embrace contradiction, "constantly linking opposites-knowledge with ignorance, cynicism with fanaticism," peace with war, truth with lies, plenty with starvation, love with torture. In this way, the Party has abandoned every basic principle of Socialism and turned its back on the original goals of the Revolution.

Winston stops reading and realizes that Julia has fallen asleep. He lies down next to her, noting that he still has not learned the "ultimate secret." He knows how, but not why. He knew all of these things before, but reading Goldstein's words showed him that he was sane. He falls asleep murmuring, "Sanity is not statistical."

Winston wakes thinking that he has slept for a long time, but the clock suggests otherwise. He hears the deep singing of the prole woman in the yard below. Julia wakes and notices that the oil stove is empty, which is strange considering she had been sure to fill it. Julia dresses, and they take a moment to observe the prole woman in her yard, performing her domestic duties and thriving in her simple life. Winston calls her beautiful, and reflects on how she must have changed quite quickly from a young, supple beauty to a hardened, wide mother of many needy children. He thinks about all the people in the world who live similarly simple lives, focused on family, children, and daily work, and again tells himself that if there is hope, it lies in the proles. He knows that this must have been Goldstein's conclusion as well, and takes heart in the notion that eventually "strength would change into consciousness," and humanity would recapture the earth.

In comparing himself to the freedom of the proles, he states aloud, "We are the dead." Julia echoes his words, and then suddenly, a voice from behind them states, "You are the dead." Winston and Julia jump apart in fear. Julia realizes that the voice is coming from behind the picture. The voice tells them to stay where they are, and then adds the final lines to the St. Clement's poem, "Here comes a candle to light you to bed/Here comes a chopper to chop off your head!" The picture falls to the ground, revealing a hidden telescreen. The Thought Police break in through the window, smash Winston's coral paperweight to the ground, and hit Julia. Mr. Charrington walks into the room, and Winston realizes that he looks younger, taller, colder, and more alert. He suddenly realizes that it was Mr. Charrington's voice on the telescreen; Mr. Charrington is a member of the Thought Police.

Analysis

Finally, Winston and Julia meet O'Brien in his home to discuss rebellion against the Party. This pivotal moment places Winston and Julia-in their minds, at least-forever on a path towards rebellion, but in reality only sends them careening towards arrest and torture. Winston's easy admission of hatred for the Party and desire to join an underground organization working against it seals his eventual downfall, but frees his spirit. Winston believes that he has finally found the anti-Party organization he has sought throughout his life. Throughout the meeting, both Winston and Julia are in awe of O'Brien's simultaneous status as a member of the Inner Party position and dedication to the Party's destruction. In expressing great confidence, knowledge and power, O'Brien is further established as a man of great wisdom and knowledge. Winston references his dream when he closes a toast with O'Brien, saying they shall meet "in the place where there is no darkness." Before leaving, Winston asks O'Brien about the St. Clement's Dane rhyme, and O'Brien is symbolically able to complete the verse, which assures Winston of O'Brien's like-mindedness. As is sadly common in Winston's experience, we later learn that O'Brien has lied to Winston and Julia in an effort to build up their hope for rebellion and trap them into arrest, torture, and deep psychological manipulation at the Ministry of Love. Through the description of Hate Week and the extra hours Winston must spend at work due to the sudden change of enemies in the middle of the propaganda-filled week, we again see the degree to which the Party can successfully manipulate people's minds.

The Party changes enemies in the middle of a speech from Eurasia to Eastasia, and immediately claims that Oceania has always been at war with Eastasia. Here, the phenomenon of doublethink is displayed clearly and powerfully. The masses accept this new enemy and the claim that Eastasia has always been the enemy with phenomenal ease.

Chapter IX consists almost entirely of excerpts from "the book," Goldstein's The Theory and Practice of Oligarchical Collectivism. When Julia arrives and finds Winston with the book, we again see the differences between them. Julia, more interested in her own personal survival than the future of the human race, is only vaguely interested, and after asking Winston to read aloud, falls asleep. Meanwhile, Winston is deeply fascinated by Goldstein's words and believes that the book will unlock the key to the mysteries behind the Party and its rule over Oceania.

This section of the book reads largely like a history

textbook, and provides a glimpse into Orwell's view of how Socialist revolutions have been abandoned by its champions to develop totalitarian regimes. We can assume that Orwell is drawing significantly from Stalin's rise to power and the institution of Stalinism in the Union of Soviet Socialist Republics. This section has often been criticized for an excess of academic analysis, but others cite it as supporting the novel's focus on the negative effects of totalitarian regimes. In this section, we can see how closely linked the world of 1984 is to historical events. During this long discourse on global political developments, Julia is lulled to sleep and Winston eventually follows, but only after he realizes that the book has not told him anything new. Winston and Julia wake in the morning with a false sense of safety and serenity that is interrupted quite dramatically with the invasion of the Thought Police. Only moments earlier, Winston and Julia had again gazed down at the singing prole woman, and Winston had imagined a world filled with simple humanity. Yet it was during this hopeful moment that the Thought Police arrived. Winston has always known he would be arrested, but the scene is a dramatic surprise for the reader. The inevitable day has come.

Summary and Analysis of Part Three I-III

Winston sits in a holding cell with white porcelain walls, no windows, and a high ceiling. He isn't sure where he is, but assumes that it is the Ministry of Love. The room is filled with light, and there is a low humming sound that Winston assumes is coming from the air system. A bench runs around the outside of the room, there is a telescreen on each of the four walls, and a lavatory pan sits in one corner. Winston is hungry, and has lost track of how long it has been since he has eaten, or even since he was arrested. Perhaps a day, perhaps two. He tries to sit as still as possible to avoid the wrath of the voices behind the telescreen, but after remembering he might have a piece of crust in his pocket, he succumbs to temptation. Immediately, the voice behind the telescreen yells, "Smith! 6079 Smith W.! Hands out of pockets in the cells!" Winston complies.

Before this cell, Winston was in another, far dirtier, cell, with at least ten to fifteen people in it at any given time. Most were proles or common criminals, and a few others were Party political prisoners. The common criminals were far less afraid. They fought against the prison guards, wrote on the walls, yelled back at the telescreen, and blatantly ate the food they had smuggled in, while the Party prisoners sat in terrified, obedient silence. Interestingly, the guards seemed to treat the common criminals more leniently. Winston gathered from what he heard in his cell that the work camps were "all right...so long as you had good contacts and knew the ropes," but the worst jobs in the forced labour camps were always given to political prisoners.

Winston observed the prisoners as they came and went. At one point, the guards brought in a very large woman, kicking and screaming, and unceremoniously dumped her across Winston's lap. She sat up, swore at the guards, and apologized to Winston by saying, "I wouldn't 'a sat on you, only the buggers put me there. They dono 'ow to treat a lady, do they?" Next, she vomited, and then, once recovered, put her arm around Winston and asked his name. Her last name was Smith as well, and she noted that is was even possible that she was his mother. Winston was struck by the possibility, but did not pursue the matter. None of the other prisoners spoke to Winston, but he overheard whispered, fearful conversations regarding Room.

In the white-walled cell, Winston thinks about what is going to happen to him. He imagines being beaten and tortured, and screaming for mercy. He rarely thinks of Julia, and finds it hard to fix her image in his mind. He wonders if O'Brien knows he has been arrested, and remembers him saying that even though the Brotherhood cannot ever help a prisoner, it might be able to smuggle him a razor blade. Winston hopes for the razor blade, imagining how quickly he might be able to end his life. Winston loses track of time completely, recognizing that with the lights always on, the Ministry of Love truly is "the place with no darkness." Suddenly, Ampleforth is thrown into the cell.

He is dirty, shoeless, and clearly in a poor state. The two

men talk, and Ampleforth says that he although he is not sure, he thinks he has been arrested because he left the word "God" in a Kipling poem. There was simply no other way to rhyme the couplet. They continue talking, but the telescreen quickly silences them. The guards return for Ampleforth, and he is sent to Room 101. Some time passes, and the guards return again, this time with Tom Parsons. Winston is shocked: he never expected Parsons to be arrested. Parsons is visibly upset, and begins asking Winston if they will shoot him. He expresses confidence that he will receive a fair trial, and hopes that his loyalty to the Party will keep his labour camp sentence short. Winston asks Parsons whether he is guilty, to which Parsons replies, "Of course I'm guilty! You don't think the Party would arrest an innocent man, do you?" He then tells Winston how his seven-year-old daughter listened at his bedroom door at night and heard him saying "Down with Big Brother!" in his sleep. He absolutely believes that he is guilty of saying it, and is proud of his daughter for doing her duty to the Party in reporting him. Parsons then uses the lavatory in a loud and obscene manner, smelling up the room for hours to come.

Parsons is eventually taken out, and other prisoners come and go. Some are relegated to Room 101, and Winston begins to notice that a few people tremble in great fear upon hearing those words. The guards bring in a man so emaciated that it seems he is being starved to death. One man offers him a piece of bread, but the telescreen quickly shouts him down, "2713 Bumstead J.! Let fall that piece of bread!" He does as he is told. Guards burst into the room, and Bumstead is punched so hard that he is sent flying across the room. Two halves of a dental plate fall out of his mouth, and blood gushes from his face. He pulls himself up to a sitting position, and Winston notices that his mouth is extremely swollen and bruised. All the other prisoners sit quietly. A guard opens the door and tells the starving man to go to Room 101.

He immediately gasps and protests, his face turning a shade of green, begging for anything but Room 101, even telling the guard he would rather they cut his wife's and children's throats than take him there. In a panic, he looks around the room, finds Bumstead, the man who tried to give him a piece of bread, and argues that the guards should take him because he is a true enemy to the Party. Finally he throws himself to the ground, grabbing a leg of one of the benches and howling, begging not to go to Room 101. Ignoring his pleas, the guards struggle with him, break his hands free, and escort him from the room while all the other prisoners sit quietly and watch. Many hours pass. Winston is desperately hungry and thirsty, and his thoughts of Julia and O'Brien wane. The doors open, and O'Brien walks in. Winston thinks O'Brien has also been captured, but O'Brien explains, "The got me a long time ago...You knew this Winston. Don't deceive yourself. You did know it-You have always known it." The guard with O'Brien hits Winston in the elbow, and he buckles in pain. The guard laughs, and Winston realizes that in the face of pain, there are no heroes. Nothing is worse than physical pain.

Winston wakes, and realizes that he is lying on a cot. O'Brien and a man with a hypodermic syringe are standing next to him. He does not know how long he has been unconscious, and has no concept of how long he has been undergoing torture. It might have been months, weeks, days, or only hours. He has been interrogated and forced to admit to a long list of crimes, and has been regularly and viciously beaten, suffering deep bruises and fractures all over his body. Sometimes, he knows, he screamed for mercy before anyone even hit him, and other times he convinced himself he would wait to confess until the pain became unbearable. After some time, the beatings became less frequent.

When his questioners became Party intellectuals, he was forced to suffer face slapping, ear ringing, and standing on one foot for long periods of time. The complicated stream of questions could go on for hours, catching him in self-contradictions and leading him to a state of nervous fatigue. Sometimes they were nice to him, and spoke to him as though he were an equal, but then they would turn on him quickly. To gain their approval, he confessed to any and everything he could think of, including the assassination of Party members and various traitorous acts.

Throughout all of this, O'Brien is always nearby, guiding and defining the extent of Winston's torture. Winston finds himself strapped into a chair with O'Brien at his side, sitting next to a dial and a lever. O'Brien turns a lever, and Winston is overcome with pain. O'Brien continues talking to Winston, warning him that the dial goes all the way up to 100. He explains to Winston that he is taking the trouble to truly work with him to correct his mental derangement and defective memory. He begins by asking Winston what country Oceania is at war with, and what country Oceania has always been at war with. He then moves on to the newspaper clipping Winston found regarding Jones, Aaronson and Rutherford. He produces a copy of the photograph, places it in a memory hole, and explains that it never existed. He forces Winston to understand that the past does not exist in space, and therefore only exists in records and in human memory. In controlling these two things, the Party controls the past. Winston argues that the Party has not controlled his memory, and O'Brien counters that in fact, Winston has not controlled his own memory. He is at the Ministry of Love because he "failed in humanity, in self-discipline...would not make the act of submission which is the price of sanity." O'Brien explains, "Reality exists in the human mind, and nowhere else."

O'Brien begins forcing Winston to destroy this last vestige of his independent spirit. He works to show him that if the Party says that two plus two makes five, it does. Throughout this entire exchange, O'Brien tortures Winston with the dial, turning it up to 60, and perhaps beyond. Finally, O'Brien releases the dial and puts his arm around Winston. In his heart, Winston still has not admitted that two and two can actually make five. O'Brien begins again, the needle travels higher, and Winston becomes increasingly desperate.

O'Brien reveals to Winston that people are brought to the Ministry of Love not to force them to confess, but to cure them. He discusses how past regimes tortured and killed their enemies, but did not work to change them. In contrast, the Party converts and changes their enemies, making them "one of their own" before killing them. He tells Winston, "We will crush you down to the point from which there is no coming back...Never again will you be capable of ordinary human feeling...friendship, or joy of living...courage or integrity."

O'Brien orders a new form of punishment similar to electroshock therapy while continuing his line of questioning. Finally, he is successful in convincing Winston that his memory is flawed. At the end of the session, when Winston is almost able to actually see five fingers where there are only four, O'Brien reveals that he likes Winston, because his mind reminds him of his own, except that Winston's mind is deranged. He then allows Winston to ask him questions, and Winston asks about Julia. She has betrayed him, and every part of her independence has been destroyed. Winston asks if Big Brother exists. O'Brien answers that he does, in the way that the Party does, but that he will never die. Winston asks if the Brotherhood exists, and O'Brien says that Winston will never know the answer to that question. Winston asks what is in Room 101. O'Brien answers, "You know what is in Room 101, Winston. Everyone knows what is in Room 101."

Winston is again tied down, flat on his back. O'Brien mentions Winston's diary entry, in which he wrote "I understand how; I do not understand why." In reference to this, O'Brien mentions Goldstein's book and reveals that he collaborated in writing it. Winston asks if it is accurate, and O'Brien replies that the book's notion of enlightenment and proletarian rebellion is nonsense. The Party can never be overthrown: "The Party is forever." After explaining this fact, O'Brien asks Winston why the Party exists. Knowing the correct answer, but not believing it, Winston replies, "You are ruling over us for our own good."

O'Brien turns the dial, and explains to Winston that the Party "seeks power entirely for its own sake...We are not interested in the good of others; we are interested solely in power." He compares the Party to the German Nazis and Russian Communists, but argues that the Party is far superior because it has no illusions of equality. The Party embraces power for the sake of power, not for any other cause. In utter submission, individuals can become part of a greater, immortal whole: the Party. As such, "Freedom is Slavery... Slavery is Freedom." O'Brien continues, explaining that the Party defines all, including the laws of nature, and explains that before man, there was no world. Without human consciousness, nothing exists. Winston argues that dinosaurs and ancient beasts lives before humans, and O'Brien counters that 19th-century scientists made those stories up. Man is the centre of the universe, the earth is the centre of the universe: "Outside man there is nothing." O'Brien pauses this philosophical discussion to return to the main issue of power over man, which is achieved through making men suffer. Progress will work towards more pain, more hatred, and more destruction. Art, science and literature will disappear. There will be no way to distinguish beauty from ugliness.

O'Brien describes "a world of victory, triumph after triumph after triumph: an endless pressing, pressing, pressing on the nerve of power." Winston disagrees, claiming that such a society would die of its own accord. He tells O'Brien that the Party will never overcome "the spirit of Man." O'Brien counters that if Winston is a man, he is the last one on earth. Winston admits feeling superior to O'Brien, at which point O'Brien plays a tape revealing the irony of Winston's statement in which Winston agrees to do anything in support of the Brotherhood, including murder, espionage, etc.

O'Brien forces Winston to look at his naked body in a mirror. Winston is horrified to see his gray, weak, bowed body. He is emaciated, has gone partially bald, is extremely dirty, and carries innumerable scars. He can barely recognize himself. O'Brien ridicules his appearance, showing him how he is rotting away, and even pulling out one of his remaining teeth. Winston breaks down, and O'Brien assures him that he can escape from this hell if he so chooses. Winston refuses to accept defeat, claiming that he still has not betrayed his love for Julia. Winston asks when he will be shot, and O'Brien says it might be a long time, but that in the end, it will happen.

Analysis

Part Two describes both the beginning and the end of

Winston and Julia's affair. Their arrest separates them for the entirety of their time at the Ministry of Love. In this way, Winston's only true act of rebellion is over. Winston's torture proves to be as horrific as he always imagined. He easily concludes that physical pain is the worst thing in the world, and entirely unbearable. During the process of torture, O'Brien quickly gains control over him and begins to penetrate his mind through deep psychological manipulation, assisted by electroshock therapy. In the hands of O'Brien and the Ministry of Love, Winston cannot stop the process of his psychological and physical destruction. O'Brien is a pivotal character throughout this section, and it is here that we finally gain insight into his thus far mysterious mind. He is an ardent Party supporter and believes deeply in the purity of his mission and work. Interestingly, Winston's fatalistic outlook continues in prison, as he acknowledges that somewhere deep down, he probably knew all along that O'Brien was a Party supporter. In truth, Winston knew he would be arrested before he met with O'Brien, and therefore the meeting neither increased nor decreased his risk.

Perhaps Winston did imagine O'Brien was a Party supporter, but wanted to trust him and believe in the Brotherhood so badly that he disregarded these thoughts. Winston's dream, seven years ago, of O'Brien's voice telling him they would "meet in the place where there is no darkness" led Winston to obsess over O'Brien and gave him hope that he might be a source of support. O'Brien becomes Winston's hero; even in his torture sessions he is calmer when O'Brien is near. As O'Brien points out, Winston once wrote in his diary that it did not matter whether O'Brien was on his side or not, because he felt the man understood him. Ironically, Winston seems to love O'Brien, even throughout the torture process, and as such comes to believe the Party propaganda he has so long rebelled against.

In this section, Winston finally gets an answer to his question, "Why?" O'Brien reveals to him that the Party pursues power for the sake of power, and for no other goal. This is why the Party is able to define the present, the past, and every facet of society. Here, we also see how the Party has broken from Socialism and the Revolution to embrace totalitarian rule. This is Orwell's greatest frustration with totalitarian regimes. Orwell watched as supposedly Socialist revolutions broke down into totalitarian regimes, specifically in the case of the Stalinist Union of Soviet Socialist Republics and Hitler's Nazi Germany. These regimes spoke of their goal of improving life for the common man, yet in actuality simply sought power. In 1984, the Party admits to its goal of power for power's sake. This totalitarian society, efficient in quelling all dissent and individuality, and in defining itself and the world, is the ultimate dystopia. Winston's torture process reveals the degree of violence prisoners are subjected to. They are starved, beaten, and deformed; brought to their weakest point, and then finally given salvation. When wholly broken, the prisoner's spirit and mind will finally give in to manipulation. Winston is almost physically destroyed in the process of his torture, but only after he sees the shell he has become does he submit to O'Brien. O'Brien becomes his savior in the next chapters, allowing him to eat, heal and grow strong. As his savior, O'Brien greatly influences Winston's mind and thought processes, guiding him to the ways of the Party and removing all sense of individuality and independence.

Summary and Analysis of Part Three IV-VI

Winston is still in the Ministry of Love, but his health is steadily improving. He is eating well and continually growing stronger. He has been given a pillow and a mattress for his wooden bed, has had a bath, and has been permitted to wash himself in a small basin. He also has new underclothes and clean overalls. Winston is unsure of the exact timeframe, but thinks that weeks or months have gone by. He has been dreaming a great deal, largely of the Golden Country, his mother, Julia, and O'Brien. He is happy and peaceful in his dreams. Eventually, he begins to exercise, walking around the cell and experimenting with carrying and lifting weight.

When he is able to complete a pushup, he feels a great sense of accomplishment. Soon, he begins to use the slate and pencil he has been given. Working through what he and O'Brien discussed, Winston analyzes his perspective of the world. He realizes that he cannot fight against the Party, and that O'Brien is correct in stating that sanity is statistical. He writes on his slate, "Freedom is Slavery, Two and Two Make Five." Then he hesitates, forgetting what comes next, reasons it out, and writes "God is Power." He accepts that the past is alterable, he accepts the Party's rule, and he accepts that he has been wrong. He thinks, "Only surrender, and everything else followed." Winston sleeps, and in his dream calls out Julia's name. He wakes himself with this exclamation and immediately realizes that he has set himself back significantly by revealing this weakness. He had surrendered his mind, but not his heart. As he expects, Winston hears boots walking up to his door. O'Brien enters and tells Winston to follow him. O'Brien explains that intellectually, there is little wrong with Winston, but emotionally, he has made no progress. Demanding honesty, O'Brien asks Winston what he thinks of Big Brother. Winston replies, "I hate him." O'Brien notes that the time has come for Winston to love Big Brother. He sends Winston to Room 101.

O'Brien meets him in Room 101, and explains to Winston that Room 101 is "the worst thing in the world," which is different for each individual. For Winston, the worst thing in the world is rats. Winston sees the cage and begins to scream protests. O'Brien picks up the cage, which houses huge rats, and sets it down next to Winston. O'Brien explains that rats are carnivorous, and are known to eat infants and attack sick or dying people. The cage has a mask that will fit over Winston's head. A lever release will force the cage door up, allowing the rats access to Winston's face. They will attack him, gouging his eye, cheeks, and tongue. Winston is in a panic. He realizes that he must put someone else between himself and the horror of the cage. He feels "blind, helpless, mindless" in his fear. When the mask is inches from his face, he screams, "Do it to Julia!" He begs O'Brien to force Julia to suffer in his place. O'Brien is satisfied.

Winston has been released from the Ministry of Love. He

sits in the Chestnut Tree Cafe drinking their special clove-flavored Victory Gin. Winston listens to the telescreen, eager for a special bulletin from the Ministry of Peace. There should be news about Central Africa. Suddenly, his mind wanders. He has trouble focusing on any single thought these days. He can smell the gin, and thinks of how it is forever mixed up with the smell of the rats he faced, although he never names the beasts. A waiter who recognizes Winston as a regular brings him a chessboard and a Times before filling his gin glass. He begins to examine the chess problem in the Times: "White to play and mate in two moves." He looks at Big Brother, thinking to himself, "White always mates." The telescreen announces that a bulletin will be given at fifteen-thirty. He is excited to think of the news. Eurasia is invading Central Africa, and if they are successful may eventually succeed in splitting Oceania in two, which could mean the destruction of the Party. Unconsciously, he traces "2+2=5" in the dust on the table, and thinks of Julia. They saw each other once after being released, purely by chance. He followed her on her walk, always a few feet behind. Eventually she stopped and he put his arm around her waist, but felt revulsion at the thought of making love to her. She did not respond; her body felt rigid and lifeless.

They sat down on a bench with some distance between them. After some time, she told him, "I betrayed you." He told her the same. They agreed, through a distant conversation, that there are some things they can do to you that make you think and care only about yourself. After that, it is impossible to ever feel the same way towards one who you loved. She made an excuse to leave, and they both feebly suggested they should meet again, knowing they never would. Winston followed her for a short time, but eventually lost her in a crowd and gave up the effort. Sitting in the Chestnut Tree Cafe, Winston feels nostalgic, and tears up when the song "Under the spreading Chestnut Tree, I sold you and you sold me" begins to play over the telescreen. The waiter brings him more gin. Winston reflects on how his life is now filled with gin. It is "his life, his death, and his resurrection." Winston is a fixture at the

Chestnut Tree Cafe, despite his new position as a sinecure, meaning he is on a sub-committee under many other sub-committees, and only goes to work a couple of days out of the week. He does little, but is paid well. Winston's thoughts turn back to the battle in Africa. He wonders if there even is a battle. Suddenly, a strong memory comes to him. Winston was nine or ten, sitting on the floor and shaking a dice box, laughing with excitement. His mother was sitting across from him, and also laughing. It was a brief moment, in their hard lives, of happiness and camaraderie. His mother had gone out in the rain to buy him the board game as a reward for behaving well. For a whole afternoon, Winston, his mother, and his sister had a wonderful, joyous time.

Winston pushes the memory out of his mind, certain that it is one of those false memories that keeps troubling him. Suddenly, a loud trumpet call sounds, signaling that the bulletin is about to be announced. Oceania has intelligently outflanked Eurasia, capturing the whole of Africa and perhaps bringing the war close to an end. It is the greatest victory in history. Winston listens to the news with excitement, thinking it has all turned out just as he had thought it would. His feet stir beneath him, and he imagines himself running with the cheering crowds out in the street. He looks at the poster of Big Brother and is in awe of his greatness. He recognizes that only ten minutes ago he had wondered if Oceania might be defeated. But now, staring into the warm, strong eyes of Big Brother, he realizes that this could never be. With tears of great understanding trickling down his face, Winston realizes he has finally defeated himself. He loves Big Brother.

Analysis

These chapters describe Winston's recovery from his near-death experience in the Ministry of Love. O'Brien continues to be his savior, allowing Winston to heal, benefit from basic comforts such as a mattress and a pillow, and gain back his strength. In this process, Winston begins to fully accept O'Brien's version of the world. Without the Party, there is nothing. Here, we see the effectiveness of the combination of

O'Brien's physical and psychological torture. Winston, a lone man, has no hope for successfully rebuffing these invasions into his body and mind. He is overcome through force and power. Knowing he has been beaten, Winston still wonders when he will be finally be killed, when the Party will finally decide his life is over.

Winston reveals that his conversion is incomplete when he yells out Julia's name in his sleep. O'Brien methodically observes Winston's behaviour, waiting to see exactly how much progress he has made. When Winston calls out in his sleep, O'Brien knows there is still some vestige of individual thought left in Winston's mind. He loves Julia, and to be a successful Party member, he can only have love for Big Brother. To remedy this dysfunction, O'Brien brings Winston to Room 101. The rat cage stretches Winston's sanity to its breaking point. To some, the rat cage might seem a simple tool, not threatening enough to demand Winston's final submission.

However, we previously learned that Winston's greatest fear was rats. This fear is innate, and lies deep in his subconscious. Therefore, presenting him with the danger of sitting fully conscious in a chair and having his face eaten by rats is the worst possible threat Winston can face. In this scene, Orwell argues yet again that physical pain is the worst thing a person can face. Winston is unable to fight against the potential horror of rats eating his face, and submits almost immediately. In this pivotal scene, Winston loses all hope of maintaining his individual spirit or his love for Julia. They once promised each other that the Party could never take away their love for each other, but now they have been proven wrong.

Although his love for Julia is removed, as we see through the failure of their accidental meeting, Winston does not yet love Big Brother. Back in Oceanian society, Winston is a shell of a man. The totalitarian regime has broken him. The reader might once have seen Winston as hope for a brighter future for Oceania, and for the end of Party rule. Here, in the final chapters, we come to understand that there is no hope for rebellion against such a regime. The Party's power is total, and once that power is obtained, there is no way to reverse it. In the last scene, Winston finally comes to love Big Brother, and in so doing notes that he has finally beaten himself. The man as we first knew him has ceased to exist. Winston has submitted to complete psychological control by the Party.

In reflecting on this conclusion, it is important to note that Winston was one of few members of Oceanian society who even remembered a time before the Revolution. Julia, although disgruntled with Party life, never believed in the potential for successful rebellion. It is easy to assume that once the last people who remember life before the Revolution die off, and once Newspeak officially takes over for Oldspeak, thus removing the citizens' ability to even think against the Party, there will be no hope for Winston's ideals. The Party's control will be absolute, and it is difficult to see any scenario that would break it. Here, we have Orwell's final warning. He suggests that allowing totalitarian regimes to develop and take hold is the equivalent of placing society on a path towards violent governance and absolute removal of individual thoughts and freedoms; in other words, towards the ultimate dystopia.

Chapter 10

Text

Part One Chapter 1

It was a bright cold day in April, and the clocks were striking thirteen. Winston Smith, his chin nuzzled into his breast in an effort to escape the vile wind, slipped quickly through the glass doors of Victory Mansions, though not quickly enough to prevent a swirl of gritty dust from entering along with him.

The hallway smelt of boiled cabbage and old rag mats. At one end of it a coloured poster, too large for indoor display, had been tacked to the wall. It depicted simply an enormous face, more than a metre wide: the face of a man of about forty-five, with a heavy black moustache and ruggedly handsome features. Winston made for the stairs. It was no use trying the lift. Even at the best of times it was seldom working, and at present the electric current was cut off during daylight hours. It was part of the economy drive in preparation for Hate Week. The flat was seven flights up, and Winston, who was thirty-nine and had a varicose ulcer above his right ankle, went slowly, resting several times on the way. On each landing, opposite the lift-shaft, the poster with the enormous face gazed from the wall. It was one of those pictures which are so contrived that the eyes follow you about when you move. BIG BROTHER IS WATCHING YOU, the caption beneath it ran.

Inside the flat a fruity voice was reading out a list of figures which had something to do with the production of pig-iron. The voice came from an oblong metal plaque like a dulled mirror which formed part of the surface of the right-hand wall.

Winston turned a switch and the voice sank somewhat, though the words were still distinguishable. The instrument (the telescreen, it was called) could be dimmed, but there was no way of shutting it off completely. He moved over to the window: a smallish, frail figure, the meagreness of his body merely emphasized by the blue overalls which were the uniform of the party. His hair was very fair, his face naturally sanguine, his skin roughened by coarse soap and blunt razor blades and the cold of the winter that had just ended.

Outside, even through the shut window-pane, the world looked cold. Down in the street little eddies of wind were whirling dust and torn paper into spirals, and though the sun was shining and the sky a harsh blue, there seemed to be no colour in anything, except the posters that were plastered everywhere. The blackmoustachio'd face gazed down from every commanding corner. There was one on the house-front immediately opposite. BIG BROTHER IS WATCHING YOU, the caption said, while the dark eyes looked deep into Winston's own. Down at streetlevel another poster, torn at one corner, flapped fitfully in the wind, alternately covering and uncovering the single word INGSOC. In the far distance a helicopter skimmed down between the roofs, hovered for an instant like a bluebottle, and darted away again with a curving flight. It was the police patrol, snooping into people's windows. The patrols did not matter, however. Only the Thought Police mattered.

Behind Winston's back the voice from the telescreen was still babbling away about pig-iron and the overfulfilment of the Ninth Three-Year Plan. The telescreen received and transmitted simultaneously. Any sound that Winston made, above the level of a very low whisper, would be picked up by it, moreover, so long as he remained within the field of vision which the metal plaque commanded, he could be seen as well as heard. There was of course no way of knowing whether you were being watched at any given moment. How often, or on what system, the Thought Police plugged in on any individual wire was guesswork. It was even conceivable that they watched everybody all the time. But at any rate they could plug in your wire whenever they wanted to. You had to live--did live, from habit that became instinct--in the assumption that every sound you made was overheard, and, except in darkness, every movement scrutinized.

Winston kept his back turned to the telescreen. It was safer, though, as he well knew, even a back can be revealing. A kilometre away the Ministry of Truth, his place of work, towered vast and white above the grimy landscape. This, he thought with a sort of vague distaste--this was London, chief city of Airstrip One, itself the third most populous of the provinces of Oceania. He tried to squeeze out some childhood memory that should tell him whether London had always been quite like this. Were there always these vistas of rotting nineteenth-century houses, their sides shored up with baulks of timber, their windows patched with cardboard and their roofs with corrugated iron, their crazy garden walls sagging in all directions? And the bombed sites where the plaster dust swirled in the air and the willow-herb straggled over the heaps of rubble; and the places where the bombs had cleared a larger patch and there had sprung up sordid colonies of wooden dwellings like chicken-houses? But it was no use, he could not remember: nothing remained of his childhood except a series of bright-lit tableaux occurring against no background and mostly unintelligible.

The Ministry of Truth--Minitrue, in Newspeak--was startlingly different from any other object in sight. It was an enormous pyramidal structure of glittering white concrete, soaring up, terrace after terrace, 300 metres into the air. From where Winston stood it was just possible to read, picked out on its white face in elegant lettering, the three slogans of the Party:

WAR IS PEACE
FREEDOM IS SLAVERY
IGNORANCE IS STRENGTH

The Ministry of Truth contained, it was said, three thousand rooms above ground level, and corresponding ramifications below. Scattered about London there were just three other buildings of similar appearance and size. So completely did they dwarf the surrounding architecture that from the roof of Victory Mansions you could see all four of them simultaneously. They were the homes of the four Ministries between which the entire apparatus of government was divided. The Ministry of Truth, which concerned itself with news, entertainment, education, and the fine arts. The Ministry of Peace, which concerned itself with war. The Ministry of Love, which maintained law and order. And the Ministry of Plenty, which was responsible for economic affairs. Their names, in Newspeak: Minitrue, Minipax, Miniluv, and Miniplenty.

The Ministry of Love was the really frightening one. There were no windows in it at all. Winston had never been inside the Ministry of Love, nor within half a kilometre of it. It was a place impossible to enter except on official business, and then only by penetrating through a maze of barbed-wire entanglements, steel doors, and hidden machine-gun nests. Even the streets leading up to its outer barriers were roamed by gorilla-faced guards in black uniforms, armed with jointed truncheons.

Winston turned round abruptly. He had set his features into the expression of quiet optimism which it was advisable to wear when facing the telescreen. He crossed the room into the tiny kitchen. By leaving the Ministry at this time of day he had sacrificed his lunch in the canteen, and he was aware that there was no food in the kitchen except a hunk of dark-coloured bread which had got to be saved for tomorrow's breakfast. He took down from the shelf a bottle of colourless liquid with a plain white label marked VICTORY GIN. It gave off a sickly, oily smell, as of Chinese ricespirit. Winston poured out nearly a teacupful, nerved himself for a shock, and gulped it down like a dose of medicine.

Instantly his face turned scarlet and the water ran out of his eyes. The stuff was like nitric acid, and moreover, in swallowing it one had the sensation of being hit on the back of the head with a rubber club. The next moment, however, the burning in his belly died down and the world began to look more cheerful. He took a cigarette from a crumpled packet marked VICTORY CIGARETTES and incautiously held it upright, whereupon the tobacco fell out on to the floor. With the next he was more successful. He went back to the living-room and sat down at a small table that stood to the left of the telescreen. From the table drawer he took out a penholder, a bottle of ink, and a thick, quarto-sized blank book with a red back and a marbled cover.

For some reason the telescreen in the living-room was in an unusual position. Instead of being placed, as was normal, in the end wall, where it could command the whole room, it was in the longer wall, opposite the window. To one side of it there was a shallow alcove in which Winston was now sitting, and which, when the flats were built, had probably been intended to hold bookshelves. By sitting in the alcove, and keeping well back, Winston was able to remain outside the range of the telescreen, so far as sight went. He could be heard, of course, but so long as he stayed in his present position he could not be seen. It was partly the unusual geography of the room that had suggested to him the thing that he was now about to do.

But it had also been suggested by the book that he had just taken out of the drawer. It was a peculiarly beautiful book. Its smooth creamy paper, a little yellowed by age, was of a kind that had not been manufactured for at least forty years past. He could guess, however, that the book was much older than that. He had seen it lying in the window of a frowsy little junk-shop in a slummy quarter of the town (just what quarter he did not now remember) and had been stricken immediately by an overwhelming desire to possess it. Party members were supposed not to go into ordinary shops ('dealing on the free market', it was called), but the rule was not strictly kept, because there were various things, such as shoelaces and razor blades, which it was impossible to get hold of in any other way. He had given a quick glance up and down the street and then had slipped inside and bought the book for two dollars fifty. At the time he was not conscious of wanting it for any particular purpose. He had carried it guiltily home in his briefcase. Even with nothing written in it, it was a compromising possession. The thing that he was about to do was to open a diary. This was not illegal (nothing was illegal, since there were no longer any laws), but if detected it was reasonably certain that it would be punished by death, or at least by twenty-five years in a forced-labour camp. Winston fitted a nib into the penholder and sucked it to get the grease off. The pen was an archaic instrument, seldom used even for signatures, and he had procured one, furtively and with some difficulty, simply because of a feeling that the beautiful creamy paper deserved to be written on with a real nib instead of being scratched with an ink-pencil. Actually he was not used to writing by hand. Apart from very short notes, it was usual to dictate everything into the speakwrite which was of course impossible for his present purpose. He dipped the pen into the ink and then faltered for just a second. A tremor had gone through his bowels. To mark the paper was the decisive act. In small clumsy letters he wrote:

April 4th, 1984: He sat back. A sense of complete helplessness had descended upon him. To begin with, he did not know with any certainty that this was 1984. It must be round about that date, since he was fairly sure that his age was thirty-nine, and he believed that he had been born in 1944 or 1945; but it was never possible nowadays to pin down any date within a year or two.

For whom, it suddenly occurred to him to wonder, was he writing this diary? For the future, for the unborn. His mind hovered for a moment round the doubtful date on the page, and then fetched up with a bump against the Newspeak word doublethink. For the first time the magnitude of what he had undertaken came home to him. How could you communicate with the future? It was of its nature impossible. Either the future would resemble the present, in which case it would not listen to him: or it would be different from it, and his predicament would be meaningless.

For some time he sat gazing stupidly at the paper. The telescreen had changed over to strident military music. It was curious that he seemed not merely to have lost the power of expressing himself, but even to have forgotten what it was that he had originally intended to say. For weeks past he had been making ready for this moment, and it had never crossed his mind that anything would be needed except courage. The actual writing would be easy. All he had to do was to transfer to paper the interminable restless monologue that had been running inside his head, literally for years. At this moment, however, even the monologue had dried up. Moreover his varicose ulcer had begun itching unbearably. He dared not scratch it, because if he did so it always became inflamed. The seconds were ticking by. He was conscious of nothing except the blankness of the page in front of him, the itching of the skin above his ankle, the blaring of the music, and a slight booziness caused by the gin.

Suddenly he began writing in sheer panic, only imperfectly aware of what he was setting down. His small but childish handwriting straggled up and down the page, shedding first its capital letters and finally even its full stops:

April 4th, 1984. Last night to the flicks. All war films. One very good one of a ship full of refugees being bombed somewhere in the Mediterranean. Audience much amused by shots of a great huge fat man trying to swim away with a helicopter after him, first you saw him wallowing along in the water like a porpoise, then you saw him through the helicopters gunsights, then he was full of holes and the sea round him turned pink and he sank as suddenly as though the holes had let in the water, audience shouting with laughter when he sank. then you saw a lifeboat full of children with a helicopter hovering over it. there was a middle-aged woman might have been a jewess sitting up in the bow with a little boy about three years old in her arms. little boy screaming with fright and hiding his head between her breasts as if he was trying to burrow right into her and the woman putting her arms round him and comforting him although she was blue with fright herself, all the time covering him up as much as possible as if she thought her arms could keep the bullets off him. then the helicopter planted a 20 kilo bomb in among them terrific flash and the boat went all to matchwood. then there was a wonderful shot of a child's arm going up up up right up into the air a helicopter with a camera in its nose must have followed it up and there was a lot of applause from the party seats but a woman down in the prole part of the house suddenly started kicking up a fuss and shouting they didnt oughter of showed it not in front of kids they didnt it aint right not in front of kids it aint until the police turned her turned her out i dont suppose anything happened to her nobody cares what the proles say typical prole reaction they never--

Winston stopped writing, partly because he was suffering from cramp. He did not know what had made him pour out this stream of rubbish. But the curious thing was that while he was doing so a totally different memory had clarified itself in his mind, to the point where he almost felt equal to writing it down. It was, he now realized, because of this other incident that he had suddenly decided to come home and begin the diary today.

It had happened that morning at the Ministry, if anything so nebulous could be said to happen.

It was nearly eleven hundred, and in the Records Department, where Winston worked, they were dragging the chairs out of the cubicles and grouping them in the centre of the hall opposite the big telescreen, in preparation for the Two Minutes Hate. Winston was just taking his place in one of the middle rows when two people whom he knew by sight, but had never spoken to, came unexpectedly into the room. One of them was a girl whom he often passed in the corridors. He did not know her name, but he knew that she worked in the Fiction Department. Presumably--since he had sometimes seen her with oily hands and carrying a spanner she had some mechanical job on one of the novel-writing machines. She was a bold-looking girl, of about twenty-seven, with thick hair, a freckled face, and swift, athletic movements. A narrow scarlet sash, emblem of the Junior Anti-Sex League, was wound several times round the waist of her overalls, just tightly enough to bring out the shapeliness of her hips. Winston had disliked her from the very first moment of seeing her. He knew the reason. It was because of the atmosphere of hockey-fields and cold baths and community hikes and general clean-mindedness which she managed to carry about with her. He disliked nearly all women, and especially the young and pretty ones. It was always the women, and above all the young ones, who were the most bigoted adherents of the Party, the swallowers of slogans, the amateur spies and nosers-out of unorthodoxy. But this particular girl gave him the impression of being more dangerous than most. Once when they passed in the corridor she gave him a quick sidelong glance which seemed to pierce right into him and for a moment had filled him with black terror. The idea had even crossed his mind that she might be an agent of the Thought Police. That, it was true, was very unlikely. Still, he continued to feel a peculiar uneasiness, which had fear mixed up in it as well as hostility, whenever she was anywhere near him.

The other person was a man named O'Brien, a member of the Inner Party and holder of some post so important and remote that Winston had only a dim idea of its nature. A momentary hush passed over the group of people round the chairs as they saw the black overalls of an Inner Party member approaching. O'Brien was a large, burly man with a thick neck and a coarse, humorous, brutal face. In spite of his formidable appearance he had a certain charm of manner. He had a trick of resettling his spectacles on his nose which was curiously disarming--in some indefinable way, curiously civilized. It was a gesture which, if anyone had still thought in such terms, might have recalled an eighteenth-century nobleman offering his snuffbox. Winston had seen O'Brien perhaps a dozen times in almost as many years.

He felt deeply drawn to him, and not solely because he was intrigued by the contrast between O'Brien's urbane manner and his prize-fighter's physique. Much more it was because of a secretly held belief--or perhaps not even a belief, merely a hope--that O'Brien's political orthodoxy was not perfect. Something in his face suggested it irresistibly. And again, perhaps it was not even unorthodoxy that was written in his face, but simply intelligence. But at any rate he had the appearance of being a person that you could talk to if somehow you could cheat the telescreen and get him alone. Winston had never made the smallest effort to verify this guess: indeed, there was no way of doing so. At this moment O'Brien glanced at his wrist-watch, saw that it was nearly eleven hundred, and evidently decided to stay in the Records Department until the Two Minutes Hate was over. He took a chair in the same row as Winston, a couple of places away. A small, sandy-haired woman who worked in the next cubicle to Winston was between them. The girl with dark hair was sitting immediately behind.

The next moment a hideous, grinding speech, as of some monstrous machine running without oil, burst from the big telescreen at the end of the room. It was a noise that set one's teeth on edge and bristled the hair at the back of one's neck. The Hate had started.

As usual, the face of Emmanuel Goldstein, the Enemy of the People, had flashed on to the screen. There were hisses here and there among the audience. The little sandy-haired woman gave a squeak of mingled fear and disgust. Goldstein was the renegade and backslider who once, long ago (how long ago, nobody quite remembered), had been one of the leading figures of the Party, almost on a level with Big Brother himself, and then had engaged in counter-revolutionary activities, had been condemned to death, and had mysteriously escaped and disappeared. The programmes of the Two Minutes Hate varied from day to day, but there was none in which Goldstein was not the principal figure. He was the primal traitor, the earliest defiler of the Party's purity. All subsequent crimes against the Party, all treacheries, acts of sabotage, heresies, deviations, sprang directly out of his teaching. Somewhere or other he was still alive and hatching his conspiracies: perhaps somewhere beyond the sea, under the protection of his foreign paymasters, perhaps even--so it was occasionally rumoured--in some hiding-place in Oceania itself.

Winston's diaphragm was constricted. He could never see the face of Goldstein without a painful mixture of emotions. It was a lean Jewish face, with a great fuzzy aureole of white hair and a small goatee beard--a clever face, and yet somehow inherently despicable, with a kind of senile silliness in the long thin nose, near the end of which a pair of spectacles was perched. It resembled the face of a sheep, and the voice, too, had a sheep-like quality. Goldstein was delivering his usual venomous attack upon the doctrines of the Party--an attack so exaggerated and perverse that a child should have been able to see through it, and yet just plausible enough to fill one with an alarmed feeling that other people, less level-headed than oneself, might be taken in by it. He was abusing Big Brother, he was denouncing the dictatorship of the Party, he was demanding the immediate conclusion of peace with Eurasia, he was advocating freedom of speech, freedom of the Press, freedom of assembly, freedom of thought, he was crying hysterically that the revolution had been betrayed--and all this in rapid polysyllabic speech which was a sort of parody of the habitual style of the orators of the Party, and even contained Newspeak words: more Newspeak words, indeed, than any Party member would normally use in real life. And all the while, lest one should be in any doubt as to the reality which Goldstein's specious claptrap covered, behind his head on the telescreen there marched the endless columns of the Eurasian army--row after row of solid-looking men with expressionless Asiatic faces, who swam up to the surface of the screen and vanished, to be replaced by others exactly similar. The dull rhythmic tramp of the soldiers' boots formed the background to Goldstein's bleating voice.

Before the Hate had proceeded for thirty seconds, uncontrollable exclamations of rage were breaking out from half the people in the room. The self-satisfied sheep-like face on the screen, and the terrifying power of the Eurasian army behind it, were too much to be borne: besides, the sight or even the thought of Goldstein produced fear and anger automatically. He was an object of hatred more constant than either Eurasia or Eastasia, since when Oceania was at war with one of these Powers it was generally at peace with the other. But what was strange was that although Goldstein was hated and despised by everybody, although every day and a thousand times a day, on platforms, on the telescreen, in newspapers, in books, his theories were refuted, smashed, ridiculed, held up to the general gaze for the pitiful rubbish that they were in spite of all this, his influence never seemed to grow less. Always there were fresh dupes waiting to be seduced by him. A day never passed when spies and saboteurs acting under his directions were not unmasked by the Thought Police. He was the commander of a vast shadowy army, an underground network of conspirators dedicated to the overthrow of the State. The Brotherhood, its name was supposed to be. There were also whispered stories of a terrible book, a compendium of all the heresies, of which Goldstein was the author and which circulated clandestinely here and there. It was a book without a title. People referred to it, if at all, simply as the book. But one knew of such things only through vague rumours. Neither the Brotherhood nor the book was a subject that any ordinary Party member would mention if there was a way of avoiding it.

In its second minute the Hate rose to a frenzy. People were leaping up and down in their places and shouting at the tops of their voices in an effort to drown the maddening bleating voice that came from the screen. The little sandy-haired woman had turned bright pink, and her mouth was opening and shutting like that of a landed fish. Even O'Brien's heavy face was flushed. He was sitting very straight in his chair, his powerful chest swelling and quivering as though he were standing up to the assault of a wave. The dark-haired girl behind Winston had begun crying out 'Swine! Swine! Swine!' and suddenly she picked up a heavy Newspeak dictionary and flung it at the screen. It struck Goldstein's nose and bounced off; the voice continued inexorably. In a lucid moment Winston found that he was shouting with the others and kicking his heel violently against the rung of his chair. The horrible thing about the Two Minutes Hate was not that one was obliged to act a part, but, on the contrary, that it was impossible to avoid joining in. Within thirty seconds any pretence was always unnecessary. A hideous ecstasy of fear and vindictiveness, a desire to kill, to torture, to smash faces in with a sledge-hammer, seemed to flow through the whole group of people like an electric current, turning one even against one's will into a grimacing, screaming lunatic. And yet the rage that one felt was an abstract, undirected emotion which could be switched from one object to another like the flame of a blowlamp. Thus, at one moment Winston's hatred was not turned against Goldstein at all, but, on the contrary, against Big Brother, the Party, and the Thought Police; and at such moments his heart went out to the lonely, derided heretic on the screen, sole guardian of truth and sanity in a world of lies. And yet the very next instant he was at one with the people about him, and all that was said of Goldstein seemed to him to be true. At those moments his secret loathing of Big Brother changed into adoration, and Big Brother seemed to tower up, an invincible, fearless protector, standing like a rock against the hordes of Asia, and Goldstein, in spite of his isolation, his helplessness, and the doubt that hung about his very existence, seemed like some sinister enchanter, capable by the mere power of his voice of wrecking the structure of civilization.

It was even possible, at moments, to switch one's hatred this way or that by a voluntary act. Suddenly, by the sort of violent effort with which one wrenches one's head away from the pillow in a nightmare, Winston succeeded in transferring his hatred from the face on the screen to the dark-haired girl behind him. Vivid, beautiful hallucinations flashed through his mind. He would flog her to death with a rubber truncheon. He would tie her naked to a stake and shoot her full of arrows like Saint Sebastian. He would ravish her and cut her throat at the moment of climax. Better than before, moreover, he realized why it was that he hated her. He hated her because she was young and pretty and sexless, because he wanted to go to bed with her and would never do so, because round her sweet supple waist, which seemed to ask you to encircle it with your arm, there was only the odious scarlet sash, aggressive symbol of chastity.

The Hate rose to its climax. The voice of Goldstein had become an actual sheep's bleat, and for an instant the face changed into that of a sheep. Then the sheep-face melted into the figure of a Eurasian soldier who seemed to be advancing, huge and terrible, his sub-machine gun roaring, and seeming to spring out of the surface of the screen, so that some of the people in the front row actually flinched backwards in their seats. But in the same moment, drawing a deep sigh of relief from everybody, the hostile figure melted into the face of Big Brother, black-haired, black-moustachio'd, full of power and mysterious calm, and so vast that it almost filled up the screen. Nobody heard what Big Brother was saying. It was merely a few words of encouragement, the sort of words that are uttered in the din of battle, not distinguishable individually but restoring confidence by the fact of being spoken. Then the face of Big Brother faded away again, and instead the three slogans of the Party stood out in bold capitals:

WAR IS PEACE
FREEDOM IS SLAVERY
IGNORANCE IS STRENGTH

But the face of Big Brother seemed to persist for several seconds on the screen, as though the impact that it had made on everyone's eyeballs was too vivid to wear off immediately. The little sandyhaired woman had flung herself forward over the back of the chair in front of her. With a tremulous murmur that sounded like 'My Saviour!' she extended her arms towards the screen. Then she buried her face in her hands. It was apparent that she was uttering a prayer.

At this moment the entire group of people broke into a deep, slow, rhythmical chant of 'B-B!...B-B!'--over and over again, very slowly, with a long pause between the first 'B' and the second-a heavy, murmurous sound, somehow curiously savage, in the background of which one seemed to hear the stamp of naked feet and the throbbing of tom-toms. For perhaps as much as thirty seconds they kept it up. It was a refrain that was often heard in moments of overwhelming emotion. Partly it was a sort of hymn to the wisdom and majesty of Big Brother, but still more it was an act of self-hypnosis, a deliberate drowning of consciousness by means of rhythmic noise. Winston's entrails seemed to grow cold. In the Two Minutes Hate he could not help sharing in the general delirium, but this sub-human chanting of 'B-B!...B-B!' always filled him with horror. Of course he chanted with the rest: it was impossible to do otherwise. To dissemble your feelings, to control your face, to do what everyone else was doing, was an instinctive reaction. But there was a space of a couple of seconds during which the expression of his eyes might conceivably have betrayed him. And it was exactly at this moment that the significant thing happened--if, indeed, it did happen.

Momentarily he caught O'Brien's eye. O'Brien had stood up. He had taken off his spectacles and was in the act of resettling them on his nose with his characteristic gesture. But there was a fraction of a second when their eyes met, and for as long as it took to happen Winston knew-yes, he knew!-that O'Brien was thinking the same thing as himself. An unmistakable message had passed. It was as though their two minds had opened and the thoughts were flowing from one into the other through their eyes. 'I am with you,' O'Brien seemed to be saying to him. 'I know precisely what you are feeling. I know all about your contempt, your hatred, your disgust. But don't worry, I am on your side!' And then the flash of intelligence was gone, and O'Brien's face was as inscrutable as everybody else's.

That was all, and he was already uncertain whether it had happened. Such incidents never had any sequel. All that they did was to keep alive in him the belief, or hope, that others besides himself were the enemies of the Party. Perhaps the rumours of vast underground conspiracies were true after all--perhaps the Brotherhood really existed! It was impossible, in spite of the endless arrests and confessions and executions, to be sure that the Brotherhood was not simply a myth. Some days he believed in it, some days not. There was no evidence, only fleeting glimpses that might mean anything or nothing: snatches of overheard conversation, faint scribbles on lavatory walls--once, even, when two strangers met, a small movement of the hand which had looked as though it might be a signal of recognition. It was all guesswork: very likely he had imagined everything. He had gone back to his cubicle without looking at O'Brien again. The idea of following up their momentary contact hardly crossed his mind. It would have been inconceivably dangerous even if he had known how to set about doing it. For a second, two seconds, they had exchanged an equivocal glance, and that was the end of the story. But even that was a memorable event, in the locked loneliness in which one had to live.

Winston roused himself and sat up straighter. He let out a belch. The gin was rising from his stomach.

His eyes re-focused on the page. He discovered that while he sat helplessly musing he had also been writing, as though by automatic action. And it was no longer the same cramped, awkward handwriting as before. His pen had slid voluptuously over the smooth paper, printing in large neat capitals:

DOWN WITH BIG BROTHER
DOWN WITH BIG BROTHER
DOWN WITH BIG BROTHER
DOWN WITH BIG BROTHER
DOWN WITH BIG BROTHER

Over and over again, filling half a page: He could not help feeling a twinge of panic. It was absurd, since the writing of those particular words was not more dangerous than the initial act of opening the diary, but for a moment he was tempted to tear out the spoiled pages and abandon the enterprise altogether.

He did not do so, however, because he knew that it was useless. Whether he wrote DOWN WITH BIG BROTHER, or whether he refrained from writing it, made no difference. Whether he went on with the diary, or whether he did not go on with it, made no difference. The Thought Police would get him just the same. He had committed--would still have committed, even if he had never set pen to paper--the essential crime that contained all others in itself. Thoughtcrime, they called it. Thoughtcrime was not a thing that could be concealed for ever. You might dodge successfully for a while, even for years, but sooner or later they were bound to get you.

It was always at night--the arrests invariably happened at night. The sudden jerk out of sleep, the rough hand shaking your shoulder, the lights glaring in your eyes, the ring of hard faces round the bed. In the vast majority of cases there was no trial, no report of the arrest. People simply disappeared, always during the night. Your name was removed from the registers, every record of everything you had ever done was wiped out, your one-time existence was denied and then forgotten. You were abolished, annihilated: vaporized was the usual word.

For a moment he was seized by a kind of hysteria. He began writing in a hurried untidy scrawl: theyll shoot me i dont care theyll shoot me in the back of the neck i dont care down with big brother they always shoot you in the back of the neck i dont care down with big brother--

He sat back in his chair, slightly ashamed of himself, and laid down the pen. The next moment he started violently. There was a knocking at the door.

Already! He sat as still as a mouse, in the futile hope that whoever it was might go away after a single attempt. But no, the knocking was repeated. The worst thing of all would be to delay. His heart was thumping like a drum, but his face, from long habit, was probably expressionless. He got up and moved heavily towards the door.

Part 1 Chapter 2

As he put his hand to the door-knob Winston saw that he had left the diary open on the table. DOWN WITH BIG BROTHER was written all over it, in letters almost big enough to be legible across the room. It was an inconceivably stupid thing to have done. But, he realized, even in his panic he had not wanted to smudge the creamy paper by shutting the book while the ink was wet.

He drew in his breath and opened the door. Instantly a warm wave of relief flowed through him. A colourless, crushed-looking woman, with wispy hair and a lined face, was standing outside.

'Oh, comrade,' she began in a dreary, whining sort of voice, 'I thought I heard you come in. Do you think you could come across and have a look at our kitchen sink? It's got blocked up and...'

It was Mrs Parsons, the wife of a neighbour on the same

floor. ('Mrs' was a word somewhat discountenanced by the Party-you were supposed to call everyone 'comrade'--but with some women one used it instinctively.) She was a woman of about thirty, but looking much older. One had the impression that there was dust in the creases of her face. Winston followed her down the passage. These amateur repair jobs were an almost daily irritation. Victory Mansions were old flats, built in 1930 or thereabouts, and were falling to pieces. The plaster flaked constantly from ceilings and walls, the pipes burst in every hard frost, the roof leaked whenever there was snow, the heating system was usually running at half steam when it was not closed down altogether from motives of economy. Repairs, except what you could do for yourself, had to be sanctioned by remote committees which were liable to hold up even the mending of a window-pane for two years.

'Of course it's only because Tom isn't home,' said Mrs Parsons vaguely. The Parsons' flat was bigger than Winston's, and dingy in a different way. Everything had a battered, trampled-on look, as though the place had just been visited by some large violent animal. Games impedimenta--hockey-sticks, boxing-gloves, a burst football, a pair of sweaty shorts turned inside out--lay all over the floor, and on the table there was a litter of dirty dishes and dog-eared exercise-books. On the walls were scarlet banners of the Youth League and the Spies, and a full-sized poster of Big Brother. There was the usual boiled-cabbage smell, common to the whole building, but it was shot through by a sharper reek of sweat, which--one knew this at the first sniff, though it was hard to say how--was the sweat of some person not present at the moment. In another room someone with a comb and a piece of toilet paper was trying to keep tune with the military music which was still issuing from the telescreen.

'It's the children,' said Mrs Parsons, casting a half-apprehensive glance at the door. 'They haven't been out today. And of course...' She had a habit of breaking off her sentences in the middle. The kitchen sink was full nearly to the brim with filthy greenish water which smelt worse than ever of cabbage. Winston knelt down and examined the angle-joint of the pipe. He hated using his hands, and he hated bending down, which was always liable to start him coughing. Mrs Parsons looked on helplessly. 'Of course if Tom was home he'd put it right in a moment,' she said. 'He loves anything like that. He's ever so good with his hands, Tom is.'

Parsons was Winston's fellow-employee at the Ministry of Truth. He was a fattish but active man of paralysing stupidity, a mass of imbecile enthusiasms--one of those completely unquestioning, devoted drudges on whom, more even than on the Thought Police, the stability of the Party depended. At thirty-five he had just been unwillingly evicted from the Youth League, and before graduating into the Youth League he had managed to stay on in the Spies for a year beyond the statutory age. At the Ministry he was employed in some subordinate post for which intelligence was not required, but on the other hand he was a leading figure on the Sports Committee and all the other committees engaged in organizing community hikes, spontaneous demonstrations, savings campaigns, and voluntary activities generally. He would inform you with quiet pride, between whiffs of his pipe, that he had put in an appearance at the Community Centre every evening for the past four years. An overpowering smell of sweat, a sort of unconscious testimony to the strenuousness of his life, followed him about wherever he went, and even remained behind him after he had gone.

'Have you got a spanner?' said Winston, fiddling with the nut on the angle-joint. 'A spanner,' said Mrs Parsons, immediately becoming invertebrate. 'I don't know, I'm sure. Perhaps the children...' There was a trampling of boots and another blast on the comb as the children charged into the living-room. Mrs Parsons brought the spanner. Winston let out the water and disgustedly removed the clot of human hair that had blocked up the pipe. He cleaned his fingers as best he could in the cold water from the tap and went back into the other room.

'Up with your hands!' yelled a savage voice.

A handsome, tough-looking boy of nine had popped up from behind the table and was menacing him with a toy automatic pistol, while his small sister, about two years younger, made the same gesture with a fragment of wood. Both of them were dressed in the blue shorts, grey shirts, and red neckerchiefs which were the uniform of the Spies. Winston raised his hands above his head, but with an uneasy feeling, so vicious was the boy's demeanour, that it was not altogether a game. 'You're a traitor!' yelled the boy. 'You're a thought-criminal! You're a Eurasian spy! I'll shoot you, I'll vaporize you, I'll send you to the salt mines!'

Suddenly they were both leaping round him, shouting 'Traitor!' and 'Thought-criminal!' the little girl imitating her brother in every movement. It was somehow slightly frightening, like the gambolling of tiger cubs which will soon grow up into man-eaters. There was a sort of calculating ferocity in the boy's eye, a quite evident desire to hit or kick Winston and a consciousness of being very nearly big enough to do so. It was a good job it was not a real pistol he was holding, Winston thought.

Mrs Parsons' eyes flitted nervously from Winston to the children, and back again. In the better light of the living-room he noticed with interest that there actually was dust in the creases of her face. 'They do get so noisy,' she said. 'They're disappointed because they couldn't go to see the hanging, that's what it is. I'm too busy to take them. and Tom won't be back from work in time.'

'Why can't we go and see the hanging?' roared the boy in his huge voice. 'Want to see the hanging! Want to see the hanging!' chanted the little girl, still capering round.

Some Eurasian prisoners, guilty of war crimes, were to be hanged in the Park that evening, Winston remembered. This happened about once a month, and was a popular spectacle. Children always clamoured to be taken to see it. He took his leave of Mrs Parsons and made for the door. But he had not gone six steps down the passage when something hit the back of his neck an agonizingly painful blow. It was as though a red-hot wire had been jabbed into him. He spun round just in time to see Mrs Parsons dragging her son back into the doorway while the boy pocketed a catapult.

'Goldstein!' bellowed the boy as the door closed on him. But what most struck Winston was the look of helpless fright on the woman's greyish face. Back in the flat he stepped quickly past the telescreen and sat down at the table again, still rubbing his neck. The music from the telescreen had stopped. Instead, a clipped military voice was reading out, with a sort of brutal relish, a description of the armaments of the new Floating Fortress which had just been anchored between Iceland and the Faroe Islands.

With those children, he thought, that wretched woman must lead a life of terror. Another year, two years, and they would be watching her night and day for symptoms of unorthodoxy. Nearly all children nowadays were horrible. What was worst of all was that by means of such organizations as the Spies they were systematically turned into ungovernable little savages, and yet this produced in them no tendency whatever to rebel against the discipline of the Party. On the contrary, they adored the Party and everything connected with it. The songs, the processions, the banners, the hiking, the drilling with dummy rifles, the yelling of slogans, the worship of Big Brother--it was all a sort of glorious game to them. All their ferocity was turned outwards, against the enemies of the State, against foreigners, traitors, saboteurs, thought-criminals. It was almost normal for people over thirty to be frightened of their own children. And with good reason, for hardly a week passed in which 'The Times' did not carry a paragraph describing how some eavesdropping little sneak--'child hero' was the phrase generally used--had overheard some compromising remark and denounced its parents to the Thought Police.

The sting of the catapult bullet had worn off. He picked up his pen half-heartedly, wondering whether he could find something more to write in the diary. Suddenly he began thinking of O'Brien again. Years ago--how long was it? Seven years it must be--he had dreamed that he was walking through a pitch-dark room. And someone sitting to one side of him had said as he passed: 'We shall meet in the place where there is no darkness.' It was said very quietly, almost casually--a statement, not a command. He had walked on without pausing. What was curious was that at the time, in the dream, the words had not made much impression on him. It was only later and by degrees that they had seemed to take on significance. He could not now remember whether it was before or after having the dream that he had seen O'Brien for the first time, nor could he remember when he had first identified the voice as O'Brien's. But at any rate the identification existed. It was O'Brien who had spoken to him out of the dark.

Winston had never been able to feel sure--even after this morning's flash of the eyes it was still impossible to be sure whether O'Brien was a friend or an enemy. Nor did it even seem to matter greatly. There was a link of understanding between them, more important than affection or partisanship. 'We shall meet in the place where there is no darkness,' he had said. Winston did not know what it meant, only that in some way or another it would come true. The voice from the telescreen paused. A trumpet call, clear and beautiful, floated into the stagnant air. The voice continued raspingly:

'Attention! Your attention, please! A newsflash has this moment arrived from the Malabar front. Our forces in South India have won a glorious victory. I am authorized to say that the action we are now reporting may well bring the war within measurable distance of its end. Here is the newsflash...'

Bad news coming, thought Winston. And sure enough, following on a gory description of the annihilation of a Eurasian army, with stupendous figures of killed and prisoners, came the announcement that, as from next week, the chocolate ration would be reduced from thirty grammes to twenty. Winston belched again. The gin was wearing off, leaving a deflated feeling. The telescreen--perhaps to celebrate the victory, perhaps to drown the memory of the lost chocolate--crashed into 'Oceania, 'tis for thee'. You were supposed to stand to attention. However, in his present position he was invisible. 'Oceania, 'tis for thee' gave way to lighter music. Winston walked over to the window, keeping his back to the telescreen. The day was still cold and clear. Somewhere far away a rocket bomb exploded with a dull, reverberating roar. About twenty or thirty of them a week were falling on London at present.

Down in the street the wind flapped the torn poster to and fro, and the word INGSOC fitfully appeared and vanished. Ingsoc. The sacred principles of Ingsoc. Newspeak, doublethink, the mutability of the past. He felt as though he were wandering in the forests of the sea bottom, lost in a monstrous world where he himself was the monster. He was alone. The past was dead, the future was unimaginable. What certainty had he that a single human creature now living was on his side? And what way of knowing that the dominion of the Party would not endure FOR EVER? Like an answer, the three slogans on the white face of the Ministry of Truth came back to him:

WAR IS PEACE
FREEDOM IS SLAVERY
IGNORANCE IS STRENGTH

He took a twenty-five cent piece out of his pocket. There, too, in tiny clear lettering, the same slogans were inscribed, and on the other face of the coin the head of Big Brother. Even from the coin the eyes pursued you. On coins, on stamps, on the covers of books, on banners, on posters, and on the wrappings of a cigarette packet--everywhere. Always the eyes watching you and the voice enveloping you. Asleep or awake, working or eating, indoors or out of doors, in the bath or in bed--no escape. Nothing was your own except the few cubic centimetres inside your skull.

The sun had shifted round, and the myriad windows of the Ministry of Truth, with the light no longer shining on them, looked grim as the loopholes of a fortress. His heart quailed before the enormous pyramidal shape. It was too strong, it could not be stormed. A thousand rocket bombs would not batter it down. He wondered again for whom he was writing the diary. For the future, for the past--for an age that might be imaginary. And in front of him there lay not death but annihilation. The diary would be reduced to ashes and himself to vapour. Only the Thought Police would read what he had written, before they wiped it out of existence and out of memory. How could you make appeal to the future when not a trace of you, not even an anonymous word scribbled on a piece of paper, could physically survive?

The telescreen struck fourteen. He must leave in ten minutes. He had to be back at work by fourteen-thirty. Curiously, the chiming of the hour seemed to have put new heart into him. He was a lonely ghost uttering a truth that nobody would ever hear. But so long as he uttered it, in some obscure way the continuity was not broken. It was not by making yourself heard but by staying sane that you carried on the human heritage. He went back to the table, dipped his pen, and wrote:

To the future or to the past, to a time when thought is free, when men are different from one another and do not live alone--to a time when truth exists and what is done cannot be undone: From the age of uniformity, from the age of solitude, from the age of Big Brother, from the age of doublethink-greetings!

He was already dead, he reflected. It seemed to him that it was only now, when he had begun to be able to formulate his thoughts, that he had taken the decisive step. The consequences of every act are included in the act itself. He wrote: Thoughtcrime does not entail death: thoughtcrime IS death.

Now he had recognized himself as a dead man it became important to stay alive as long as possible. Two fingers of his right hand were inkstained. It was exactly the kind of detail that might betray you. Some nosing zealot in the Ministry (a woman, probably: someone like the little sandy-haired woman or the dark-haired girl from the Fiction Department) might start wondering why he had been writing during the lunch interval, why he had used an old-fashioned pen, WHAT he had been writing--and then drop a hint in the appropriate quarter. He went to the bathroom and carefully scrubbed the ink away with the gritty dark-brown soap which rasped your skin like sandpaper and was therefore well adapted for this purpose.

He put the diary away in the drawer. It was quite useless to think of hiding it, but he could at least make sure whether or not its existence had been discovered. A hair laid across the page-ends was too obvious. With the tip of his finger he picked up an identifiable grain of whitish dust and deposited it on the corner of the cover, where it was bound to be shaken off if the book was moved.

Part 1 Chapter 3

Winston was dreaming of his mother: He must, he thought, have been ten or eleven years old when his mother had disappeared. She was a tall, statuesque, rather silent woman with slow movements and magnificent fair hair. His father he remembered more vaguely as dark and thin, dressed always in neat dark clothes (Winston remembered especially the very thin soles of his father's shoes) and wearing spectacles. The two of them must evidently have been swallowed up in one of the first great purges of the fifties.

At this moment his mother was sitting in some place deep down beneath him, with his young sister in her arms. He did not remember his sister at all, except as a tiny, feeble baby, always silent, with large, watchful eyes. Both of them were looking up at him. They were down in some subterranean place--the bottom of a well, for instance, or a very deep grave--but it was a place which, already far below him, was itself moving downwards. They were in the saloon of a sinking ship, looking up at him through the darkening water.

There was still air in the saloon, they could still see him and he them, but all the while they were sinking down, down into the green waters which in another moment must hide them from sight for ever. He was out in the light and air while they were being sucked down to death, and they were down there because he was up here. He knew it and they knew it, and he could see the knowledge in their faces. There was no reproach either in their faces or in their hearts, only the knowledge that they must die in order that he might remain alive, and that this was part of the unavoidable order of things.

He could not remember what had happened, but he knew

in his dream that in some way the lives of his mother and his sister had been sacrificed to his own. It was one of those dreams which, while retaining the characteristic dream scenery, are a continuation of one's intellectual life, and in which one becomes aware of facts and ideas which still seem new and valuable after one is awake. The thing that now suddenly struck Winston was that his mother's death, nearly thirty years ago, had been tragic and sorrowful in a way that was no longer possible. Tragedy, he perceived, belonged to the ancient time, to a time when there was still privacy, love, and friendship, and when the members of a family stood by one another without needing to know the reason.

His mother's memory tore at his heart because she had died loving him, when he was too young and selfish to love her in return, and because somehow, he did not remember how, she had sacrificed herself to a conception of loyalty that was private and unalterable. Such things, he saw, could not happen today. Today there were fear, hatred, and pain, but no dignity of emotion, no deep or complex sorrows. All this he seemed to see in the large eyes of his mother and his sister, looking up at him through the green water, hundreds of fathoms down and still sinking.

Suddenly he was standing on short springy turf, on a summer evening when the slanting rays of the sun gilded the ground. The landscape that he was looking at recurred so often in his dreams that he was never fully certain whether or not he had seen it in the real world. In his waking thoughts he called it the Golden Country. It was an old, rabbit-bitten pasture, with a foot-track wandering across it and a molehill here and there. In the ragged hedge on the opposite side of the field the boughs of the elm trees were swaying very faintly in the breeze, their leaves just stirring in dense masses like women's hair. Somewhere near at hand, though out of sight, there was a clear, slow-moving stream where dace were swimming in the pools under the willow trees.

The girl with dark hair was coming towards them across the field. With what seemed a single movement she tore off her clothes and flung them disdainfully aside. Her body was white and smooth, but it aroused no desire in him, indeed he barely looked at it. What overwhelmed him in that instant was admiration for the gesture with which she had thrown her clothes aside. With its grace and carelessness it seemed to annihilate a whole culture, a whole system of thought, as though Big Brother and the Party and the Thought Police could all be swept into nothingness by a single splendid movement of the arm. That too was a gesture belonging to the ancient time. Winston woke up with the word 'Shakespeare' on his lips. The telescreen was giving forth an ear-splitting whistle which continued on the same note for thirty seconds. It was nought seven fifteen, getting-up time for office workers. Winston wrenched his body out of bed--naked, for a member of the Outer Party received only 3,000 clothing coupons annually, and a suit of pyjamas was 600--and seized a dingy singlet and a pair of shorts that were lying across a chair. The Physical Jerks would begin in three minutes. The next moment he was doubled up by a violent coughing fit which nearly always attacked him soon after waking up. It emptied his lungs so completely that he could only begin breathing again by lying on his back and taking a series of deep gasps. His veins had swelled with the effort of the cough, and the varicose ulcer had started itching.

'Thirty to forty group!' yapped a piercing female voice. 'Thirty to forty group! Take your places, please. Thirties to forties!' Winston sprang to attention in front of the telescreen, upon which the image of a youngish woman, scrawny but muscular, dressed in tunic and gym-shoes, had already appeared.

'Arms bending and stretching!' she rapped out. 'Take your time by me. ONE, two, three, four! ONE, two, three, four! Come on, comrades, put a bit of life into it! ONE, two, three four! ONE two, three, four!...' The pain of the coughing fit had not quite driven out of Winston's mind the impression made by his dream, and the rhythmic movements of the exercise restored it somewhat. As he mechanically shot his arms back and forth, wearing on his face the look of grim enjoyment which was considered proper during the Physical Jerks, he was struggling to think his way backward into the dim period of his early childhood. It was extraordinarily difficult. Beyond the late fifties everything faded. When there were no external records that you could refer to, even the outline of your own life lost its sharpness. You remembered huge events which had quite probably not happened, you remembered the detail of incidents without being able to recapture their atmosphere, and there were long blank periods to which you could assign nothing. Everything had been different then. Even the names of countries, and their shapes on the map, had been different. Airstrip One, for instance, had not been so called in those days: it had been called England or Britain, though London, he felt fairly certain, had always been called London.

Winston could not definitely remember a time when his country had not been at war, but it was evident that there had been a fairly long interval of peace during his childhood, because one of his early memories was of an air raid which appeared to take everyone by surprise. Perhaps it was the time when the atomic bomb had fallen on Colchester. He did not remember the raid itself, but he did remember his father's hand clutching his own as they hurried down, down, down into some place deep in the earth, round and round a spiral staircase which rang under his feet and which finally so wearied his legs that he began whimpering and they had to stop and rest. His mother, in her slow, dreamy way, was following a long way behind them. She was carrying his baby sister--or perhaps it was only a bundle of blankets that she was carrying: he was not certain whether his sister had been born then. Finally they had emerged into a noisy, crowded place which he had realized to be a Tube station.

There were people sitting all over the stone-flagged floor, and other people, packed tightly together, were sitting on metal bunks, one above the other. Winston and his mother and father found themselves a place on the floor, and near them an old man and an old woman were sitting side by side on a bunk. The old man had on a decent dark suit and a black cloth cap pushed back from very white hair: his face was scarlet and his eyes were blue and full of tears. He reeked of gin. It seemed to breathe out of his skin in place of sweat, and one could have fancied that the tears welling from his eyes were pure gin. But though slightly drunk he was also suffering under some grief that was genuine and unbearable. In his childish way Winston grasped that some terrible thing, something that was beyond forgiveness and could never be remedied, had just happened. It also seemed to him that he knew what it was. Someone whom the old man loved--a little granddaughter, perhaps--had been killed. Every few minutes the old man kept repeating: 'We didn't ought to 'ave trusted 'em. I said so, Ma, didn't I? That's what comes of trusting 'em. I said so all along. We didn't ought to 'ave trusted the buggers.'

But which buggers they didn't ought to have trusted Winston could not now remember. Since about that time, war had been literally continuous, though strictly speaking it had not always been the same war. For several months during his childhood there had been confused street fighting in London itself, some of which he remembered vividly. But to trace out the history of the whole period, to say who was fighting whom at any given moment, would have been utterly impossible, since no written record, and no spoken word, ever made mention of any other alignment than the existing one. At this moment, for example, in 1984, Oceania was at war with Eurasia and in alliance with Eastasia.

In no public or private utterance was it ever admitted that the three powers had at any time been grouped along different lines. Actually, as Winston well knew, it was only four years since Oceania had been at war with Eastasia and in alliance with Eurasia. But that was merely a piece of furtive knowledge which he happened to possess because his memory was not satisfactorily under control. Officially the change of partners had never happened. Oceania was at war with Eurasia: therefore Oceania had always been at war with Eurasia. The enemy of the moment always represented absolute evil, and it followed that any past or future agreement with him was impossible. The frightening thing, he reflected for the ten thousandth time as he forced his shoulders painfully backward (with hands on hips, they were gyrating their bodies from the waist, an exercise that was supposed to be good for the back muscles)--the frightening thing was that it might all be true. If the Party could thrust its hand into the past and say of this or that event, IT NEVER HAPPENED--that, surely, was more terrifying than mere torture and death?

The Party said that Oceania had never been in alliance with Eurasia. He, Winston Smith, knew that Oceania had been in alliance with Eurasia as short a time as four years ago. But where did that knowledge exist? Only in his own consciousness, which in any case must soon be annihilated. And if all others accepted the lie which the Party imposed--if all records told the same tale--then the lie passed into history and became truth. 'Who controls the past,' ran the Party slogan, 'controls the future: who controls the present controls the past.' And yet the past, though of its nature alterable, never had been altered. Whatever was true now was true from everlasting to everlasting. It was quite simple. All that was needed was an unending series of victories over your own memory. 'Reality control', they called it: in Newspeak, 'doublethink'. 'Stand easy!' barked the instructress, a little more genially.

Winston sank his arms to his sides and slowly refilled his lungs with air. His mind slid away into the labyrinthine world of doublethink. To know and not to know, to be conscious of complete truthfulness while telling carefully constructed lies, to hold simultaneously two opinions which cancelled out, knowing them to be contradictory and believing in both of them, to use logic against logic, to repudiate morality while laying claim to it, to believe that democracy was impossible and that the Party was the guardian of democracy, to forget whatever it was necessary to forget, then to draw it back into memory again at the moment when it was needed, and then promptly to forget it again: and above all, to apply the same process to the process itself. That was the ultimate subtlety: consciously to induce unconsciousness, and then, once again, to become unconscious of the act of hypnosis you had just performed. Even to understand the word 'doublethink' involved the use of doublethink.

The instructress had called them to attention again. 'And

now let's see which of us can touch our toes!' she said enthusiastically. 'Right over from the hips, please, comrades. ONE-two! ONE-two!...'

Winston loathed this exercise, which sent shooting pains all the way from his heels to his buttocks and often ended by bringing on another coughing fit. The half-pleasant quality went out of his meditations. The past, he reflected, had not merely been altered, it had been actually destroyed. For how could you establish even the most obvious fact when there existed no record outside your own memory? He tried to remember in what year he had first heard mention of Big Brother. He thought it must have been at some time in the sixties, but it was impossible to be certain. In the Party histories, of course, Big Brother figured as the leader and guardian of the Revolution since its very earliest days. His exploits had been gradually pushed backwards in time until already they extended into the fabulous world of the forties and the thirties, when the capitalists in their strange cylindrical hats still rode through the streets of London in great gleaming motor-cars or horse carriages with glass sides.

There was no knowing how much of this legend was true and how much invented. Winston could not even remember at what date the Party itself had come into existence. He did not believe he had ever heard the word Ingsoc before 1960, but it was possible that in its Oldspeak form--'English Socialism', that is to say--it had been current earlier. Everything melted into mist. Sometimes, indeed, you could put your finger on a definite lie. It was not true, for example, as was claimed in the Party history books, that the Party had invented aeroplanes. He remembered aeroplanes since his earliest childhood. But you could prove nothing. There was never any evidence. Just once in his whole life he had held in his hands unmistakable documentary proof of the falsification of an historical fact. And on that occasion----'Smith!' screamed the shrewish voice from the telescreen. '6079 Smith W.! Yes, YOU! Bend lower, please! You can do better than that. You're not trying. Lower, please! THAT'S better, comrade. Now stand at ease, the whole squad, and watch me.'

A sudden hot sweat had broken out all over Winston's body. His face remained completely inscrutable. Never show dismay! Never show resentment! A single flicker of the eyes could give you away. He stood watching while the instructress raised her arms above her head and--one could not say gracefully, but with remarkable neatness and efficiency--bent over and tucked the first joint of her fingers under her toes.

'THERE, comrades! THAT'S how I want to see you doing it. Watch me again. I'm thirty-nine and I've had four children. Now look.' She bent over again. 'You see MY knees aren't bent. You can all do it if you want to,' she added as she straightened herself up. 'Anyone under forty-five is perfectly capable of touching his toes. We don't all have the privilege of fighting in the front line, but at least we can all keep fit. Remember our boys on the Malabar front! And the sailors in the Floating Fortresses! Just think what THEY have to put up with. Now try again. That's better, comrade, that's MUCH better,' she added encouragingly as Winston, with a violent lunge, succeeded in touching his toes with knees unbent, for the first time in several years.

Part 1 Chapter 6

Winston was writing in his diary: It was three years ago. It was on a dark evening, in a narrow side-street near one of the big railway stations. She was standing near a doorway in the wall, under a street lamp that hardly gave any light. She had a young face, painted very thick. It was really the paint that appealed to me, the whiteness of it, like a mask, and the bright red lips. Party women never paint their faces. There was nobody else in the street, and no telescreens. She said two dollars. I...

For the moment it was too difficult to go on. He shut his eyes and pressed his fingers against them, trying to squeeze out the vision that kept recurring. He had an almost overwhelming temptation to shout a string of filthy words at the top of his voice. Or to bang his head against the wall, to kick over the table, and hurl the inkpot through the window--to do any violent or noisy or painful thing that might black out the memory that was tormenting him. Your worst enemy, he reflected, was your own nervous system. At any moment the tension inside you was liable to translate itself into some visible symptom. He thought of a man whom he had passed in the street a few weeks back; a quite ordinary-looking man, a Party member, aged thirty-five to forty, tallish and thin, carrying a brief-case. They were a few metres apart when the left side of the man's face was suddenly contorted by a sort of spasm. It happened again just as they were passing one another: it was only a twitch, a quiver, rapid as the clicking of a camera shutter, but obviously habitual. He remembered thinking at the time: That poor devil is done for. And what was frightening was that the action was quite possibly unconscious. The most deadly danger of all was talking in your sleep. There was no way of guarding against that, so far as he could see.

He drew his breath and went on writing: I went with her through the doorway and across a backyard into a basement kitchen. There was a bed against the wall, and a lamp on the table, turned down very low. She...

His teeth were set on edge. He would have liked to spit. Simultaneously with the woman in the basement kitchen he thought of Katharine, his wife. Winston was married--had been married, at any rate: probably he still was married, so far as he knew his wife was not dead. He seemed to breathe again the warm stuffy odour of the basement kitchen, an odour compounded of bugs and dirty clothes and villainous cheap scent, but nevertheless alluring, because no woman of the Party ever used scent, or could be imagined as doing so. Only the proles used scent. In his mind the smell of it was inextricably mixed up with fornication.

When he had gone with that woman it had been his first lapse in two years or thereabouts. Consorting with prostitutes was forbidden, of course, but it was one of those rules that you could occasionally nerve yourself to break. It was dangerous, but it was not a life-and-death matter. To be caught with a prostitute might mean five years in a forced-labour camp: not more, if you had committed no other offence. And it was easy enough, provided that you could avoid being caught in the act. The poorer quarters swarmed with women who were ready to sell themselves. Some could even be purchased for a bottle of gin, which the proles were not supposed to drink. Tacitly the Party was even inclined to encourage prostitution, as an outlet for instincts which could not be altogether suppressed. Mere debauchery did not matter very much, so long as it was furtive and joyless and only involved the women of a submerged and despised class. The unforgivable crime was promiscuity between Party members. But--though this was one of the crimes that the accused in the great purges invariably confessed to--it was difficult to imagine any such thing actually happening.

The aim of the Party was not merely to prevent men and women from forming loyalties which it might not be able to control. Its real, undeclared purpose was to remove all pleasure from the sexual act. Not love so much as eroticism was the enemy, inside marriage as well as outside it. All marriages between Party members had to be approved by a committee appointed for the purpose, and--though the principle was never clearly stated--permission was always refused if the couple concerned gave the impression of being physically attracted to one another.

The only recognized purpose of marriage was to beget children for the service of the Party. Sexual intercourse was to be looked on as a slightly disgusting minor operation, like having an enema. This again was never put into plain words, but in an indirect way it was rubbed into every Party member from childhood onwards. There were even organizations such as the Junior Anti-Sex League, which advocated complete celibacy for both sexes. All children were to be begotten by artificial insemination (ARTSEM, it was called in Newspeak) and brought up in public institutions. This, Winston was aware, was not meant altogether seriously, but somehow it fitted in with the general ideology of the Party. The Party was trying to kill the sex instinct, or, if it could not be killed, then to distort it and dirty it. He did not know why this was so, but it seemed natural that it should be so. And as far as the women were concerned, the Party's efforts were largely successful.

He thought again of Katharine. It must be nine, ten--nearly eleven years since they had parted. It was curious how seldom he thought of her. For days at a time he was capable of forgetting that he had ever been married. They had only been together for about fifteen months. The Party did not permit divorce, but it rather encouraged separation in cases where there were no children.

Katharine was a tall, fair-haired girl, very straight, with splendid movements. She had a bold, aquiline face, a face that one might have called noble until one discovered that there was as nearly as possible nothing behind it. Very early in her married life he had decided--though perhaps it was only that he knew her more intimately than he knew most people--that she had without exception the most stupid, vulgar, empty mind that he had ever encountered. She had not a thought in her head that was not a slogan, and there was no imbecility, absolutely none that she was not capable of swallowing if the Party handed it out to her. 'The human sound-track' he nicknamed her in his own mind. Yet he could have endured living with her if it had not been for just one thing--sex.

As soon as he touched her she seemed to wince and stiffen. To embrace her was like embracing a jointed wooden image. And what was strange was that even when she was clasping him against her he had the feeling that she was simultaneously pushing him away with all her strength. The rigidity of her muscles managed to convey that impression. She would lie there with shut eyes, neither resisting nor co-operating but SUBMITTING. It was extraordinarily embarrassing, and, after a while, horrible. But even then he could have borne living with her if it had been agreed that they should remain celibate. But curiously enough it was Katharine who refused this. They must, she said, produce a child if they could. So the performance continued to happen, once a week quite regularly, whenever it was not impossible. She even used to remind him of it in the morning, as something which had to be done that evening and which must not be forgotten. She had two names for it. One was 'making a baby', and the other was 'our duty to the Party' (yes, she had actually used that phrase). Quite soon he grew to have a feeling of positive dread when the appointed day came round. But luckily no child appeared, and in the end she agreed to give up trying, and soon afterwards they parted.

Winston sighed inaudibly. He picked up his pen again and wrote: She threw herself down on the bed, and at once, without any kind of preliminary in the most coarse, horrible way you can imagine, pulled up her skirt. I...

He saw himself standing there in the dim lamplight, with the smell of bugs and cheap scent in his nostrils, and in his heart a feeling of defeat and resentment which even at that moment was mixed up with the thought of Katharine's white body, frozen for ever by the hypnotic power of the Party. Why did it always have to be like this? Why could he not have a woman of his own instead of these filthy scuffles at intervals of years? But a real love affair was an almost unthinkable event. The women of the Party were all alike. Chastity was as deep ingrained in them as Party loyalty.

By careful early conditioning, by games and cold water, by the rubbish that was dinned into them at school and in the Spies and the Youth League, by lectures, parades, songs, slogans, and martial music, the natural feeling had been driven out of them. His reason told him that there must be exceptions, but his heart did not believe it. They were all impregnable, as the Party intended that they should be. And what he wanted, more even than to be loved, was to break down that wall of virtue, even if it were only once in his whole life. The sexual act, successfully performed, was rebellion. Desire was thoughtcrime. Even to have awakened Katharine, if he could have achieved it, would have been like a seduction, although she was his wife.

But the rest of the story had got to be written down. He wrote: I turned up the lamp. When I saw her in the light...

After the darkness the feeble light of the paraffin lamp had seemed very bright. For the first time he could see the woman properly. He had taken a step towards her and then halted, full of lust and terror. He was painfully conscious of the risk he had taken in coming here. It was perfectly possible that the patrols would catch him on the way out: for that matter they might be waiting outside the door at this moment.

If he went away without even doing what he had come here to do It had got to be written down, it had got to be confessed. What he had suddenly seen in the lamplight was that the woman was OLD. The paint was plastered so thick on her face that it looked as though it might crack like a cardboard mask. There were streaks of white in her hair; but the truly dreadful detail was that her mouth had fallen a little open, revealing nothing except a cavernous blackness. She had no teeth at all. *He wrote hurriedly, in scrabbling handwriting:* When I saw her in the light she was quite an old woman, fifty years old at least. But I went ahead and did it just the same. He pressed his fingers against his eyelids again. He had written it down at last, but it made no difference. The therapy had not worked. The urge to shout filthy words at the top of his voice was as strong as ever.

Part 1 Chapter 7

'If there is hope,' wrote Winston, 'it lies in the proles.' If there was hope, it MUST lie in the proles, because only there in those swarming disregarded masses, 85 per cent of the population of Oceania, could the force to destroy the Party ever be generated. The Party could not be overthrown from within. Its enemies, if it had any enemies, had no way of coming together or even of identifying one another. Even if the legendary Brotherhood existed, as just possibly it might, it was inconceivable that its members could ever assemble in larger numbers than twos and threes. Rebellion meant a look in the eyes, an inflexion of the voice, at the most, an occasional whispered word. But the proles, if only they could somehow become conscious of their own strength. would have no need to conspire. They needed only to rise up and shake themselves like a horse shaking off flies. If they chose they could blow the Party to pieces tomorrow morning. Surely sooner or later it must occur to them to do it? And yet...!

He remembered how once he had been walking down a crowded street when a tremendous shout of hundreds of voices women's voices--had burst from a side-street a little way ahead. It was a great formidable cry of anger and despair, a deep, loud 'Oh-o-o-o-oh!' that went humming on like the reverberation of a bell. His heart had leapt. It's started! he had thought. A riot! The proles are breaking loose at last! When he had reached the spot it was to see a mob of two or three hundred women crowding round the stalls of a street market, with faces as tragic as though they had been the doomed passengers on a sinking ship. But at this moment the general despair broke down into a multitude of individual quarrels. It appeared that one of the stalls had been selling tin saucepans. They were wretched, flimsy things, but cooking-pots of any kind were always difficult to get. Now the supply had unexpectedly given out. The successful women, bumped and jostled by the rest, were trying to make off with their saucepans while dozens of others clamoured round the stall, accusing the stall-keeper of favouritism and of having more saucepans somewhere in reserve.

There was a fresh outburst of yells. Two bloated women, one of them with her hair coming down, had got hold of the same saucepan and were trying to tear it out of one another's hands. For a moment they were both tugging, and then the handle came off. Winston watched them disgustedly. And yet, just for a moment, what almost frightening power had sounded in that cry from only a few hundred throats! Why was it that they could never shout like that about anything that mattered?

He wrote: Until they become conscious they will never rebel, and until after they have rebelled they cannot become conscious. That, he reflected, might almost have been a transcription from one of the Party textbooks. The Party claimed, of course, to have liberated the proles from bondage. Before the Revolution they had been hideously oppressed by the capitalists, they had been starved and flogged, women had been forced to work in the coal mines (women still did work in the coal mines, as a matter of fact), children had been sold into the factories at the age of six. But simultaneously, true to the Principles of doublethink, the Party taught that the proles were natural inferiors who must be kept in subjection, like animals, by the application of a few simple rules.

In reality very little was known about the proles. It was not necessary to know much. So long as they continued to work and breed, their other activities were without importance. Left to themselves, like cattle turned loose upon the plains of Argentina, they had reverted to a style of life that appeared to be natural to them, a sort of ancestral pattern. They were born, they grew up in the gutters, they went to work at twelve, they passed through a brief blossoming-period of beauty and sexual desire, they married at twenty, they were middle-aged at thirty, they died, for the most part, at sixty. Heavy physical work, the care of home and children, petty quarrels with neighbours, films, football, beer, and above all, gambling, filled up the horizon of their minds. To keep them in control was not difficult. A few agents of the Thought Police moved always among them, spreading false rumours and marking down and eliminating the few individuals who were judged capable of becoming dangerous; but no attempt was made to indoctrinate them with the ideology of the Party.

It was not desirable that the proles should have strong political feelings. All that was required of them was a primitive patriotism which could be appealed to whenever it was necessary to make them accept longer working-hours or shorter rations. And even when they became discontented, as they sometimes did, their discontent led nowhere, because being without general ideas, they could only focus it on petty specific grievances. The larger evils invariably escaped their notice. The great majority of proles did not even have telescreens in their homes.

Even the civil police interfered with them very little. There was a vast amount of criminality in London, a whole world-within-a-world of thieves, bandits, prostitutes, drug-peddlers, and racketeers of every description; but since it all happened among the proles themselves, it was of no importance. In all questions of morals they were allowed to follow their ancestral code. The sexual puritanism of the Party was not imposed upon them. Promiscuity went unpunished, divorce was permitted. For that matter, even religious worship would have been permitted if the proles had shown any sign of needing or wanting it. They were beneath suspicion. As the Party slogan put it: 'Proles and animals are free.'

Winston reached down and cautiously scratched his varicose ulcer. It had begun itching again. The thing you invariably came back to was the impossibility of knowing what life before the Revolution had really been like. He took out of the drawer a copy of a children's history textbook which he had borrowed from Mrs Parsons, and began copying a passage into the diary: In the old days, before the glorious Revolution, London was not the beautiful city that we know today. It was a dark, dirty, miserable place where hardly anybody had enough to eat and where hundreds and thousands of poor people had no boots on their feet and not even a roof to sleep under. Children no older than you had to work twelve hours a day for cruel masters who flogged them with whips if they worked too slowly and fed them on nothing but stale breadcrusts and water.

But in among all this terrible poverty there were just a few great big beautiful houses that were lived in by rich men who had as many as thirty servants to look after them. These rich men were called capitalists. They were fat, ugly men with wicked faces, like the one in the picture on the opposite page. You can see that he is dressed in a long black coat which was called a frock coat, and a queer, shiny hat shaped like a stovepipe, which was called a top hat. This was the uniform of the capitalists, and no one else was allowed to wear it. The capitalists owned everything in the world, and everyone else was their slave. They owned all the land, all the houses, all the factories, and all the money. If anyone disobeyed them they could throw them into prison, or they could take his job away and starve him to death. When any ordinary person spoke to a capitalist he had to cringe and bow to him, and take off his cap and address him as 'Sir'. The chief of all the capitalists was called the King, and...

But he knew the rest of the catalogue. There would be mention of the bishops in their lawn sleeves, the judges in their ermine robes, the pillory, the stocks, the treadmill, the cat-o'-nine tails, the Lord Mayor's Banquet, and the practice of kissing the Pope's toe. There was also something called the JUS PRIMAE NOCTIS, which would probably not be mentioned in a textbook for children. It was the law by which every capitalist had the right to sleep with any woman working in one of his factories.

How could you tell how much of it was lies? It MIGHT be true that the average human being was better off now than he had been before the Revolution. The only evidence to the contrary was the mute protest in your own bones, the instinctive feeling that the conditions you lived in were intolerable and that at some other time they must have been different. It struck him that the truly characteristic thing about modern life was not its cruelty and insecurity, but simply its bareness, its dinginess, its listlessness.

Life, if you looked about you, bore no resemblance not only to the lies that streamed out of the telescreens, but even to the ideals that the Party was trying to achieve. Great areas of it, even for a Party member, were neutral and non-political, a matter of slogging through dreary jobs, fighting for a place on the Tube, darning a worn-out sock, cadging a saccharine tablet, saving a cigarette end. The ideal set up by the Party was something huge, terrible, and glittering--a world of steel and concrete, of monstrous machines and terrifying weapons--a nation of warriors and fanatics, marching forward in perfect unity, all thinking the same thoughts and shouting the same slogans, perpetually working, fighting, triumphing, persecuting--three hundred million people all with the same face. The reality was decaying, dingy cities where underfed people shuffled to and fro in leaky shoes, in patched-up nineteenth-century houses that smelt always of cabbage and bad lavatories. He seemed to see a vision of London, vast and ruinous, city of a million dustbins, and mixed up with it was a picture of Mrs Parsons, a woman with lined face and wispy hair, fiddling helplessly with a blocked waste-pipe.

He reached down and scratched his ankle again. Day and night the telescreens bruised your ears with statistics proving that people today had more food, more clothes, better houses, better recreations--that they lived longer, worked shorter hours, were bigger, healthier, stronger, happier, more intelligent, better educated, than the people of fifty years ago. Not a word of it could ever be proved or disproved. The Party claimed, for example, that today 40 per cent of adult proles were literate: before the Revolution, it was said, the number had only been 15 per cent. The Party claimed that the infant mortality rate was now only 160 per thousand, whereas before the Revolution it had been 300--and so it went on. It was like a single equation with two unknowns. It might very well be that literally every word in the history books, even the things that one accepted without question, was pure fantasy. For all he knew there might never have been any such law as the JUS PRIMAE NOCTIS, or any such creature as a capitalist, or any such garment as a top hat.

Everything faded into mist. The past was erased, the erasure was forgotten, the lie became truth. Just once in his life he had possessed--AFTER the event: that was what counted--concrete, unmistakable evidence of an act of falsification. He had held it between his fingers for as long as thirty seconds. In 1973, it must have been--at any rate, it was at about the time when he and Katharine had parted. But the really relevant date was seven or eight years earlier.

The story really began in the middle sixties, the period of the great purges in which the original leaders of the Revolution were wiped out once and for all. By 1970 none of them was left, except Big Brother himself. All the rest had by that time been exposed as traitors and counter-revolutionaries. Goldstein had fled and was hiding no one knew where, and of the others, a few had simply disappeared, while the majority had been executed after spectacular public trials at which they made confession of their crimes. Among the last survivors were three men named Jones, Aaronson, and Rutherford. It must have been in 1965 that these three had been arrested.

As often happened, they had vanished for a year or more,

so that one did not know whether they were alive or dead, and then had suddenly been brought forth to incriminate themselves in the usual way. They had confessed to intelligence with the enemy (at that date, too, the enemy was Eurasia), embezzlement of public funds, the murder of various trusted Party members, intrigues against the leadership of Big Brother which had started long before the Revolution happened, and acts of sabotage causing the death of hundreds of thousands of people. After confessing to these things they had been pardoned, reinstated in the Party, and given posts which were in fact sinecures but which sounded important. All three had written long, abject articles in 'The Times', analysing the reasons for their defection and promising to make amends.

Some time after their release Winston had actually seen all three of them in the Chestnut Tree Cafe. He remembered the sort of terrified fascination with which he had watched them out of the corner of his eye. They were men far older than himself, relics of the ancient world, almost the last great figures left over from the heroic days of the Party. The glamour of the underground struggle and the civil war still faintly clung to them. He had the feeling, though already at that time facts and dates were growing blurry, that he had known their names years earlier than he had known that of Big Brother. But also they were outlaws, enemies, untoucha-bles, doomed with absolute certainty to extinction within a year or two. No one who had once fallen into the hands of the Thought Police ever escaped in the end. They were corpses waiting to be sent back to the grave.

There was no one at any of the tables nearest to them. It was not wise even to be seen in the neighbourhood of such people. They were sitting in silence before glasses of the gin flavoured with cloves which was the speciality of the cafe. Of the three, it was Rutherford whose appearance had most impressed Winston. Rutherford had once been a famous caricaturist, whose brutal cartoons had helped to inflame popular opinion before and during the Revolution. Even now, at long intervals, his cartoons were appearing in The Times.

They were simply an imitation of his earlier manner, and curiously lifeless and unconvincing.

Always they were a rehashing of the ancient themes--slum tenements, starving children, street battles, capitalists in top hats--even on the barricades the capitalists still seemed to cling to their top hats an endless, hopeless effort to get back into the past. He was a monstrous man, with a mane of greasy grey hair, his face pouched and seamed, with thick negroid lips. At one time he must have been immensely strong; now his great body was sagging, sloping, bulging, falling away in every direction. He seemed to be breaking up before one's eyes, like a mountain crumbling.

It was the lonely hour of fifteen. Winston could not now remember how he had come to be in the cafe at such a time. The place was almost empty. A tinny music was trickling from the telescreens. The three men sat in their corner almost motionless, never speaking. Uncommanded, the waiter brought fresh glasses of gin. There was a chessboard on the table beside them, with the pieces set out but no game started. And then, for perhaps half a minute in all, something happened to the telescreens. The tune that they were playing changed, and the tone of the music changed too. There came into it--but it was something hard to describe. It was a peculiar, cracked, braying, jeering note: in his mind Winston called it a yellow note. And then a voice from the telescreen was singing:

Under the spreading chestnut tree
I sold you and you sold me:
There lie they, and here lie we
Under the spreading chestnut tree.

The three men never stirred. But when Winston glanced again at Rutherford's ruinous face, he saw that his eyes were full of tears. And for the first time he noticed, with a kind of inward shudder, and yet not knowing AT WHAT he shuddered, that both Aaronson and Rutherford had broken noses. A little later all three were re-arrested. It appeared that they had engaged in fresh conspiracies from the very moment of their release. At their second trial they confessed to all their old crimes over again, with a whole string of new ones. They were executed, and their fate was recorded in the Party histories, a warning to posterity.

About five years after this, in 1973, Winston was unrolling a wad of documents which had just flopped out of the pneumatic tube on to his desk when he came on a fragment of paper which had evidently been slipped in among the others and then forgotten. The instant he had flattened it out he saw its significance. It was a half-page torn out of 'The Times' of about ten years earlier--the top half of the page, so that it included the date--and it contained a photograph of the delegates at some Party function in New York. Prominent in the middle of the group were Jones, Aaronson, and Rutherford. There was no mistaking them, in any case their names were in the caption at the bottom. The point was that at both trials all three men had confessed that on that date they had been on Eurasian soil. They had flown from a secret airfield in Canada to a rendezvous somewhere in Siberia, and had conferred with members of the Eurasian General Staff, to whom they had betrayed important military secrets. The date had stuck in Winston's memory because it chanced to be midsummer day; but the whole story must be on record in countless other places as well. There was only one possible conclusion: the confessions were lies.

Of course, this was not in itself a discovery. Even at that time Winston had not imagined that the people who were wiped out in the purges had actually committed the crimes that they were accused of. But this was concrete evidence; it was a fragment of the abolished past, like a fossil bone which turns up in the wrong stratum and destroys a geological theory. It was enough to blow the Party to atoms, if in some way it could have been published to the world and its significance made known.

He had gone straight on working. As soon as he saw what the photograph was, and what it meant, he had covered it up with another sheet of paper. Luckily, when he unrolled it, it had been upside-down from the point of view of the telescreen.

He took his scribbling pad on his knee and pushed back his chair so as to get as far away from the telescreen as possible.

To keep your face expressionless was not difficult, and even your breathing could be controlled, with an effort: but you could not control the beating of your heart, and the telescreen was quite delicate enough to pick it up. He let what he judged to be ten minutes go by, tormented all the while by the fear that some accident--a sudden draught blowing across his desk, for instance--would betray him. Then, without uncovering it again, he dropped the photograph into the memory hole, along with some other waste papers. Within another minute, perhaps, it would have crumbled into ashes.

That was ten--eleven years ago. Today, probably, he would have kept that photograph. It was curious that the fact of having held it in his fingers seemed to him to make a difference even now, when the photograph itself, as well as the event it recorded, was only memory. Was the Party's hold upon the past less strong, he wondered, because a piece of evidence which existed no longer HAD ONCE existed?

But today, supposing that it could be somehow resurrected from its ashes, the photograph might not even be evidence. Already, at the time when he made his discovery, Oceania was no longer at war with Eurasia, and it must have been to the agents of Eastasia that the three dead men had betrayed their country. Since then there had been other changes--two, three, he could not remember how many. Very likely the confessions had been rewritten and rewritten until the original facts and dates no longer had the smallest significance. The past not only changed, but changed continuously. What most afflicted him with the sense of nightmare was that he had never clearly understood why the huge imposture was undertaken. The immediate advantages of falsifying the past were obvious, but the ultimate motive was mysterious. He took up his pen again and wrote: I understand HOW: I do not understand WHY.

He wondered, as he had many times wondered before, whether he himself was a lunatic. Perhaps a lunatic was simply a minority of one. At one time it had been a sign of madness to believe that the earth goes round the sun; today, to believe that the past is unalterable. He might be ALONE in holding that belief, and if alone, then a lunatic. But the thought of being a lunatic did not greatly trouble him: the horror was that he might also be wrong.

He picked up the children's history book and looked at the portrait of Big Brother which formed its frontispiece. The hypnotic eyes gazed into his own. It was as though some huge force were pressing down upon you--something that penetrated inside your skull, battering against your brain, frightening you out of your beliefs, persuading you, almost, to deny the evidence of your senses. In the end the Party would announce that two and two made five, and you would have to believe it.

It was inevitable that they should make that claim sooner or later: the logic of their position demanded it. Not merely the validity of experience, but the very existence of external reality, was tacitly denied by their philosophy. The heresy of heresies was common sense. And what was terrifying was not that they would kill you for thinking otherwise, but that they might be right. For, after all, how do we know that two and two make four? Or that the force of gravity works? Or that the past is unchangeable? If both the past and the external world exist only in the mind, and if the mind itself is controllable what then?

But no! His courage seemed suddenly to stiffen of its own accord. The face of O'Brien, not called up by any obvious association, had floated into his mind. He knew, with more certainty than before, that O'Brien was on his side. He was writing the diary for O'Brien--TO O'Brien: it was like an interminable letter which no one would ever read, but which was addressed to a particular person and took its colour from that fact.

The Party told you to reject the evidence of your eyes and ears. It was their final, most essential command. His heart sank as he thought of the enormous power arrayed against him, the ease with which any Party intellectual would overthrow him in debate, the subtle arguments which he would not be able to understand, much less answer. And yet he was in the right! They were wrong and he was right. The obvious, the silly, and the true had got to be defended. Truisms are true, hold on to that! The solid world exists, its laws do not change. Stones are hard, water is wet, objects unsupported fall towards the earth's centre. With the feeling that he was speaking to O'Brien, and also that he was setting forth an important axiom, he wrote:

Freedom is the freedom to say that two plus two make four. If that is granted, all else follows.

Part 2 Chapter 1

It was the middle of the morning, and Winston had left the cubicle to go to the lavatory.

A solitary figure was coming towards him from the other end of the long, brightly-lit corridor. It was the girl with dark hair. Four days had gone past since the evening when he had run into her outside the junk-shop. As she came nearer he saw that her right arm was in a sling, not noticeable at a distance because it was of the same colour as her overalls. Probably she had crushed her hand while swinging round one of the big kaleidoscopes on which the plots of novels were 'roughed in'. It was a common accident in the Fiction Department.

They were perhaps four metres apart when the girl stumbled and fell almost flat on her face. A sharp cry of pain was wrung out of her. She must have fallen right on the injured arm. Winston stopped short. The girl had risen to her knees. Her face had turned a milky yellow colour against which her mouth stood out redder than ever. Her eyes were fixed on his, with an appealing expression that looked more like fear than pain.

A curious emotion stirred in Winston's heart. In front of him was an enemy who was trying to kill him: in front of him, also, was a human creature, in pain and perhaps with a broken bone. Already he had instinctively started forward to help her. In the moment when he had seen her fall on the bandaged arm, it had been as though he felt the pain in his own body.

'You're hurt?' he said.

'It's nothing. My arm. It'll be all right in a second.'

She spoke as though her heart were fluttering. She had certainly turned very pale.

'You haven't broken anything?'

'No, I'm all right. It hurt for a moment, that's all.'

She held out her free hand to him, and he helped her up. She had regained some of her colour, and appeared very much better. 'It's nothing,' she repeated shortly. 'I only gave my wrist a bit of a bang. Thanks, comrade!'

And with that she walked on in the direction in which she had been going, as briskly as though it had really been nothing. The whole incident could not have taken as much as half a minute. Not to let one's feelings appear in one's face was a habit that had acquired the status of an instinct, and in any case they had been standing straight in front of a telescreen when the thing happened. Nevertheless it had been very difficult not to betray a momentary surprise, for in the two or three seconds while he was helping her up the girl had slipped something into his hand. There was no question that she had done it intentionally. It was something small and flat. As he passed through the lavatory door he transferred it to his pocket and felt it with the tips of his fingers. It was a scrap of paper folded into a square.

While he stood at the urinal he managed, with a little more fingering, to get it unfolded. Obviously there must be a message of some kind written on it. For a moment he was tempted to take it into one of the water-closets and read it at once. But that would be shocking folly, as he well knew. There was no place where you could be more certain that the telescreens were watched continuously.

He went back to his cubicle, sat down, threw the fragment of paper casually among the other papers on the desk, put on his spectacles and hitched the speakwrite towards him. 'Five minutes,' he told himself, 'five minutes at the very least!' His heart bumped in his breast with frightening loudness. Fortunately the piece of work he was engaged on was mere routine, the rectification of a long list of figures, not needing close attention.

Whatever was written on the paper, it must have some kind of political meaning. So far as he could see there were two possibilities. One, much the more likely, was that the girl was an agent of the Thought Police, just as he had feared. He did not know why the Thought Police should choose to deliver their messages in such a fashion, but perhaps they had their reasons. The thing that was written on the paper might be a threat, a summons, an order to commit suicide, a trap of some description. But there was another, wilder possibility that kept raising its head, though he tried vainly to suppress it. This was, that the message did not come from the Thought Police at all, but from some kind of underground organization.

Perhaps the Brotherhood existed after all! Perhaps the girl was part of it! No doubt the idea was absurd, but it had sprung into his mind in the very instant of feeling the scrap of paper in his hand. It was not till a couple of minutes later that the other, more probable explanation had occurred to him. And even now, though his intellect told him that the message probably meant death--still, that was not what he believed, and the unreasonable hope persisted, and his heart banged, and it was with difficulty that he kept his voice from trembling as he murmured his figures into the speakwrite.

He rolled up the completed bundle of work and slid it into the pneumatic tube. Eight minutes had gone by. He re-adjusted his spectacles on his nose, sighed, and drew the next batch of work towards him, with the scrap of paper on top of it. He flattened it out. On it was written, in a large unformed handwriting:

I LOVE YOU: For several seconds he was too stunned even to throw the incriminating thing into the memory hole. When he did so, although he knew very well the danger of showing too much interest, he could not resist reading it once again, just to make sure that the words were really there.

For the rest of the morning it was very difficult to work. What was even worse than having to focus his mind on a series of niggling jobs was the need to conceal his agitation from the telescreen. He felt as though a fire were burning in his belly. Lunch in the hot, crowded, noise-filled canteen was torment. He had hoped to be alone for a little while during the lunch hour, but as bad luck would have it the imbecile Parsons flopped down beside him, the tang of his sweat almost defeating the tinny smell of stew, and kept up a stream of talk about the preparations for Hate Week. He was particularly enthusiastic about a papier-mache model of Big Brother's head, two metres wide, which was being made for the occasion by his daughter's troop of Spies. The irritating thing was that in the racket of voices Winston could hardly hear what Parsons was saying, and was constantly having to ask for some fatuous remark to be repeated. Just once he caught a glimpse of the girl, at a table with two other girls at the far end of the room. She appeared not to have seen him, and he did not look in that direction again.

The afternoon was more bearable. Immediately after lunch there arrived a delicate, difficult piece of work which would take several hours and necessitated putting everything else aside. It consisted in falsifying a series of production reports of two years ago, in such a way as to cast discredit on a prominent member of the Inner Party, who was now under a cloud. This was the kind of thing that Winston was good at, and for more than two hours he succeeded in shutting the girl out of his mind altogether. Then the memory of her face came back, and with it a raging, intolerable desire to be alone.

Until he could be alone it was impossible to think this new development out. Tonight was one of his nights at the Community Centre. He wolfed another tasteless meal in the canteen, hurried off to the Centre, took part in the solemn foolery of a 'discussion group', played two games of table tennis, swallowed several glasses of gin, and sat for half an hour through a lecture entitled 'Ingsoc in relation to chess'. His soul writhed with boredom, but for once he had had no impulse to shirk his evening at the Centre. At the sight of the words I LOVE YOU the desire to stay alive had welled up in him, and the taking of minor risks suddenly seemed stupid. It was not till twenty-three hours, when he was home and in bed--in the darkness, where you were safe even from the telescreen so long as you kept silent--that he was able to think continuously.

It was a physical problem that had to be solved: how to get in touch with the girl and arrange a meeting. He did not consider any longer the possibility that she might be laying some kind of trap for him. He knew that it was not so, because of her unmistakable agitation when she handed him the note. Obviously she had been frightened out of her wits, as well she might be. Nor did the idea of refusing her advances even cross his mind. Only five nights ago he had contemplated smashing her skull in with a cobblestone, but that was of no importance. He thought of her naked, youthful body, as he had seen it in his dream. He had imagined her a fool like all the rest of them, her head stuffed with lies and hatred, her belly full of ice. A kind of fever seized him at the thought that he might lose her, the white youthful body might slip away from him! What he feared more than anything else was that she would simply change her mind if he did not get in touch with her quickly. But the physical difficulty of meeting was enormous. It was like trying to make a move at chess when you were already mated. Whichever way you turned, the telescreen faced you. Actually, all the possible ways of communicating with her had occurred to him within five minutes of reading the note; but now, with time to think, he went over them one by one, as though laying out a row of instruments on a table.

Obviously the kind of encounter that had happened this morning could not be repeated. If she had worked in the Records Department it might have been comparatively simple, but he had only a very dim idea whereabouts in the building the Fiction Department lay, and he had no pretext for going there. If he had known where she lived, and at what time she left work, he could have contrived to meet her somewhere on her way home; but to try to follow her home was not safe, because it would mean loitering about outside the Ministry, which was bound to be noticed. As for sending a letter through the mails, it was out of the question.

By a routine that was not even secret, all letters were opened in transit. Actually, few people ever wrote letters. For the messages that it was occasionally necessary to send, there were printed postcards with long lists of phrases, and you struck out the ones that were inapplicable. In any case he did ' know the girl's name, let alone her address. Finally he decided that the safest place was the canteen. If he could get her at a table by herself, somewhere in the middle of the room, not too near the telescreens, and with a sufficient buzz of conversation all round--if these conditions endured for, say, thirty seconds, it might be possible to exchange a few words.

For a week after this, life was like a restless dream. On the next day she did not appear in the canteen until he was leaving it, the whistle having already blown. Presumably she had been changed on to a later shift. They passed each other without a glance. On the day after that she was in the canteen at the usual time, but with three other girls and immediately under a telescreen. Then for three dreadful days she did not appear at all. His whole mind and body seemed to be afflicted with an unbearable sensitivity, a sort of transparency, which made every movement, every sound, every contact, every word that he had to speak or listen to, an agony. Even in sleep he could not altogether escape from her image. He did not touch the diary during those days. If there was any relief, it was in his work, in which he could sometimes forget himself for ten minutes at a stretch. He had absolutely no clue as to what had happened to her. There was no enquiry he could make. She might have been vaporized, she might have committed suicide, she might have been transferred to the other end of Oceania: worst and likeliest of all, she might simply have changed her mind and decided to avoid him.

The next day she reappeared. Her arm was out of the sling and she had a band of sticking-plaster round her wrist. The relief of seeing her was so great that he could not resist staring directly at her for several seconds. On the following day he very nearly succeeded in speaking to her. When he came into the canteen she was sitting at a table well out from the wall, and was quite alone. It was early, and the place was not very full. The queue edged forward till Winston was almost at the counter, then was held up for two minutes because someone in front was complaining that he had not received his tablet of saccharine. But the girl was still alone when Winston secured his tray and began to make for her table. He walked casually towards her, his eyes searching for a place at some table beyond her. She was perhaps three metres away from him. Another two seconds would do it.

Then a voice behind him called, 'Smith!' He pretended not to hear. 'Smith!' repeated the voice, more loudly. It was no use. He turned round. A blond-headed, silly-faced young man named Wilsher, whom he barely knew, was inviting him with a smile to a vacant place at his table. It was not safe to refuse. After having been recognized, he could not go and sit at a table with an unattended girl. It was too noticeable. He sat down with a friendly smile. The silly blond face beamed into his. Winston had a hallucination of himself smashing a pick-axe right into the middle of it. The girl's table filled up a few minutes later.

But she must have seen him coming towards her, and perhaps she would take the hint. Next day he took care to arrive early. Surely enough, she was at a table in about the same place, and again alone. The person immediately ahead of him in the queue was a small, swiftly-moving, beetle-like man with a flat face and tiny, suspicious eyes. As Winston turned away from the counter with his tray, he saw that the little man was making straight for the girl's table. .

His hopes sank again. There was a vacant place at a table further away, but something in the little man's appearance suggested that he would be sufficiently attentive to his own comfort to choose the emptiest table. With ice at his heart Winston followed. It was no use unless he could get the girl alone. At this moment there was a tremendous crash. The little man was sprawling on all fours, his tray had gone flying, two streams of soup and coffee were flowing across the floor. He started to his feet with a malignant glance at Winston, whom he evidently suspected of having tripped him up. But it was all right. Five seconds later, with a thundering heart, Winston was sitting at the girl's table.

He did not look at her. He unpacked his tray and promptly began eating. It was all-important to speak at once, before anyone else came, but now a terrible fear had taken possession of him. A week had gone by since she had first approached him. She would have changed her mind, she must have changed her mind! It was impossible that this affair should end successfully; such things did not happen in real life. He might have flinched altogether from speaking if at this moment he had not seen Ampleforth, the hairy-eared poet, wandering limply round the room with a tray, looking for a place to sit down. In his vague way Ampleforth was attached to Winston, and would certainly sit down at his table if he caught sight of him. There was perhaps a minute in which to act. Both Winston and the girl were eating steadily. The stuff they were eating was a thin stew, actually a soup, of haricot beans. In a low murmur Winston began speaking. Neither of them looked up; steadily they spooned the watery stuff into their mouths, and between spoonfuls exchanged the few necessary words in low expressionless voices.

'What time do you leave work?'

'Eighteen-thirty.'

'Where can we meet?'

'Victory Square, near the monument.'

'It's full of telescreens.'

'It doesn't matter if there's a crowd.'

'Any signal?'

'No. Don't come up to me until you see me among a lot of people. And don't look at me. Just keep somewhere near me.'

'What time?'

'Nineteen hours.'

'All right.'

Ampleforth failed to see Winston and sat down at another table. They did not speak again, and, so far as it was possible for two people sitting on opposite sides of the same table, they did not look at one another. The girl finished her lunch quickly and made off, while Winston stayed to smoke a cigarette.

Winston was in Victory Square before the appointed time. He wandered round the base of the enormous fluted column, at the top of which Big Brother's statue gazed southward towards the skies where he had vanquished the Eurasian aeroplanes (the Eastasian aeroplanes, it had been, a few years ago) in the Battle of Airstrip One. In the street in front of it there was a statue of a man on horseback which was supposed to represent Oliver Cromwell. At five minutes past the hour the girl had still not appeared. Again the terrible fear seized upon Winston. She was not coming, she had changed her mind! He walked slowly up to the north side of the square and got a sort of pale-coloured pleasure from identifying St Martin's Church, whose bells, when it had bells, had chimed 'You owe me three farthings.'

Then he saw the girl standing at the base of the monument, reading or pretending to read a poster which ran spirally up the column. It was not safe to go near her until some more people had accumulated. There were telescreens all round the pediment. But at this moment there was a din of shouting and a zoom of heavy vehicles from somewhere to the left. Suddenly everyone seemed to be running across the square. The girl nipped nimbly round the lions at the base of the monument and joined in the rush. Winston followed. As he ran, he gathered from some shouted remarks that a convoy of Eurasian prisoners was passing.

Already a dense mass of people was blocking the south side of the square. Winston, at normal times the kind of person who gravitates to the outer edge of any kind of scrimmage, shoved, butted, squirmed his way forward into the heart of the crowd. Soon he was within arm's length of the girl, but the way was blocked by an enormous prole and an almost equally enormous woman, presumably his wife, who seemed to form an impenetrable wall of flesh. Winston wriggled himself sideways, and with a violent lunge managed to drive his shoulder between them. For a moment it felt as though his entrails were being ground to pulp between the two muscular hips, then he had broken through, sweating a little. He was next to the girl. They were shoulder to shoulder, both staring fixedly in front of them.

A long line of trucks, with wooden-faced guards armed with sub-machine guns standing upright in each corner, was passing slowly down the street. In the trucks little yellow men in shabby greenish uniforms were squatting, jammed close together. Their sad, Mongolian faces gazed out over the sides of the trucks utterly incurious. Occasionally when a truck jolted there was a clank-clank of metal: all the prisoners were wearing leg-irons. Truck-load after truck-load of the sad faces passed. Winston knew they were there but he saw them only intermittently. The girl's shoulder, and her arm right down to the elbow, were pressed against his. Her cheek was almost near enough for him to feel its warmth. She had immediately taken charge of the situation, just as she had done in the canteen. She began speaking in the same expressionless voice as before, with lips barely moving, a mere murmur easily drowned by the din of voices and the rumbling of the trucks.

'Can you hear me?'

'Yes.'

'Can you get Sunday afternoon off?'

'Yes.'

'Then listen carefully. You'll have to remember this. Go to Paddington Station----'

With a sort of military precision that astonished him, she outlined the route that he was to follow. A half-hour railway journey; turn left outside the station; two kilometres along the road; a gate with the top bar missing; a path across a field; a grass-grown lane; a track between bushes; a dead tree with moss on it. It was as though she had a map inside her head. 'Can you remember all that?' she murmured finally.

'Yes.'

'You turn left, then right, then left again.
And the gate's got no top bar.'

'Yes. What time?'

'About fifteen. You may have to wait.
I'll get there by another way.
Are you sure you remember everything?'

'Yes.'

'Then get away from me as quick as you can.'

She need not have told him that. But for the moment they could not extricate themselves from the crowd. The trucks were still filing past, the people still insatiably gaping. At the start there had been a few boos and hisses, but it came only from the Party members among the crowd, and had soon stopped. The prevailing emotion was simply curiosity.

Foreigners, whether from Eurasia or from Eastasia, were a kind of strange animal. One literally never saw them except in the guise of prisoners, and even as prisoners one never got more than a momentary glimpse of them. Nor did one know what became of them, apart from the few who were hanged as war-criminals: the others simply vanished, presumably into forced-labour camps. The round Mogol faces had given way to faces of a more European type, dirty, bearded and exhausted.

From over scrubby cheekbones eyes looked into Winston's, sometimes with strange intensity, and flashed away again. The convoy was drawing to an end. In the last truck he could see an aged man, his face a mass of grizzled hair, standing upright with wrists crossed in front of him, as though he were used to having them bound together. It was almost time for Winston and the girl to part. But at the last moment, while the crowd still hemmed them in, her hand felt for his and gave it a fleeting squeeze. It could not have been ten seconds, and yet it seemed a long time that their hands were clasped together. He had time to learn every detail of her hand. He explored the long fingers, the shapely nails, the work-hardened palm with its row of callouses, the smooth flesh under the wrist. Merely from feeling it he would have known it by sight. In the same instant it occurred to him that he did not know what colour the girl's eyes were. They were probably brown, but people with dark hair sometimes had blue eyes. To turn his head and look at her would have been inconceivable folly. With hands locked together, invisible among the press of bodies, they stared steadily in front of them, and instead of the eyes of the girl, the eyes of the aged prisoner gazed mournfully at Winston out of nests of hair.

Part 2 Chapter 2

Winston picked his way up the lane through dappled light and shade, stepping out into pools of gold wherever the boughs parted. Under the trees to the left of him the ground was misty with bluebells. The air seemed to kiss one's skin. It was the second of May. From somewhere deeper in the heart of the wood came the droning of ring-doves.

He was a bit early. There had been no difficulties about the journey, and the girl was so evidently experienced that he was less frightened than he would normally have been. Presumably she could be trusted to find a safe place. In general you could not assume that you were much safer in the country than in London. There were no telescreens, of course, but there was always the danger of concealed microphones by which your voice might be picked up and recognized; besides, it was not easy to make a journey by yourself without attracting attention. For distances of less than 100 kilometres it was not necessary to get your passport endorsed, but sometimes there were patrols hanging about the railway stations, who examined the papers of any Party member they found there and asked awkward questions. However, no patrols had appeared, and on the walk from the station he had made sure by cautious backward glances that he was not being followed. The train was full of proles, in holiday mood because of the summery weather. The wooden-seated carriage in which he travelled was filled to overflowing by a single enormous family, ranging from a toothless great-grandmother to a month-old baby, going out to spend an afternoon with 'in-laws' in the country, and, as they freely explained to Winston, to get hold of a little black-market butter.

The lane widened, and in a minute he came to the footpath she had told him of, a mere cattle-track which plunged between the bushes. He had no watch, but it could not be fifteen yet. The bluebells were so thick underfoot that it was impossible not to tread on them. He knelt down and began picking some partly to pass the time away, but also from a vague idea that he would like to have a bunch of flowers to offer to the girl when they met. He had got together a big bunch and was smelling their faint sickly scent when a sound at his back froze him, the unmistakable crackle of a foot on twigs. He went on picking bluebells. It was the best thing to do. It might be the girl, or he might have been followed after all. To look round was to show guilt. He picked another and another. A hand fell lightly on his shoulder.

He looked up. It was the girl. She shook her head,

evidently as a warning that he must keep silent, then parted the bushes and quickly led the way along the narrow track into the wood. Obviously she had been that way before, for she dodged the boggy bits as though by habit. Winston followed, still clasping his bunch of flowers. His first feeling was relief, but as he watched the strong slender body moving in front of him, with the scarlet sash that was just tight enough to bring out the curve of her hips, the sense of his own inferiority was heavy upon him. Even now it seemed quite likely that when she turned round and looked at him she would draw back after all. The sweetness of the air and the greenness of the leaves daunted him. Already on the walk from the station the May sunshine had made him feel dirty and etiolated, a creature of indoors, with the sooty dust of London in the pores of his skin. It occurred to him that till now she had probably never seen him in broad daylight in the open. They came to the fallen tree that she had spoken of. The girl hopped over and forced apart the bushes, in which there did not seem to be an opening. When Winston followed her, he found that they were in a natural clearing, a tiny grassy knoll surrounded by tall saplings that shut it in completely. The girl stopped and turned.

'Here we are,' she said.

He was facing her at several paces' distance. As yet he did not dare move nearer to her.

'I didn't want to say anything in the lane,' she went on, 'in case there's a mike hidden there. I don't suppose there is, but there could be. There's always the chance of one of those swine recognizing your voice. We're all right here.'

He still had not the courage to approach her. 'We're all right here?' he repeated stupidly.

'Yes. Look at the trees.' They were small ashes, which at some time had been cut down and had sprouted up again into a forest of poles, none of them thicker than one's wrist. 'There's nothing big enough to hide a mike in. Besides, I've been here before.'

They were only making conversation. He had managed to move closer to her now. She stood before him very upright, with a smile on her face that looked faintly ironical, as though she were wondering why he was so slow to act. The bluebells had cascaded on to the ground. They seemed to have fallen of their own accord. He took her hand.

'Would you believe,' he said, 'that till this moment I didn't know what colour your eyes were?' They were brown, he noted, a rather light shade of brown, with dark lashes. 'Now that you've seen what I'm really like, can you still bear to look at me?'

'Yes, easily.'

'I'm thirty-nine years old. I've got a wife that I can't get rid of. I've got varicose veins. I've got five false teeth.'

'I couldn't care less,' said the girl.

The next moment, it was hard to say by whose act, she was in his his arms. At the beginning he had no feeling except sheer incredulity. The youthful body was strained against his own, the mass of dark hair was against his face, and yes! actually she had turned her face up and he was kissing the wide red mouth.

She had clasped her arms about his neck, she was calling him darling, precious one, loved one. He had pulled her down on to the ground, she was utterly unresisting, he could do what he liked with her. But the truth was that he had no physical sensation, except that of mere contact. All he felt was incredulity and pride. He was glad that this was happening, but he had no physical desire. It was too soon, her youth and prettiness had frightened him, he was too much used to living without women--he did not know the reason. The girl picked herself up and pulled a bluebell out of her hair. She sat against him, putting her arm round his waist.

'Never mind, dear. There's no hurry. We've got the whole afternoon. Isn't this a splendid hide-out? I found it when I got lost once on a community hike. If anyone was coming you could hear them a hundred metres away.'

'What is your name?' said Winston.

'Julia. I know yours. It's Winston--Winston Smith.'

'How did you find that out?'

'I expect I'm better at finding things out than you are, dear.

Tell me, what did you think of me before that day I gave you the note?'

He did not feel any temptation to tell lies to her. It was even a sort of love-offering to start off by telling the worst.

'I hated the sight of you,' he said. 'I wanted to rape you and then murder you afterwards. Two weeks ago I thought seriously of smashing your head in with a cobblestone. If you really want to know, I imagined that you had something to do with the Thought Police.'

The girl laughed delightedly, evidently taking this as a tribute to the excellence of her disguise.

'Not the Thought Police! You didn't honestly think that?'

'Well, perhaps not exactly that. But from your general appearance--merely because you're young and fresh and healthy, you understand--I thought that probably----'

'You thought I was a good Party member. Pure in word and deed. Banners, processions, slogans, games, community hikes all that stuff. And you thought that if I had a quarter of a chance I'd denounce you as a thought-criminal and get you killed off?' 'Yes, something of that kind. A great many young girls are like that, you know.' 'It's this bloody thing that does it,' she said, ripping off the scarlet sash of the Junior Anti-Sex League and flinging it on to a bough.

Then, as though touching her waist had reminded her of something, she felt in the pocket of her overalls and produced a small slab of chocolate. She broke it in half and gave one of the pieces to Winston. Even before he had taken it he knew by the smell that it was very unusual chocolate. It was dark and shiny, and was wrapped in silver paper. Chocolate normally was dull-brown crumbly stuff that tasted, as nearly as one could describe it, like the smoke of a rubbish fire. But at some time or another he had tasted chocolate like the piece she had given him. The first whiff of its scent had stirred up some memory which he could not pin down, but which was powerful and troubling.

'Where did you get this stuff?' he said. 'Black market,' she said indifferently. 'Actually I am that sort of girl, to look at. I'm good at games. I was a troop-leader in the Spies. I do voluntary work three evenings a week for the Junior Anti-Sex League. Hours and hours I've spent pasting their bloody rot all over London. I always carry one end of a banner in the processions. I always look cheerful and I never shirk anything. Always yell with the crowd, that's what I say. It's the only way to be safe.'

The first fragment of chocolate had melted on Winston's tongue. The taste was delightful. But there was still that memory moving round the edges of his consciousness, something strongly felt but not reducible to definite shape, like an object seen out of the corner of one's eye. He pushed it away from him, aware only that it was the memory of some action which he would have liked to undo but could not. 'You are very young,' he said. 'You are ten or fifteen years younger than I am. What could you see to attract you in a man like me?'

'It was something in your face. I thought I'd take a chance. I'm good at spotting people who don't belong. As soon as I saw you I knew you were against THEM.'

THEM, it appeared, meant the Party, and above all the Inner Party, about whom she talked with an open jeering hatred which made Winston feel uneasy, although he knew that they were safe here if they could be safe anywhere. A thing that astonished him about her was the coarseness of her language. Party members were supposed not to swear, and Winston himself very seldom did swear, aloud, at any rate. Julia, however, seemed unable to mention the Party, and especially the Inner Party, without using the kind of words that you saw chalked up in dripping alley-ways.

He did not dislike it. It was merely one symptom of her revolt against the Party and all its ways, and somehow it seemed natural and healthy, like the sneeze of a horse that smells bad hay. They had left the clearing and were wandering again through the chequered shade, with their arms round each other's waists whenever it was wide enough to walk two abreast. He noticed how much softer her waist seemed to feel now that the sash was gone. They did not speak above a whisper. Outside the clearing, Julia said, it was better to go quietly. Presently they had reached the edge of the little wood.

She stopped him. 'Don't go out into the open. There might be someone watching. We're all right if we keep behind the boughs.' They were standing in the shade of hazel bushes.

The sunlight, filtering through innumerable leaves, was still hot on their faces. Winston looked out into the field beyond, and underwent a curious, slow shock of recognition. He knew it by sight. An old, close-bitten pasture, with a footpath wandering across it and a molehill here and there. In the ragged hedge on the opposite side the boughs of the elm trees swayed just perceptibly in the breeze, and their leaves stirred faintly in dense masses like women's hair. Surely somewhere nearby, but out of sight, there must be a stream with green pools where dace were swimming?

'Isn't there a stream somewhere near here?' he whispered.

'That's right, there is a stream. It's at the edge of the next field, actually. There are fish in it, great big ones. You can watch them lying in the pools under the willow trees, waving their tails.'

'It's the Golden Country--almost,' he murmured.

'The Golden Country?'

'It's nothing, really. A landscape I've seen sometimes in a dream.'

'Look!' whispered Julia.

A thrush had alighted on a bough not five metres away, almost at the level of their faces. Perhaps it had not seen them. It was in the sun, they in the shade. It spread out its wings, fitted them carefully into place again, ducked its head for a moment, as though making a sort of obeisance to the sun, and then began to pour forth a torrent of song. In the afternoon hush the volume of sound was startling. Winston and Julia clung together, fascinated. The music went on and on, minute after minute, with astonishing variations, never once repeating itself, almost as though the bird were deliberately showing off its virtuosity. Sometimes it stopped for a few seconds, spread out and resettled its wings, then swelled its speckled breast and again burst into song. Winston watched it with a sort of vague reverence. For whom, for what, was that bird singing? No mate, no rival was watching it.

What made it sit at the edge of the lonely wood and pour its music into nothingness? He wondered whether after all there was a microphone hidden somewhere near. He and Julia had spoken only in low whispers, and it would not pick up what they had said, but it would pick up the thrush. Perhaps at the other end of the instrument some small, beetle-like man was listening intently--listening to that. But by degrees the flood of music drove all speculations out of his mind. It was as though it were a kind of liquid stuff that poured all over him and got mixed up with the sunlight that filtered through the leaves. He stopped thinking and merely felt. The girl's waist in the bend of his arm was soft and warm. He pulled her round so that they were breast to breast; her body seemed to melt into his. Wherever his hands moved it was all as yielding as water. Their mouths clung together; it was quite different from the hard kisses they had exchanged earlier. When they moved their faces apart again both of them sighed deeply. The bird took fright and fled with a clatter of wings.

Winston put his lips against her ear. 'NOW,' he whispered.

'Not here,' she whispered back. 'Come back to the hide-out. It's safer.'

Quickly, with an occasional crackle of twigs, they threaded their way back to the clearing. When they were once inside the ring of saplings she turned and faced him. They were both breathing fast, but the smile had reappeared round the corners of her mouth. She stood looking at him for an instant, then felt at the zipper of her overalls. And, yes! it was almost as in his dream. Almost as swiftly as he had imagined it, she had torn her clothes off, and when she flung them aside it was with that same magnificent gesture by which a whole civilization seemed to be annihilated. Her body gleamed white in the sun. But for a moment he did not look at her body; his eyes were anchored by the freckled face with its faint, bold smile. He knelt down before her and took her hands in his.

'Have you done this before?'

'Of course. Hundreds of times--well, scores of times, anyway.'

'With Party members?'

'Yes, always with Party members.'

'With members of the Inner Party?'

'Not with those swine, no. But there's plenty that WOULD if they got half a chance. They're not so holy as they make out.'

His heart leapt. Scores of times she had done it: he wished it had been hundreds--thousands. Anything that hinted at corruption always filled him with a wild hope. Who knew, perhaps the Party was rotten under the surface, its cult of strenuousness and self-denial simply a sham concealing iniquity. If he could have infected the whole lot of them with leprosy or syphilis, how gladly he would have done so! Anything to rot, to weaken, to undermine! He pulled her down so that they were kneeling face to face.

'Listen. The more men you've had, the more I love you. Do you understand that?'

'Yes, perfectly.'

'I hate purity, I hate goodness! I don't want any virtue to exist anywhere. I want everyone to be corrupt to the bones.'

'Well then, I ought to suit you, dear. I'm corrupt to the bones.'

'You like doing this? I don't mean simply me: I mean the thing in itself?'

'I adore it.'

That was above all what he wanted to hear. Not merely the love of one person but the animal instinct, the simple undifferentiated desire: that was the force that would tear the Party to pieces. He pressed her down upon the grass, among the fallen bluebells. This time there was no difficulty. Presently the rising and falling of their breasts slowed to normal speed, and in a sort of pleasant helplessness they fell apart. The sun seemed to have grown hotter. They were both sleepy. He reached out for the discarded overalls and pulled them partly over her. Almost immediately they fell asleep and slept for about half an hour.

Winston woke first. He sat up and watched the freckled face, still peacefully asleep, pillowed on the palm of her hand. Except for her mouth, you could not call her beautiful. There was a line or two round the eyes, if you looked closely. The short dark hair was extraordinarily thick and soft. It occurred to him that he still did not know her surname or where she lived. The young, strong body, now helpless in sleep, awoke in him a pitying, protecting feeling. But the mindless tenderness that he had felt under the hazel tree, while the thrush was singing, had not quite come back. He pulled the overalls aside and studied her smooth white flank. In the old days, he thought, a man looked at a girl's body and saw that it was desirable, and that was the end of the story. But you could not have pure love or pure lust nowadays. No emotion was pure, because everything was mixed up with fear and hatred. Their embrace had been a battle, the climax a victory. It was a blow struck against the Party. It was a political act.

Part 2 Chapter 3

'We can come here once again,' said Julia. 'It's generally safe to use any hide-out twice. But not for another month or two, of course.'

As soon as she woke up her demeanour had changed. She became alert and business-like, put her clothes on, knotted the scarlet sash about her waist, and began arranging the details of the journey home. It seemed natural to leave this to her. She obviously had a practical cunning which Winston lacked, and she seemed also to have an exhaustive knowledge of the countryside round London, stored away from innumerable community hikes. The route she gave him was quite different from the one by which he had come, and brought him out at a different railway station. 'Never go home the same way as you went out,' she said, as though enunciating an important general principle. She would leave first, and Winston was to wait half an hour before following her.

She had named a place where they could meet after work, four evenings hence. It was a street in one of the poorer quarters, where there was an open market which was generally crowded and noisy. She would be hanging about among the stalls, pretending to be in search of shoelaces or sewing-thread. If she judged that the coast was clear she would blow her nose when he approached; otherwise he was to walk past her without recognition. But with luck, in the middle of the crowd, it would be safe to talk for a quarter of an hour and arrange another meeting.

'And now I must go,' she said as soon as he had mastered his instructions. 'I'm due back at nineteen-thirty. I've got to put in two hours for the Junior Anti-Sex League, handing out leaflets, or something. Isn't it bloody? Give me a brush-down, would you? Have I got any twigs in my hair? Are you sure? Then good-bye, my love, good-bye!' She flung herself into his arms, kissed him almost violently, and a moment later pushed her way through the saplings and disappeared into the wood with very little noise.

Even now he had not found out her surname or her address. However, it made no difference, for it was inconceivable that they could ever meet indoors or exchange any kind of written communication.

As it happened, they never went back to the clearing in the wood. During the month of May there was only one further occasion on which they actually succeeded in making love. That was in another hiding-place known to Julia, the belfry of a ruinous church in an almost-deserted stretch of country where an atomic bomb had fallen thirty years earlier. It was a good hiding-place when once you got there, but the getting there was very dangerous. For the rest they could meet only in the streets, in a different place every evening and never for more than half an hour at a time. In the street it was usually possible to talk, after a fashion.

As they drifted down the crowded pavements, not quite abreast and never looking at one another, they carried on a curious, intermittent conversation which flicked on and off like the beams of a lighthouse, suddenly nipped into silence by the approach of a Party uniform or the proximity of a telescreen, then taken up again minutes later in the middle of a sentence, then abruptly cut short as they parted at the agreed spot, then continued almost without introduction on the following day.

Julia appeared to be quite used to this kind of conversation, which she called 'talking by instalments'. She was also surprisingly adept at speaking without moving her lips. Just once in almost a month of nightly meetings they managed to exchange a kiss. They were passing in silence down a side-street (Julia would never speak when they were away from the main streets) when there was a deafening roar, the earth heaved, and the air darkened, and Winston found himself lying on his side, bruised and terrified.

A rocket bomb must have dropped quite near at hand. Suddenly he became aware of Julia's face a few centimetres from his own, deathly white, as white as chalk. Even her lips were white. She was dead! He clasped her against him and found that he was kissing a live warm face. But there was some powdery stuff that got in the way of his lips. Both of their faces were thickly coated with plaster. There were evenings when they reached their rendezvous and then had to walk past one another without a sign, because a patrol had just come round the corner or a helicopter was hovering overhead. Even if it had been less dangerous, it would still have been difficult to find time to meet. Winston's working week was sixty hours, Julia's was even longer, and their free days varied according to the pressure of work and did not often coincide.

Julia, in any case, seldom had an evening completely free. She spent an astonishing amount of time in attending lectures and demonstrations, distributing literature for the junior Anti-Sex League, preparing banners for Hate Week, making collections for the savings campaign, and such-like activities. It paid, she said, it was camouflage. If you kept the small rules, you could break the big ones. She even induced Winston to mortgage yet another of his evenings by enrolling himself for the part-time munition work which was done voluntarily by zealous Party members. So, one evening every week, Winston spent four hours of paralysing boredom, screwing together small bits of metal which were probably parts of bomb fuses, in a draughty, ill-lit workshop where the knocking of hammers mingled drearily with the music of the telescreens.

When they met in the church tower the gaps in their fragmentary conversation were filled up. It was a blazing afternoon. The air in the little square chamber above the bells was hot and stagnant, and smelt overpoweringly of pigeon dung. They sat talking for hours on the dusty, twig-littered floor, one or other of them getting up from time to time to cast a glance through the arrowslits and make sure that no one was coming.

Julia was twenty-six years old. She lived in a hostel with thirty other girls ('Always in the stink of women! How I hate women!' she said parenthetically), and she worked, as he had guessed, on the novel-writing machines in the Fiction Department. She enjoyed her work, which consisted chiefly in running and servicing a powerful but tricky electric motor. She was 'not clever', but was fond of using her hands and felt at home with machinery. She could describe the whole process of composing a novel, from the general directive issued by the Planning Committee down to the final touching-up by the Rewrite Squad. But she was not interested in the finished product. She 'didn't much care for reading,' she said. Books were just a commodity that had to be produced, like jam or bootlaces.

She had no memories of anything before the early sixties and the only person she had ever known who talked frequently of the days before the Revolution was a grandfather who had disappeared when she was eight. At school she had been captain of the hockey team and had won the gymnastics trophy two years running. She had been a troop-leader in the Spies and a branch secretary in the Youth League before joining the Junior Anti-Sex League.

She had always borne an excellent character. She had even (an infallible mark of good reputation) been picked out to work in Pornosec, the sub-section of the Fiction Department which turned out cheap pornography for distribution among the proles. It was nicknamed Muck House by the people who worked in it, she remarked. There she had remained for a year, helping to produce booklets in sealed packets with titles like 'Spanking Stories' or 'One Night in a Girls' School', to be bought furtively by proletarian youths who were under the impression that they were buying something illegal.

'What are these books like?' said Winston curiously.

'Oh, ghastly rubbish. They're boring, really. They only have six plots, but they swap them round a bit. Of course I was only on the kaleidoscopes. I was never in the Rewrite Squad. I'm not literary, dear--not even enough for that.'

He learned with astonishment that all the workers in Pornosec, except the heads of the departments, were girls. The theory was that men, whose sex instincts were less controllable than those of women, were in greater danger of being corrupted by the filth they handled.

'They don't even like having married women there,' she added. Girls are always supposed to be so pure. Here's one who isn't, anyway.

She had had her first love-affair when she was sixteen, with a Party member of sixty who later committed suicide to avoid arrest. 'And a good job too,' said Julia, 'otherwise they'd have had my name out of him when he confessed.' Since then there had been various others. Life as she saw it was quite simple. You wanted a good time; 'they', meaning the Party, wanted to stop you having it; you broke the rules as best you could. She seemed to think it just as natural that 'they' should want to rob you of your pleasures as that you should want to avoid being caught. She hated the Party, and said so in the crudest words, but she made no general criticism of it.

Except where it touched upon her own life she had no interest in Party doctrine. He noticed that she never used Newspeak words except the ones that had passed into everyday use. She had never heard of the Brotherhood, and refused to believe in its existence. Any kind of organized revolt against the Party, which was bound to be a failure, struck her as stupid. The clever thing was to break the rules and stay alive all the same. He wondered vaguely how many others like her there might be in the younger generation people who had grown up in the world of the Revolution, knowing nothing else, accepting the Party as something unalterable, like the sky, not rebelling against its authority but simply evading it, as a rabbit dodges a dog.

They did not discuss the possibility of getting married. It was too remote to be worth thinking about. No imaginable committee would ever sanction such a marriage even if Katharine, Winston's wife, could somehow have been got rid of. It was hopeless even as a daydream.

'What was she like, your wife?' said Julia.

'She was--do you know the Newspeak word GOODTHINKFUL? Meaning naturally orthodox, incapable of thinking a bad thought?'

'No, I didn't know the word, but I know the kind of person, right enough.'

He began telling her the story of his married life, but curiously enough she appeared to know the essential parts of it already. She described to him, almost as though she had seen or felt it, the stiffening of Katharine's body as soon as he touched her, the way in which she still seemed to be pushing him from her with all her strength, even when her arms were clasped tightly round him. With Julia he felt no difficulty in talking about such things: Katharine, in any case, had long ceased to be a painful memory and became merely a distasteful one. 'I could have stood it if it hadn't been for one thing,' he said. He told her about the frigid little ceremony that Katharine had forced him to go through on the same night every week. 'She hated it, but nothing would make her stop doing it. She used to call it--but you'll never guess.'

'Our duty to the Party,' said Julia promptly.

'How did you know that?'

'I've been at school too, dear. Sex talks once a month for the over-sixteens. And in the Youth Movement. They rub it into you for years. I dare say it works in a lot of cases. But of course you can never tell; people are such hypocrites.'

She began to enlarge upon the subject. With Julia, everything came back to her own sexuality. As soon as this was touched upon in any way she was capable of great acuteness. Unlike Winston, she had grasped the inner meaning of the Party's sexual puritanism. It was not merely that the sex instinct created a world of its own which was outside the Party's control and which therefore had to be destroyed if possible. What was more important was that sexual privation induced hysteria, which was desirable because it could be transformed into war-fever and leader-worship. The way she put it was:

'When you make love you're using up energy; and afterwards you feel happy and don't give a damn for anything. They can't bear you to feel like that. They want you to be bursting with energy all the time. All this marching up and down and cheering and waving flags is simply sex gone sour. If you're happy inside yourself, why should you get excited about Big Brother and the Three-Year Plans and the Two Minutes Hate and all the rest of their bloody rot?'

That was very true, he thought. There was a direct intimate connexion between chastity and political orthodoxy. For how could the fear, the hatred, and the lunatic credulity which the Party needed in its members be kept at the right pitch, except by bottling down some powerful instinct and using it as a driving force? The sex impulse was dangerous to the Party, and the Party had turned it to account. They had played a similar trick with the instinct of parenthood. The family could not actually be abolished, and, indeed, people were encouraged to be fond of their children, in almost the old-fashioned way. The children, on the other hand, were systematically turned against their parents and taught to spy on them and report their deviations. The family had become in effect an extension of the Thought Police. It was a device by means of which everyone could be surrounded night and day by informers who knew him intimately.

Abruptly his mind went back to Katharine. Katharine would unquestionably have denounced him to the Thought Police if she had not happened to be too stupid to detect the unorthodoxy of his opinions. But what really recalled her to him at this moment was the stifling heat of the afternoon, which had brought the sweat out on his forehead. He began telling Julia of something that had happened, or rather had failed to happen, on another sweltering summer afternoon, eleven years ago.

It was three or four months after they were married. They had lost their way on a community hike somewhere in Kent. They had only lagged behind the others for a couple of minutes, but they took a wrong turning, and presently found themselves pulled up short by the edge of an old chalk quarry. It was a sheer drop of ten or twenty metres, with boulders at the bottom. There was nobody of whom they could ask the way. As soon as she realized that they were lost Katharine became very uneasy. To be away from the noisy mob of hikers even for a moment gave her a feeling of wrong-doing.

She wanted to hurry back by the way they had come and start searching in the other direction. But at this moment Winston noticed some tufts of loosestrife growing in the cracks of the cliff beneath them. One tuft was of two colours, magenta and brick-red, apparently growing on the same root. He had never seen anything of the kind before, and he called to Katharine to come and look at it.

'Look, Katharine! Look at those flowers. That clump down near the bottom. Do you see they're two different colours?' She had already turned to go, but she did rather fretfully come back for a moment. She even leaned out over the cliff face to see where he was pointing. He was standing a little behind her, and he put his hand on her waist to steady her. At this moment it suddenly occurred to him how completely alone they were. There was not a human creature anywhere, not a leaf stirring, not even a bird awake. In a place like this the danger that there would be a hidden microphone was very small, and even if there was a microphone it would only pick up sounds. It was the hottest sleepiest hour of the afternoon. The sun blazed down upon them, the sweat tickled his face. And the thought struck him...

'Why didn't you give her a good shove?' said Julia. 'I would have.' 'Yes, dear, you would have. I would, if I'd been the same person then as I am now. Or perhaps I would--I'm not certain.'

'Are you sorry you didn't?'

'Yes. On the whole I'm sorry I didn't.'

They were sitting side by side on the dusty floor. He pulled her closer against him. Her head rested on his shoulder, the pleasant smell of her hair conquering the pigeon dung. She was very young, he thought, she still expected something from life, she did not understand that to push an inconvenient person over a cliff solves nothing.

'Actually it would have made no difference,' he said.

'Then why are you sorry you didn't do it?'

'Only because I prefer a positive to a negative. In this game that we're playing, we can't win. Some kinds of failure are better than other kinds, that's all.'

He felt her shoulders give a wriggle of dissent. She always contradicted him when he said anything of this kind. She would not accept it as a law of nature that the individual is always defeated. In a way she realized that she herself was doomed, that sooner or later the Thought Police would catch her and kill her, but with another part of her mind she believed that it was somehow possible to construct a secret world in which you could live as you chose. All you needed was luck and cunning and boldness. She did not understand that there was no such thing as happiness, that the only victory lay in the far future, long after you were dead, that from the moment of declaring war on the Party it was better to think of yourself as a corpse.

'We are the dead,' he said.

'We're not dead yet,' said Julia prosaically.

'Not physically. Six months, a year--five years, conceivably. I am afraid of death. You are young, so presumably you're more afraid of it than I am. Obviously we shall put it off as long as we can. But it makes very little difference. So long as human beings stay human, death and life are the same thing.'

'Oh, rubbish! Which would you sooner sleep with, me or a skeleton? Don't you enjoy being alive? Don't you like feeling: This is me, this is my hand, this is my leg, I'm real, I'm solid, I'm alive! Don't you like THIS?'

She twisted herself round and pressed her bosom against him. He could feel her breasts, ripe yet firm, through her overalls. Her body seemed to be pouring some of its youth and vigour into his.

'Yes, I like that,' he said.

'Then stop talking about dying. And now listen, dear,

we've got to fix up about the next time we meet. We may as well go back to the place in the wood. We've given it a good long rest. But you must get there by a different way this time. I've got it all planned out. You take the train--but look, I'll draw it out for you.' And in her practical way she scraped together a small square of dust, and with a twig from a pigeon's nest began drawing a map on the floor.

It had happened at last. The expected message had come. All his life, it seemed to him, he had been waiting for this to happen.

He was walking down the long corridor at the Ministry and he was almost at the spot where Julia had slipped the note into his hand when he became aware that someone larger than himself was walking just behind him. The person, whoever it was, gave a small cough, evidently as a prelude to speaking. Winston stopped abruptly and turned. It was O'Brien.

At last they were face to face, and it seemed that his only impulse was to run away. His heart bounded violently. He would have been incapable of speaking. O'Brien, however, had continued forward in the same movement, laying a friendly hand for a moment on Winston's arm, so that the two of them were walking side by side. He began speaking with the peculiar grave courtesy that differentiated him from the majority of Inner Party members.

'I had been hoping for an opportunity of talking to you,' he said. 'I was reading one of your Newspeak articles in 'The Times' the other day. You take a scholarly interest in Newspeak, I believe?'

Winston had recovered part of his self-possession. 'Hardly scholarly,' he said. 'I'm only an amateur. It's not my subject. I have never had anything to do with the actual construction of the language.' 'But you write it very elegantly,' said O'Brien. 'That is not only my own opinion. I was talking recently to a friend of yours who is certainly an expert. His name has slipped my memory for the moment.'

Again Winston's heart stirred painfully. It was inconceivable that this was anything other than a reference to Syme. But Syme was not only dead, he was abolished, an unperson. Any identifiable reference to him would have been mortally dangerous. O'Brien's remark must obviously have been intended as a signal, a codeword. By sharing a small act of thoughtcrime he had turned the two of them into accomplices. They had continued to stroll slowly down the corridor, but now O'Brien halted. With the curious, disarming friendliness that he always managed to put in to the gesture he resettled his spectacles on his nose. Then he went on:

'What I had really intended to say was that in your article I noticed you had used two words which have become obsolete. But they have only become so very recently. Have you seen the tenth edition of the Newspeak Dictionary?'

'No,' said Winston. 'I didn't think it had been issued yet. We are still using the ninth in the Records Department.'

'The tenth edition is not due to appear for some months, I believe. But a few advance copies have been circulated. I have one myself. It might interest you to look at it, perhaps?'

'Very much so,' said Winston, immediately seeing where this tended. 'Some of the new developments are most ingenious. The reduction in the number of verbs--that is the point that will appeal to you, I think. Let me see, shall I send a messenger to you with the dictionary? But I am afraid I invariably forget anything of that kind. Perhaps you could pick it up at my flat at some time that suited you? Wait. Let me give you my address.'

They were standing in front of a telescreen. Somewhat absent-mindedly O'Brien felt two of his pockets and then produced a small leather-covered notebook and a gold ink-pencil. Immediately beneath the telescreen, in such a position that anyone who was watching at the other end of the instrument could read what he was writing, he scribbled an address, tore out the page and handed it to Winston.

'I am usually at home in the evenings,' he said. 'If not, my servant will give you the dictionary.' He was gone, leaving Winston holding the scrap of paper, which this time there was no need to conceal. Nevertheless he carefully memorized what was written on it, and some hours later dropped it into the memory hole along with a mass of other papers.

They had been talking to one another for a couple of minutes at the most. There was only one meaning that the episode could possibly have. It had been contrived as a way of letting Winston know O'Brien's address. This was necessary, because except by direct enquiry it was never possible to discover where anyone lived. There were no directories of any kind. 'If you ever want to see me, this is where I can be found,' was what O'Brien had been saying to him. Perhaps there would even be a message concealed somewhere in the dictionary. But at any rate, one thing was certain. The conspiracy that he had dreamed of did exist, and he had reached the outer edges of it.

He knew that sooner or later he would obey O'Brien's summons. Perhaps tomorrow, perhaps after a long delay--he was not certain. What was happening was only the working-out of a process that had started years ago. The first step had been a secret, involuntary thought, the second had been the opening of the diary. He had moved from thoughts to words, and now from words to actions. The last step was something that would happen in the Ministry of Love. He had accepted it. The end was contained in the beginning. But it was frightening: or, more exactly, it was like a foretaste of death, like being a little less alive. Even while he was speaking to O'Brien, when the meaning of the words had sunk in, a chilly shuddering feeling had taken possession of his body. He had the sensation of stepping into the dampness of a grave, and it was not much better because he had always known that the grave was there and waiting for him.

Part 2 Chapter 7

Winston had woken up with his eyes full of tears. Julia rolled sleepily against him, murmuring something that might have been 'What's the matter?' 'I dreamt--' he began, and stopped short. It was too complex to be put into words. There was the dream itself, and there was a memory connected with it that had swum into his mind in the few seconds after waking.

He lay back with his eyes shut, still sodden in the atmosphere of the dream. It was a vast, luminous dream in which his whole life seemed to stretch out before him like a landscape on a summer evening after rain. It had all occurred inside the glass paperweight, but the surface of the glass was the dome of the sky, and inside the dome everything was flooded with clear soft light in which one could see into interminable distances. The dream had also been comprehended by--indeed, in some sense it had consisted in--a gesture of the arm made by his mother, and made again thirty years later by the Jewish woman he had seen on the news film, trying to shelter the small boy from the bullets, before the helicopter blew them both to pieces. 'Do you know,' he said, 'that until this moment I believed I had murdered my mother?'

'Why did you murder her?' said Julia, almost asleep.

'I didn't murder her. Not physically.'

In the dream he had remembered his last glimpse of his mother, and within a few moments of waking the cluster of small events surrounding it had all come back. It was a memory that he must have deliberately pushed out of his consciousness over many years. He was not certain of the date, but he could not have been less than ten years old, possibly twelve, when it had happened.

His father had disappeared some time earlier, how much earlier he could not remember. He remembered better the rackety, uneasy circumstances of the time: the periodical panics about air-raids and the sheltering in Tube stations, the piles of rubble everywhere, the unintelligible proclamations posted at street corners, the gangs of youths in shirts all the same colour, the enormous queues outside the bakeries, the intermittent machine-gun fire in the distance--above all, the fact that there was never enough to eat. He remembered long afternoons spent with other boys in scrounging round dustbins and rubbish heaps, picking out the ribs of cabbage leaves, potato peelings, sometimes even scraps of stale breadcrust from which they carefully scraped away the cinders; and also in waiting for the passing of trucks which travelled over a certain route and were known to carry cattle feed, and which, when they jolted over the bad patches in the road, sometimes

the chocolate he felt somewhat ashamed of himself and hung about in the streets for several hours, until hunger drove him home. When he came back his mother had disappeared. This was already becoming normal at that time. Nothing was gone from the room except his mother and his sister. They had not taken any clothes, not even his mother's overcoat. To this day he did not know with any certainty that his mother was dead. It was perfectly possible that she had merely been sent to a forced-labour camp. As for his sister, she might have been removed, like Winston himself, to one of the colonies for homeless children (Reclamation Centres, they were called) which had grown up as a result of the civil war, or she might have been sent to the labour camp along with his mother, or simply left somewhere or other to die.

The dream was still vivid in his mind, especially the enveloping protecting gesture of the arm in which its whole meaning seemed to be contained. His mind went back to another dream of two months ago. Exactly as his mother had sat on the dingy white-quilted bed, with the child clinging to her, so she had sat in the sunken ship, far underneath him, and drowning deeper every minute, but still looking up at him through the darkening water.

He told Julia the story of his mother's disappearance. Without opening her eyes she rolled over and settled herself into a more comfortable position.

'I expect you were a beastly little swine in those days,' she said indistinctly. 'All children are swine.'

'Yes. But the real point of the story----'

From her breathing it was evident that she was going off to sleep again. He would have liked to continue talking about his mother. He did not suppose, from what he could remember of her, that she had been an unusual woman, still less an intelligent one; and yet she had possessed a kind of nobility, a kind of purity, simply because the standards that she obeyed were private ones. Her feelings were her own, and could not be altered from outside. It would not have occurred to her that an action which is ineffectual thereby becomes meaningless. If you loved someone, you loved him, and when you had nothing else to give, you still gave him love. When the last of the chocolate was gone, his mother had clasped the child in her arms. It was no use, it changed nothing, it did not produce more chocolate, it did not avert the child's death or her own; but it seemed natural to her to do it.

The refugee woman in the boat had also covered the little boy with her arm, which was no more use against the bullets than a sheet of paper. The terrible thing that the Party had done was to persuade you that mere impulses, mere feelings, were of no account, while at the same time robbing you of all power over the material world. When once you were in the grip of the Party, what you felt or did not feel, what you did or refrained from doing, made literally no difference. Whatever happened you vanished, and neither you nor your actions were ever heard of again. You were lifted clean out of the stream of history. And yet to the people of only two generations ago this would not have seemed all-important, because they were not attempting to alter history. They were governed by private loyalties which they did not question. What mattered were individual relationships, and a completely helpless gesture, an embrace, a tear, a word spoken to a dying man, could have value in itself. The proles, it suddenly occurred to him, had remained in this condition.

They were not loyal to a party or a country or an idea, they were loyal to one another. For the first time in his life he did not despise the proles or think of them merely as an inert force which would one day spring to life and regenerate the world. The proles had stayed human. They had not become hardened inside. They had held on to the primitive emotions which he himself had to re-learn by conscious effort. And in thinking this he remembered, without apparent relevance, how a few weeks ago he had seen a severed hand lying on the pavement and had kicked it into the gutter as though it had been a cabbage-stalk.

'The proles are human beings,' he said aloud. 'We are not human.' 'Why not?' said Julia, who had woken up again.

He thought for a little while. 'Has it ever occurred to you,' he said, 'that the best thing for us to do would be simply to walk out of here before it's too late, and never see each other again?'

'Yes, dear, it has occurred to me, several times. But I'm not going to do it, all the same.'

'We've been lucky,' he said 'but it can't last much longer. You're young. You look normal and innocent. If you keep clear of people like me, you might stay alive for another fifty years.'

'No. I've thought it all out. What you do, I'm going to do. And don't be too downhearted. I'm rather good at staying alive.'

'We may be together for another six months--a year--there's no knowing. At the end we're certain to be apart. Do you realise how utterly alone we shall be? When once they get hold of us there will be nothing, literally nothing, that either of us can do for the other. If I confess, they'll shoot you, and if I refuse to confess, they'll shoot you just the same. Nothing that I can do or say, or stop myself from saying, will put off your death for as much as five minutes. Neither of us will even know whether the other is alive or dead. We shall be utterly without power of any kind. The one thing that matters is that we shouldn't betray one another, although even that can't make the slightest difference.'

'If you mean confessing,' she said, 'we shall do that, right enough. Everybody always confesses. You can't help it. They torture you.' 'I don't mean confessing. Confession is not betrayal. What you say or do doesn't matter: only feelings matter. If they could make me stop loving you--that would be the real betrayal.' She thought it over. 'They can't do that,' she said finally. 'It's the one thing they can't do. They can make you say anything--ANYTHING--but they can't make you believe it. They can't get inside you.'

'No,' he said a little more hopefully, 'no; that's quite true. They can't get inside you. If you can FEEL that staying human is worth while, even when it can't have any result whatever, you've beaten them.'

He thought of the telescreen with its never-sleeping ear. They could spy upon you night and day, but if you kept your head you could still outwit them. With all their cleverness they had never mastered the secret of finding out what another human being was thinking. Perhaps that was less true when you were actually in their hands. One did not know what happened inside the Ministry of Love, but it was possible to guess: tortures, drugs, delicate instruments that registered your nervous reactions, gradual wearing-down by sleeplessness and solitude and persistent questioning. Facts, at any rate, could not be kept hidden. They could be tracked down by enquiry, they could be squeezed out of you by torture. But if the object was not to stay alive but to stay human, what difference did it ultimately make? They could not alter your feelings: for that matter you could not alter them yourself, even if you wanted to. They could lay bare in the utmost detail everything that you had done or said or thought; but the inner heart, whose workings were mysterious even to yourself, remained impregnable.

Part 2 Chapter 8

They had done it, they had done it at last!

The room they were standing in was long-shaped and softly lit. The telescreen was dimmed to a low murmur; the richness of the dark-blue carpet gave one the impression of treading on velvet. At the far end of the room O'Brien was sitting at a table under a green-shaded lamp, with a mass of papers on either side of him. He had not bothered to look up when the servant showed Julia and Winston in.

Winston's heart was thumping so hard that he doubted whether he would be able to speak. They had done it, they had done it at last, was all he could think. It had been a rash act to come here at all, and sheer folly to arrive together; though it was true that they had come by different routes and only met on O'Brien's doorstep. But merely to walk into such a place needed an effort of the nerve. It was only on very rare occasions that one saw inside the dwelling-places of the Inner Party, or even penetrated into the quarter of the town where they lived. The whole atmosphere of the huge block of flats, the richness and spaciousness of everything, the unfamiliar smells of good food and good tobacco, the silent and incredibly rapid lifts sliding up and down, the white-jacketed servants hurrying to and fro--everything was intimidating.

Although he had a good pretext for coming here, he was haunted at every step by the fear that a black-uniformed guard would suddenly appear from round the corner, demand his papers, and order him to get out. O'Brien's servant, however, had admitted the two of them without demur. He was a small, dark-haired man in a white jacket, with a diamond-shaped, completely expressionless face which might have been that of a Chinese. The passage down which he led them was softly carpeted, with cream-papered walls and white wainscoting, all exquisitely clean. That too was intimidating. Winston could not remember ever to have seen a passageway whose walls were not grimy from the contact of human bodies.

O'Brien had a slip of paper between his fingers and seemed to be studying it intently. His heavy face, bent down so that one could see the line of the nose, looked both formidable and intelligent. For perhaps twenty seconds he sat without stirring. Then he pulled the speakwrite towards him and rapped out a message in the hybrid jargon of the Ministries: 'Items one comma five comma seven approved fullwise stop suggestion contained item six doubleplus ridiculous verging crimethink cancel stop unproceed constructionwise antegetting plusfull estimates machinery overheads stop end message.'

He rose deliberately from his chair and came towards them across the soundless carpet. A little of the official atmosphere seemed to have fallen away from him with the Newspeak words, but his expression was grimmer than usual, as though he were not pleased at being disturbed. The terror that Winston already felt was suddenly shot through by a streak of ordinary embarrassment. It seemed to him quite possible that he had simply made a stupid mistake. For what evidence had he in reality that O'Brien was any kind of political conspirator? Nothing but a flash of the eyes and a single equivocal remark: beyond that, only his own secret imaginings, founded on a dream. He could not even fall back on the pretence that he had come to borrow the dictionary, because in that case Julia's presence was impossible to explain. As O'Brien passed the telescreen a thought seemed to strike him. He stopped, turned aside and pressed a switch on the wall. There was a sharp snap. The voice had stopped.

Julia uttered a tiny sound, a sort of squeak of surprise. Even in the midst of his panic, Winston was too much taken aback to be able to hold his tongue.

'You can turn it off!' he said.

'Yes,' said O'Brien, 'we can turn it off. We have that privilege.'

He was opposite them now. His solid form towered over the pair of them, and the expression on his face was still indecipherable. He was waiting, somewhat sternly, for Winston to speak, but about what? Even now it was quite conceivable that he was simply a busy man wondering irritably why he had been interrupted. Nobody spoke. After the stopping of the telescreen the room seemed deadly silent. The seconds marched past, enormous. With difficulty Winston continued to keep his eyes fixed on O'Brien's. Then suddenly the grim face broke down into what might have been the beginnings of a smile. With his characteristic gesture O'Brien resettled his spectacles on his nose.

'Shall I say it, or will you?' he said.

'I will say it,' said Winston promptly. 'That thing is really turned off?'

'Yes, everything is turned off. We are alone.'

'We have come here because----'

He paused, realizing for the first time the vagueness of his own motives. Since he did not in fact know what kind of help he expected from O'Brien, it was not easy to say why he had come here. He went on, conscious that what he was saying must sound both feeble and pretentious:

'We believe that there is some kind of conspiracy, some kind of secret organization working against the Party, and that you are involved in it. We want to join it and work for it. We are enemies of the Party. We disbelieve in the principles of Ingsoc. We are thought-criminals. We are also adulterers. I tell you this because we want to put ourselves at your mercy. If you want us to incriminate ourselves in any other way, we are ready.'

He stopped and glanced over his shoulder, with the feeling that the door had opened. Sure enough, the little yellow-faced servant had come in without knocking. Winston saw that he was carrying a tray with a decanter and glasses.

'Martin is one of us,' said O'Brien impassively. 'Bring the drinks over here, Martin. Put them on the round table. Have we enough chairs? Then we may as well sit down and talk in comfort. Bring a chair for yourself, Martin. This is business. You can stop being a servant for the next ten minutes.'

The little man sat down, quite at his ease, and yet still with a servant-like air, the air of a valet enjoying a privilege. Winston regarded him out of the corner of his eye. It struck him that the man's whole life was playing a part, and that he felt it to be dangerous to drop his assumed personality even for a moment. O'Brien took the decanter by the neck and filled up the glasses with a dark-red liquid. It aroused in Winston dim memories of something seen long ago on a wall or a hoarding--a vast bottle composed of electric lights which seemed to move up and down and pour its contents into a glass. Seen from the top the stuff looked almost black, but in the decanter it gleamed like a ruby.

It had a sour-sweet smell. He saw Julia pick up her glass and sniff at it with frank curiosity. 'It is called wine,' said O'Brien with a faint smile. 'You will have read about it in books, no doubt. Not much of it gets to the Outer Party, I am afraid.' His face grew solemn again, and he raised his glass: 'I think it is fitting that we should begin by drinking a health. To our Leader: To Emmanuel Goldstein.' Winston took up his glass with a certain eagerness. Wine was a thing he had read and dreamed about. Like the glass paperweight or Mr Charrington's half-remembered rhymes, it belonged to the vanished, romantic past, the olden time as he liked to call it in his secret thoughts. For some reason he had always thought of wine as having an intensely sweet taste, like that of blackberry jam and an immediate intoxicating effect. Actually, when he came to swallow it, the stuff was distinctly disappointing. The truth was that after years of gin-drinking he could barely taste it. He set down the empty glass.

'Then there is such a person as Goldstein?' he said. 'Yes, there is such a person, and he is alive. Where, I do not know.'

'And the conspiracy--the organization? Is it real? It is not simply an invention of the Thought Police?'

'No, it is real. The Brotherhood, we call it. You will never learn much more about the Brotherhood than that it exists and that you belong to it. I will come back to that presently.' He looked at his wrist-watch. 'It is unwise even for members of the Inner Party to turn off the telescreen for more than half an hour. You ought not to have come here together, and you will have to leave separately. You, comrade'--he bowed his head to Julia--'will leave first. We have about twenty minutes at our disposal. You will understand that I must start by asking you certain questions. In general terms, what are you prepared to do?'

'Anything that we are capable of,' said Winston.

O'Brien had turned himself a little in his chair so that he was facing Winston. He almost ignored Julia, seeming to take it for granted that Winston could speak for her. For a moment the lids flitted down over his eyes. He began asking his questions in a low, expressionless voice, as though this were a routine, a sort of catechism, most of whose answers were known to him already.

'You are prepared to give your lives?'

'Yes.'

'You are prepared to commit murder?'

'Yes.'

'To commit acts of sabotage which may cause the death of hundreds of innocent people?'

'Yes.'

'To betray your country to foreign powers?'

'Yes.'

'You are prepared to cheat, to forge, to blackmail, to corrupt the minds of children, to distribute habit-forming drugs, to encourage prostitution, to disseminate venereal diseases--to do anything which is likely to cause demoralization and weaken the power of the Party?'

'Yes.'

'If, for example, it would somehow serve our interests to throw sulphuric acid in a child's face--are you prepared to do that?'

'Yes.'

'You are prepared to lose your identity and live out the rest of your life as a waiter or a dock-worker?'

'Yes.'

'You are prepared to commit suicide, if and when we order you to do so?'

'Yes.'

'You are prepared, the two of you, to separate and never see one another again?'

'No!' broke in Julia.

It appeared to Winston that a long time passed before he answered. For a moment he seemed even to have been deprived of the power of speech. His tongue worked soundlessly, forming the opening syllables first of one word, then of the other, over and over again. Until he had said it, he did not know which word he was going to say. 'No,' he said finally.

'You did well to tell me,' said O'Brien. 'It is necessary for us to know everything.'

He turned himself toward Julia and added in a voice with somewhat more expression in it:

'Do you understand that even if he survives, it may be as a different person? We may be obliged to give him a new identity. His face, his movements, the shape of his hands, the colour of his hair--even his voice would be different. And you yourself might have become a different person. Our surgeons can alter people beyond recognition. Sometimes it is necessary. Sometimes we even amputate a limb.'

Winston could not help snatching another sidelong glance at Martin's Mongolian face. There were no scars that he could see. Julia had turned a shade paler, so that her freckles were showing, but she faced O'Brien boldly. She murmured something that seemed to be assent.

'Good. Then that is settled.'

There was a silver box of cigarettes on the table. With a rather absent-minded air O'Brien pushed them towards the others, took one himself, then stood up and began to pace slowly to and fro, as though he could think better standing. They were very good cigarettes, very thick and well-packed, with an unfamiliar silkiness in the paper. O'Brien looked at his wrist-watch again.

'You had better go back to your Pantry, Martin,' he said. 'I shall switch on in a quarter of an hour. Take a good look at these comrades' faces before you go. You will be seeing them again. I may not.'

Exactly as they had done at the front door, the little man's dark eyes flickered over their faces. There was not a trace of friendliness in his manner. He was memorizing their appearance, but he felt no interest in them, or appeared to feel none. It occurred to Winston that a synthetic face was perhaps incapable of changing its expression. Without speaking or giving any kind of salutation, Martin went out, closing the door silently behind him. O'Brien was strolling up and down, one hand in the pocket of his black overalls, the other holding his cigarette.

'You understand,' he said, 'that you will be fighting in the dark. You will always be in the dark. You will receive orders and you will obey them, without knowing why. Later I shall send you a book from which you will learn the true nature of the society we live in, and the strategy by which we shall destroy it. When you have read the book, you will be full members of the Brotherhood. But between the general aims that we are fighting for and the immediate tasks of the moment, you will never know anything.]

I tell you that the Brotherhood exists, but I cannot tell you whether it numbers a hundred members, or ten million. From your personal knowledge you will never be able to say that it numbers even as many as a dozen. You will have three or four contacts, who will be renewed from time to time as they disappear. As this was your first contact, it will be preserved. When you receive orders, they will come from me. If we find it necessary to communicate with you, it will be through

Martin. When you are finally caught, you will confess. That is unavoidable. But you will have very little to confess, other than your own actions. You will not be able to betray more than a handful of unimportant people. Probably you will not even betray me. By that time I may be dead, or I shall have become a different person, with a different face.'

He continued to move to and fro over the soft carpet. In spite of the bulkiness of his body there was a remarkable grace in his movements. It came out even in the gesture with which he thrust a hand into his pocket, or manipulated a cigarette. More even than of strength, he gave an impression of confidence and of an understanding tinged by irony. However much in earnest he might be, he had nothing of the single-mindedness that belongs to a fanatic. When he spoke of murder, suicide, venereal disease, amputated limbs, and altered faces, it was with a faint air of persiflage. 'This is unavoidable,' his voice seemed to say; 'this is what we have got to do, unflinchingly. But this is not what we shall be doing when life is worth living again.' A wave of admiration, almost of worship, flowed out from Winston towards O'Brien. For the moment he had forgotten the shadowy figure of Goldstein. When you looked at O'Brien's powerful shoulders and his blunt-featured face, so ugly and yet so civilized, it was impossible to believe that he could be defeated. There was no stratagem that he was not equal to, no danger that he could not foresee. Even Julia seemed to be impressed. She had let her cigarette go out and was listening intently. O'Brien went on: 'You will have heard rumours of the existence of the Brotherhood. No doubt you have formed your own picture of it. You have imagined, probably, a huge underworld of conspirators, meeting secretly in cellars, scribbling messages on walls, recognizing one another by codewords or by special movements of the hand. Nothing of the kind exists.

The members of the Brotherhood have no way of recognizing one another, and it is impossible for any one member to be aware of the identity of more than a few others. Goldstein himself, if he fell into the hands of the Thought Police, could not give them a complete list of members, or any information that would lead them to a complete list. No such list exists. The Brotherhood cannot be wiped out because it is not an organization in the ordinary sense. Nothing holds it together except an idea which is indestructible. You will never have anything to sustain you, except the idea. You will get no comradeship and no encouragement.

When finally you are caught, you will get no help. We never help our members. At most, when it is absolutely necessary that someone should be silenced, we are occasionally able to smuggle a razor blade into a prisoner's cell. You will have to get used to living without results and without hope. You will work for a while, you will be caught, you will confess, and then you will die. Those are the only results that you will ever see. There is no possibility that any perceptible change will happen within our own lifetime. We are the dead. Our only true life is in the future. We shall take part in it as handfuls of dust and splinters of bone. But how far away that future may be, there is no knowing. It might be a thousand years. At present nothing is possible except to extend the area of sanity little by little. We cannot act collectively. We can only spread our knowledge outwards from individual to individual, generation after generation. In the face of the Thought Police there is no other way.'

He halted and looked for the third time at his wrist-watch.

'It is almost time for you to leave, comrade,' he said to Julia. 'Wait. The decanter is still half full.'

He filled the glasses and raised his own glass by the stem.

'What shall it be this time?' he said, still with the same faint suggestion of irony. 'To the confusion of the Thought Police? To the death of Big Brother? To humanity? To the future?' 'To the past,' said Winston.

'The past is more important,' agreed O'Brien gravely.

They emptied their glasses, and a moment later Julia stood up to go. O'Brien took a small box from the top of a cabinet and handed her a flat white tablet which he told her to place on her tongue. It was important, he said, not to go out smelling of wine: the lift attendants were very observant. As soon as the door had shut behind her he appeared to forget her existence. He took another pace or two up and down, then stopped. 'There are details to be settled,' he said. 'I assume that you have a hiding-place of some kind?' Winston explained about the room over Mr Charrington's shop.

'That will do for the moment. Later we will arrange something else for you. It is important to change one's hiding-place frequently. Meanwhile I shall send you a copy of THE BOOK'--even O'Brien, Winston noticed, seemed to pronounce the words as though they were in italics--'Goldstein's book, you understand, as soon as possible. It may be some days before I can get hold of one. There are not many in existence, as you can imagine. The Thought Police hunt them down and destroy them almost as fast as we can produce them. It makes very little difference. The book is indestructible. If the last copy were gone, we could reproduce it almost word for word. Do you carry a brief-case to work with you?' he added.

'As a rule, yes.'

'What is it like?'

'Black, very shabby. With two straps.'

'Black, two straps, very shabby--good. One day in the fairly near future--I cannot give a date--one of the messages among your morning's work will contain a misprinted word, and you will have to ask for a repeat. On the following day you will go to work without your brief-case. At some time during the day, in the street, a man will touch you on the arm and say "I think you have dropped your brief-case." The one he gives you will contain a copy of Goldstein's book. You will return it within fourteen days.'

They were silent for a moment.

'There are a couple of minutes before you need go,' said O'Brien. 'We shall meet again--if we do meet again----' Winston looked up at him. 'In the place where there is no darkness?' he said hesitantly.

O'Brien nodded without appearance of surprise. 'In the place where there is no darkness,' he said, as though he had recognized the allusion. 'And in the meantime, is there anything that you wish to say before you leave? Any message? Any question?.'

Winston thought. There did not seem to be any further question that he wanted to ask: still less did he feel any impulse to utter high-sounding generalities. Instead of anything directly connected with O'Brien or the Brotherhood, there came into his mind a sort of composite picture of the dark bedroom where his mother had spent her last days, and the little room over Mr Charrington's shop, and the glass paperweight, and the steel engraving in its rosewood frame. Almost at random he said: 'Did you ever happen to hear an old rhyme that begins "Oranges and lemons, say the bells of St Clement's"?'

Again O'Brien nodded. With a sort of grave courtesy he completed the stanza:

'Oranges and lemons, say the bells of St Clement's,
You owe me three farthings, say the bells of St Martin's,
When will you pay me? say the bells of Old Bailey,
When I grow rich, say the bells of Shoreditch.'

'You knew the last line!' said Winston.

'Yes, I knew the last line. And now, I am afraid, it is time for you to go. But wait. You had better let me give you one of these tablets.'

As Winston stood up O'Brien held out a hand. His powerful grip crushed the bones of Winston's palm. At the door Winston looked back, but O'Brien seemed already to be in process of putting him out of mind. He was waiting with his hand on the switch that controlled the telescreen. Beyond him Winston could see the writing-table with its green-shaded lamp and the speakwrite and the wire baskets deep-laden with papers. The incident was closed. Within thirty seconds, it occurred to him, O'Brien would be back at his interrupted and important work on behalf of the Party.

Part 2 Chapter 9

Winston was gelatinous with fatigue. Gelatinous was the right word. It had come into his head spontaneously. His body seemed to have not only the weakness of a jelly, but its translucency. He felt that if he held up his hand he would be able to see the light through it. All the blood and lymph had been drained out of him by an enormous debauch of work, leaving only a frail structure of nerves, bones, and skin. All sensations seemed to be magnified. His overalls fretted his shoulders, the pavement tickled his feet, even the opening and closing of a hand was an effort that made his joints creak.

He had worked more than ninety hours in five days. So had everyone else in the Ministry. Now it was all over, and he had literally nothing to do, no Party work of any description, until tomorrow morning. He could spend six hours in the hiding-place and another nine in his own bed. Slowly, in mild afternoon sunshine, he walked up a dingy street in the direction of Mr Charrington's shop, keeping one eye open for the patrols, but irrationally convinced that this afternoon there was no danger of anyone interfering with him. The heavy brief-case that he was carrying bumped against his knee at each step, sending a tingling sensation up and down the skin of his leg. Inside it was the book, which he had now had in his possession for six days and had not yet opened, nor even looked at. On the sixth day of Hate Week, after the processions, the speeches, the shouting, the singing, the banners, the posters, the films, the waxworks, the rolling of drums and squealing of trumpets, the tramp of marching feet, the grinding of the caterpillars of tanks, the roar of massed planes, the booming of guns--after six days of this, when the great orgasm was quivering to its climax and the general hatred of Eurasia had boiled up into such delirium that if the crowd could have got their hands on the 2,000 Eurasian war-criminals who were to be publicly hanged on the last day of the proceedings, they would unquestionably have torn them to pieces--at just this moment it had been announced that Oceania was not after all at war with Eurasia.

Oceania was at war with Eastasia. Eurasia was an ally. There was, of course, no admission that any change had taken place. Merely it became known, with extreme suddenness and everywhere at once, that Eastasia and not Eurasia was the enemy. Winston was taking part in a demonstration in one of the central London squares at the moment when it happened. It was night, and the white faces and the scarlet banners were luridly floodlit. The square was packed with several thousand people, including a block of about a thousand schoolchildren in the uniform of the Spies. On a scarlet-draped platform an orator of the Inner Party, a small lean man with disproportionately long arms and a large bald skull over which a few lank locks straggled, was haranguing the crowd.

A little Rumpelstiltskin figure, contorted with hatred, he gripped the neck of the microphone with one hand while the other, enormous at the end of a bony arm, clawed the air menacingly above his head. His voice, made metallic by the amplifiers, boomed forth an endless catalogue of atrocities, massacres, deportations, lootings, rapings, torture of prisoners, bombing of civilians, lying propaganda, unjust aggressions, broken treaties. It was almost impossible to listen to him without being first convinced and then maddened. At every few moments the fury of the crowd boiled over and the voice of the speaker was drowned by a wild beast-like roaring that rose uncontrollably from thousands of throats. The most savage yells of all came from the schoolchildren. The speech had been proceeding for perhaps twenty minutes when a messenger hurried on to the platform and a scrap of paper was slipped into the speaker's hand. He unrolled and read it without pausing in his speech.

Nothing altered in his voice or manner, or in the content of what he was saying, but suddenly the names were different. Without words said, a wave of understanding rippled through the crowd. Oceania was at war with Eastasia! The next moment there was a tremendous commotion. The banners and posters with which the square was decorated were all wrong! Quite half of them had the wrong faces on them. It was sabotage! The agents of Goldstein had been at work! There was a riotous interlude while posters were ripped from the walls, banners torn to shreds and trampled underfoot.

The Spies performed prodigies of activity in clambering over the rooftops and cutting the streamers that fluttered from the chimneys. But within two or three minutes it was all over. The orator, still gripping the neck of the microphone, his shoulders hunched forward, his free hand clawing at the air, had gone straight on with his speech. One minute more, and the feral roars of rage were again bursting from the crowd. The Hate continued exactly as before, except that the target had been changed.

The thing that impressed Winston in looking back was that the speaker had switched from one line to the other actually in midsentence, not only without a pause, but without even breaking the syntax. But at the moment he had other things to preoccupy him. It was during the moment of disorder while the posters were being torn down that a man whose face he did not see had tapped him on the shoulder and said, 'Excuse me, I think you've dropped your brief-case.' He took the brief-case abstractedly, without speaking.

He knew that it would be days before he had an opportunity to look inside it. The instant that the demonstration was over he went straight to the Ministry of Truth, though the time was now nearly twenty-three hours. The entire staff of the Ministry had done likewise. The orders already issuing from the telescreen, recalling them to their posts, were hardly necessary. Oceania was at war with Eastasia: Oceania had always been at war with Eastasia. A large part of the political literature of five years was now completely obsolete. Reports and records of all kinds, newspapers, books, pamphlets, films, sound-tracks, photographs--all had to be rectified at lightning speed. Although no directive was ever issued, it was known that the chiefs of the Department intended that within one week no reference to the war with Eurasia, or the alliance with Eastasia, should remain in existence anywhere. The work was overwhelming, all the more so because the processes that it involved could not be called by their true names.

Everyone in the Records Department worked eighteen hours in the twenty-four, with two three-hour snatches of sleep. Mattresses were brought up from the cellars and pitched all over the corridors: meals consisted of sandwiches and Victory Coffee wheeled round on trolleys by attendants from the canteen. Each time that Winston broke off for one of his spells of sleep he tried to leave his desk clear of work, and each time that he crawled back sticky-eyed and aching, it was to find that another shower of paper cylinders had covered the desk like a snowdrift, half-burying the speakwrite and overflowing on to the floor, so that the first job was always to stack them into a neat enough pile to give him room to work. What was worst of all was that the work was by no means purely mechanical. Often it was enough merely to substitute one name for another, but any detailed report of events demanded care and imagination. Even the geographical knowledge that one needed in transferring the war from one part of the world to another was considerable.

By the third day his eyes ached unbearably and his spectacles needed wiping every few minutes. It was like struggling with some crushing physical task, something which one had the right to refuse and which one was nevertheless neurotically anxious to accomplish. In so far as he had time to remember it, he was not troubled by the fact that every word he murmured into the speakwrite, every stroke of his ink-pencil, was a deliberate lie. He was as anxious as anyone else in the Department that the forgery should be perfect. On the morning of the sixth day the dribble of cylinders slowed down. For as much as half an hour nothing came out of the tube; then one more cylinder, then nothing. Everywhere at about the same time the work was easing off. A deep and as it were secret sigh went through the Department.

A mighty deed, which could never be mentioned, had been achieved. It was now impossible for any human being to prove by documentary evidence that the war with Eurasia had ever happened. At twelve hundred it was unexpectedly announced that all workers in the Ministry were free till tomorrow morning. Winston, still carrying the brief-case containing the book, which had remained between his feet while he worked and under his body while he slept, went home, shaved himself, and almost fell asleep in his bath, although the water was barely more than tepid.

With a sort of voluptuous creaking in his joints he climbed the stair above Mr Charrington's shop. He was tired, but not sleepy any longer. He opened the window, lit the dirty little oilstove and put on a pan of water for coffee. Julia would arrive presently: meanwhile there was the book. He sat down in the sluttish armchair and undid the straps of the brief-case.

A heavy black volume, amateurishly bound, with no name or title on the cover. The print also looked slightly irregular. The pages were worn at the edges, and fell apart, easily, as though the book had passed through many hands. The inscription on the title-page ran:

Part 3Chapter 1

He did not know where he was. Presumably he was in the Ministry of Love, but there was no way of making certain. He was in a high-ceilinged windowless cell with walls of glittering white porcelain. Concealed lamps flooded it with cold light, and there was a low, steady humming sound which he supposed had something to do with the air supply. A bench, or shelf, just wide enough to sit on ran round the wall, broken only by the door and, at the end opposite the door, a lavatory pan with no wooden seat. There were four telescreens, one in each wall.

There was a dull aching in his belly. It had been there ever since they had bundled him into the closed van and driven him away. But he was also hungry, with a gnawing, unwholesome kind of hunger. It might be twenty-four hours since he had eaten, it might be thirty-six. He still did not know, probably never would know, whether it had been morning or evening when they arrested him. Since he was arrested he had not been fed. He sat as still as he could on the narrow bench, with his hands crossed on his knee. He had already learned to sit still. If you made unexpected movements they yelled at you from the telescreen. But the craving for food was growing upon him. What he longed for above all was a piece of bread. He had an idea that there were a few breadcrumbs in the pocket of his overalls. It was even possible--he thought this because from time to time something seemed to tickle his leg--that there might be a sizeable bit of crust there. In the end the temptation to find out overcame his fear; he slipped a hand into his pocket

'Smith!' yelled a voice from the telescreen. '6079 Smith W.! Hands out of pockets in the cells!' He sat still again, his hands crossed on his knee. Before being brought here he had been taken to another place which must have been an ordinary prison or a temporary lock-up used by the patrols. He did not know how long he had been there; some hours at any rate; with no clocks and no daylight it was hard to gauge the time. It was a noisy, evil-smelling place. They had put him into a cell similar to the one he was now in, but filthily dirty and at all times crowded by ten or fifteen people. The majority of them were common criminals, but there were a few political prisoners among them. He had sat silent against the wall, jostled by dirty bodies, too preoccupied by fear and the pain in his belly to take much interest in his surroundings, but still noticing the astonishing difference in demeanour between the Party prisoners and the others. The Party prisoners were always silent and terrified, but the ordinary criminals seemed to care nothing for anybody.

They yelled insults at the guards, fought back fiercely when their belongings were impounded, wrote obscene words on the floor, ate smuggled food which they produced from mysterious hiding-places in their clothes, and even shouted down the telescreen when it tried to restore order. On the other hand some of them seemed to be on good terms with the guards, called them by nicknames, and tried to wheedle cigarettes through the spyhole in the door. The guards, too, treated the common criminals with a certain forbearance, even when they had to handle them roughly.

There was much talk about the forced-labour camps to which most of the prisoners expected to be sent. It was 'all right' in the camps, he gathered, so long as you had good contacts and knew the ropes. There was bribery, favouritism, and racketeering of every kind, there was homosexuality and prostitution, there was even illicit alcohol distilled from potatoes. The positions of trust were given only to the common criminals, especially the gangsters and the murderers, who formed a sort of aristocracy. All the dirty jobs were done by the politicals.

There was a constant come-and-go of prisoners of every description: drug-peddlers, thieves, bandits, black-marketeers, drunks, prostitutes. Some of the drunks were so violent that the other prisoners had to combine to suppress them. An enormous wreck of a woman, aged about sixty, with great tumbling breasts and thick coils of white hair which had come down in her struggles, was carried in, kicking and shouting, by four guards, who had hold of her one at each corner. They wrenched off the boots with which she had been trying to kick them, and dumped her down across Winston's lap, almost breaking his thigh-bones. The woman hoisted herself upright and followed them out with a yell of 'F--bastards!' Then, noticing that she was sitting on something uneven, she slid off Winston's knees on to the bench.

'Beg pardon, dearie,' she said. 'I wouldn't 'a sat on you, only the buggers put me there. They dono 'ow to treat a lady, do they?' She paused, patted her breast, and belched. 'Pardon,' she said, 'I ain't meself, quite.' She leant forward and vomited copiously on the floor.

'Thass better,' she said, leaning back with closed eyes. 'Never keep it down, thass what I say. Get it up while it's fresh on your stomach, like.'

She revived, turned to have another look at Winston and seemed immediately to take a fancy to him. She put a vast arm round his shoulder and drew him towards her, breathing beer and vomit into his face.

'Wass your name, dearie?' she said.

'Smith,' said Winston.

'Smith?' said the woman. 'Thass funny. My name's Smith too. Why,' she added sentimentally, 'I might be your mother!'

She might, thought Winston, be his mother. She was about the right age and physique, and it was probable that people changed somewhat after twenty years in a forced-labour camp.

No one else had spoken to him. To a surprising extent the ordinary criminals ignored the Party prisoners. 'The polits,' they called them, with a sort of uninterested contempt. The Party prisoners seemed terrified of speaking to anybody, and above all of speaking to one another. Only once, when two Party members, both women, were pressed close together on the bench, he overheard amid the din of voices a few hurriedly-whispered words; and in particular a reference to something called 'room one-oh-one', which he did not understand.

It might be two or three hours ago that they had brought him here. The dull pain in his belly never went away, but sometimes it grew better and sometimes worse, and his thoughts expanded or contracted accordingly. When it grew worse he thought only of the pain itself, and of his desire for food. When it grew better, panic took hold of him. There were moments when he foresaw the things that would happen to him with such actuality that his heart galloped and his breath stopped. He felt the smash of truncheons on his elbows and iron-shod boots on his shins; he saw himself grovelling on the floor, screaming for mercy through broken teeth. He hardly thought of Julia. He could not fix his mind on her. He loved her and would not betray her; but that was only a fact, known as he knew the rules of arithmetic. He felt no love for her, and he hardly even wondered what was happening to her.

He thought oftener of O'Brien, with a flickering hope. O'Brien might know that he had been arrested. The Brotherhood, he had said, never tried to save its members. But there was the razor blade; they would send the razor blade if they could. There would be perhaps five seconds before the guard could rush into the cell. The blade would bite into him with a sort of burning coldness, and even the fingers that held it would be cut to the bone. Everything came back to his sick body, which shrank trembling from the smallest pain. He was not certain that he would use the razor blade even if he got the chance. It was more natural to exist from moment to moment, accepting another ten minutes' life even with the certainty that there was torture at the end of it.

Sometimes he tried to calculate the number of porcelain bricks in the walls of the cell. It should have been easy, but he always lost count at some point or another. More often he wondered where he was, and what time of day it was. At one moment he felt certain that it was broad daylight outside, and at the next equally certain that it was pitch darkness. In this place, he knew instinctively, the lights would never be turned out. It was the place with no darkness: he saw now why

O'Brien had seemed to recognize the allusion. In the Ministry of Love there were no windows. His cell might be at the heart of the building or against its outer wall; it might be ten floors below ground, or thirty above it. He moved himself mentally from place to place, and tried to determine by the feeling of his body whether he was perched high in the air or buried deep underground.

There was a sound of marching boots outside. The steel door opened with a clang. A young officer, a trim black-uniformed figure who seemed to glitter all over with polished leather, and whose pale, straight-featured face was like a wax mask, stepped smartly through the doorway. He motioned to the guards outside to bring in the prisoner they were leading. The poet Ampleforth shambled into the cell. The door clanged shut again. Ampleforth made one or two uncertain movements from side to side, as though having some idea that there was another door to go out of, and then began to wander up and down the cell. He had not yet noticed Winston's presence. His troubled eyes were gazing at the wall about a metre above the level of Winston's head. He was shoeless; large, dirty toes were sticking out of the holes in his socks. He was also several days away from a shave. A scrubby beard covered his face to the cheekbones, giving him an air of ruffianism that went oddly with his large weak frame and nervous movements.

Winston roused hirnself a little from his lethargy. He must speak to Ampleforth, and risk the yell from the telescreen. It was even conceivable that Ampleforth was the bearer of the razor blade.

'Ampleforth,' he said.

There was no yell from the telescreen. Ampleforth paused, mildly startled. His eyes focused themselves slowly on Winston. 'Ah, Smith!' he said. 'You too!'

'What are you in for?'

'To tell you the truth--' He sat down awkwardly on the bench opposite Winston. 'There is only one offence, is there not?'he said.

'And have you committed it?'

'Apparently I have.'

He put a hand to his forehead and pressed his temples for a moment, as though trying to remember something.

'These things happen,' he began vaguely. 'I have been able to recall one instance--a possible instance. It was an indiscretion, undoubtedly. We were producing a definitive edition of the poems of Kipling. I allowed the word "God" to remain at the end of a line. I could not help it!' he added almost indignantly, raising his face to look at Winston. 'It was impossible to change the line. The rhyme was "rod". Do you realise that there are only twelve rhymes to "rod" in the entire language? For days I had racked my brains. There was no other rhyme.' The expression on his face changed. The annoyance passed out of it and for a moment he looked almost pleased. A sort of intellectual warmth, the joy of the pedant who has found out some useless fact, shone through the dirt and scrubby hair.

'Has it ever occurred to you,' he said, 'that the whole history of English poetry has been determined by the fact that the English language lacks rhymes?'

No, that particular thought had never occurred to Winston. Nor, in the circumstances, did it strike him as very important or interesting.

'Do you know what time of day it is?' he said.

Ampleforth looked startled again. 'I had hardly thought about it. They arrested me--it could be two days ago--perhaps three.' His eyes flitted round the walls, as though he half expected to find a window somewhere. 'There is no difference between night and day in this place. I do not see how one can calculate the time.'

They talked desultorily for some minutes, then, without apparent reason, a yell from the telescreen bade them be silent. Winston sat quietly, his hands crossed. Ampleforth, too large to sit in comfort on the narrow bench, fidgeted from side to side, clasping his lank hands first round one knee, then round the other. The telescreen barked at him to keep still. Time passed. Twenty minutes, an hour--it was difficult to judge. Once more there was a sound of boots outside. Winston's entrails contracted. Soon, very soon, perhaps in five minutes, perhaps now, the tramp of boots would mean that his own turn had come.

The door opened. The cold-faced young officer stepped into the cell. With a brief movement of the hand he indicated Ampleforth.

'Room 101,' he said: Ampleforth marched clumsily out between the guards, his face vaguely perturbed, but uncomprehending.

What seemed like a long time passed. The pain in Winston's belly had revived. His mind sagged round and round on the same trick, like a ball falling again and again into the same series of slots. He had only six thoughts. The pain in his belly; a piece of bread; the blood and the screaming; O'Brien; Julia; the razor blade. There was another spasm in his entrails, the heavy boots were approaching. As the door opened, the wave of air that it created brought in a powerful smell of cold sweat. Parsons walked into the cell. He was wearing khaki shorts and a sports-shirt.

This time Winston was startled into self-forgetfulness.

'You here!' he said.

Parsons gave Winston a glance in which there was neither interest nor surprise, but only misery. He began walking jerkily up and down, evidently unable to keep still. Each time he straightened his pudgy knees it was apparent that they were trembling. His eyes had a wide-open, staring look, as though he could not prevent himself from gazing at something in the middle distance.

'What are you in for?' said Winston.

'Thoughtcrime!' said Parsons, almost blubbering. The tone of his voice implied at once a complete admission of his guilt and a sort of incredulous horror that such a word could be applied to himself. He paused opposite Winston and began eagerly appealing to him: 'You don't think they'll shoot me, do you, old chap? They don't shoot you if you haven't actually done anything--only thoughts, which you can't help? I know they give you a fair hearing. Oh, I trust them for that! They'll know my record, won't they? You know what kind of chap I was. Not a bad chap in my way. Not brainy, of course, but keen. I tried to do my best for the Party, didn't I? I'll get off with five years, don't you think? Or even ten years? A chap like me could make himself pretty useful in a labour-camp. They wouldn't shoot me for going off the rails just once?'

'Are you guilty?' said Winston.: 'Of course I'm guilty!' cried Parsons with a servile glance at the telescreen. 'You don't think the Party would arrest an innocent man, do you?' His frog-like face grew calmer, and even took on a slightly sanctimonious expression. 'Thoughtcrime is a dreadful thing, old man,' he said sententiously. 'It's insidious. It can get hold of you without your even knowing it. Do you know how it got hold of me? In my sleep! Yes, that's a fact. There I was, working away, trying to do my bit--never knew I had any bad stuff in my mind at all. And then I started talking in my sleep. Do you know what they heard me saying?'

He sank his voice, like someone who is obliged for medical reasons to utter an obscenity.

"Down with Big Brother!" Yes, I said that! Said it over and over again, it seems. Between you and me, old man, I'm glad they got me before it went any further. Do you know what I'm going to say to them when I go up before the tribunal? "Thank you," I'm going to say, "thank you for saving me before it was too late."

'Who denounced you?' said Winston.

'It was my little daughter,' said Parsons with a sort of doleful pride. 'She listened at the keyhole. Heard what I was saying, and nipped off to the patrols the very next day. Pretty smart for a nipper of seven, eh? I don't bear her any grudge for it. In fact I'm proud of her. It shows I brought her up in the right spirit, anyway.'

He made a few more jerky movements up and down, several times, casting a longing glance at the lavatory pan. Then he suddenly ripped down his shorts.

'Excuse me, old man,' he said. 'I can't help it. It's the waiting.' He plumped his large posterior into the lavatory pan. Winston covered his face with his hands.

'Smith!' yelled the voice from the telescreen. '6079 Smith W! Uncover your face. No faces covered in the cells.'

Winston uncovered his face. Parsons used the lavatory, loudly and abundantly. It then turned out that the plug was defective and the cell stank abominably for hours afterwards.

Parsons was removed. More prisoners came and went, mysteriously. One, a woman, was consigned to 'Room 101', and, Winston noticed, seemed to shrivel and turn a different colour when she heard the words. A time came when, if it had been morning when he was brought here, it would be afternoon; or if it had been afternoon, then it would be midnight.

There were six prisoners in the cell, men and women. All sat very still. Opposite Winston there sat a man with a chinless, toothy face exactly like that of some large, harmless rodent. His fat, mottled cheeks were so pouched at the bottom that it was difficult not to believe that he had little stores of food tucked away there. His pale-grey eyes flitted timorously from face to face and turned quickly away again when he caught anyone's eye.

The door opened, and another prisoner was brought in whose appearance sent a momentary chill through Winston. He was a commonplace, mean-looking man who might have been an engineer or technician of some kind. But what was startling was the emaciation of his face. It was like a skull. Because of its thinness the mouth and eyes looked disproportionately large, and the eyes seemed filled with a murderous, unappeasable hatred of somebody or something.

The man sat down on the bench at a little distance from Winston. Winston did not look at him again, but the tormented, skull-like face was as vivid in his mind as though it had been straight in front of his eyes. Suddenly he realized what was the matter. The man was dying of starvation. The same thought seemed to occur almost simultaneously to everyone in the cell. There was a very faint stirring all the way round the bench. The eyes of the chinless man kept flitting towards the skull-faced man, then turning guiltily away, then being dragged back by an irresistible attraction. Presently he began to fidget on his seat. At last he stood up, waddled clumsily across the cell, dug down into the pocket of his overalls, and, with an abashed air, held out a grimy piece of bread to the skull-faced man.

There was a furious, deafening roar from the telescreen. The chinless man jumped in his tracks. The skull-faced man had quickly thrust his hands behind his back, as though demonstrating to all the world that he refused the gift. 'Bumstead!' roared the voice. '2713 Bumstead J.! Let fall that piece of bread!'

The chinless man dropped the piece of bread on the floor. 'Remain standing where you are,' said the voice. 'Face the door. Make no movement.' The chinless man obeyed. His large pouchy cheeks were quivering uncontrollably. The door clanged open. As the young officer entered and stepped aside, there emerged from behind him a short stumpy guard with enormous arms and shoulders. He took his stand opposite the chinless man, and then, at a signal from the officer, let free a frightful blow, with all the weight of his body behind it, full in the chinless man's mouth. The force of it seemed almost to knock him clear of the floor. His body was flung across the cell and fetched up against the base of the lavatory seat. For a moment he lay as though stunned, with dark blood oozing from his mouth and nose. A very faint whimpering or squeaking, which seemed unconscious, came out of him. Then he rolled over and raised himself unsteadily on hands and knees.

Amid a stream of blood and saliva, the two halves of a dental plate fell out of his mouth. The prisoners sat very still, their hands crossed on their knees. The chinless man climbed back into his place. Down one side of his face the flesh was darkening. His mouth had swollen into a shapeless cherry-coloured mass with a black hole in the middle of it.

From time to time a little blood dripped on to the breast of his overalls. His grey eyes still flitted from face to face, more guiltily than ever, as though he were trying to discover how much the others despised him for his humiliation.

The door opened. With a small gesture the officer indicated the skull-faced man. 'Room 101,' he said.

There was a gasp and a flurry at Winston's side. The man

had actually flung himself on his knees on the floor, with his hand clasped together.

'Comrade! Officer!' he cried. 'You don't have to take me to that place! Haven't I told you everything already? What else is it you want to know? There's nothing I wouldn't confess, nothing! Just tell me what it is and I'll confess straight off. Write it down and I'll sign it--anything! Not room 101!'

'Room 101,' said the officer: The man's face, already very pale, turned a colour Winston would not have believed possible. It was definitely, unmistakably, a shade of green. 'Do anything to me!' he yelled. 'You've been starving me for weeks. Finish it off and let me die. Shoot me. Hang me. Sentence me to twenty-five years. Is there somebody else you want me to give away? Just say who it is and I'll tell you anything you want. I don't care who it is or what you do to them. I've got a wife and three children. The biggest of them isn't six years old. You can take the whole lot of them and cut their throats in front of my eyes, and I'll stand by and watch it. But not Room 101!'

'Room 101,' said the office: The man looked frantically round at the other prisoners, as though with some idea that he could put another victim in his own place. His eyes settled on the smashed face of the chinless man. He flung out a lean arm.

'That's the one you ought to be taking, not me!' he shouted. 'You didn't hear what he was saying after they bashed his face. Give me a chance and I'll tell you every word of it. He's the one that's against the Party, not me.' The guards stepped forward. The man's voice rose to a shriek. 'You didn't hear him!' he repeated. 'Something went wrong with the telescreen. He's the one you want. Take him, not me!'

The two sturdy guards had stooped to take him by the arms. But just at this moment he flung himself across the floor of the cell and grabbed one of the iron legs that supported the bench. He had set up a wordless howling, like an animal. The guards took hold of him to wrench him loose, but he clung on with astonishing strength. For perhaps twenty seconds they were hauling at him. The prisoners sat quiet, their hands crossed on their knees, looking straight in front of them. The howling stopped; the man had no breath left for anything except hanging on. Then there was a different kind of cry. A kick from a guard's boot had broken the fingers of one of his hands. They dragged him to his feet.

'Room 101,' said the officer: The man was led out, walking unsteadily, with head sunken, nursing his crushed hand, all the fight had gone out of him. A long time passed. If it had been midnight when the skull-faced man was taken away, it was morning: if morning, it was afternoon. Winston was alone, and had been alone for hours. The pain of sitting on the narrow bench was such that often he got up and walked about, unreproved by the telescreen. The piece of bread still lay where the chinless man had dropped it. At the beginning it needed a hard effort not to look at it, but presently hunger gave way to thirst.

His mouth was sticky and evil-tasting. The humming sound and the unvarying white light induced a sort of faintness, an empty feeling inside his head. He would get up because the ache in his bones was no longer bearable, and then would sit down again almost at once because he was too dizzy to make sure of staying on his feet. Whenever his physical sensations were a little under control the terror returned. Sometimes with a fading hope he thought of O'Brien and the razor blade. It was thinkable that the razor blade might arrive concealed in his food, if he were ever fed. More dimly he thought of Julia. Somewhere or other she was suffering perhaps far worse than he. She might be screaming with pain at this moment. He thought: 'If I could save Julia by doubling my own pain, would I do it? Yes, I would.' But that was merely an intellectual decision, taken because he knew that he ought to take it. He did not feel it. In this place you could not feel anything, except pain and foreknowledge of pain. Besides, was it possible, when you were actually suffering it, to wish for any reason that your own pain should increase? But that question was not answerable yet.

The boots were approaching again. The door opened. O'Brien came in. Winston started to his feet. The shock of the sight had driven all caution out of him. For the first time in many years he forgot the presence of the telescreen.

'They've got you too!' he cried.

'They got me a long time ago,' said O'Brien with a mild, almost regretful irony. He stepped aside. From behind him there emerged a broad-chested guard with a long black truncheon in his hand.

'You know him, Winston,' said O'Brien. 'Don't deceive yourself. You did know it--you have always known it.'

Yes, he saw now, he had always known it. But there was no time to think of that. All he had eyes for was the truncheon in the guard's hand. It might fall anywhere; on the crown, on the tip of the ear, on the upper arm, on the elbow--

The elbow! He had slumped to his knees, almost paralysed, clasping the stricken elbow with his other hand. Everything had exploded into yellow light. Inconceivable, inconceivable that one blow could cause such pain! The light cleared and he could see the other two looking down at him. The guard was laughing at his contortions. One question at any rate was answered. Never, for any reason on earth, could you wish for an increase of pain. Of pain you could wish only one thing: that it should stop. Nothing in the world was so bad as physical pain. In the face of pain there are no heroes, no heroes, he thought over and over as he writhed on the floor, clutching uselessly at his disabled left arm.

Part 3 Chapter 2

He was lying on something that felt like a camp bed, except that it was higher off the ground and that he was fixed down in some way so that he could not move. Light that seemed stronger than usual was falling on his face. O'Brien was standing at his side, looking down at him intently. At the other side of him stood a man in a white coat, holding a hypodermic syringe.

Even after his eyes were open he took in his surroundings only gradually. He had the impression of swimming up into this room from some quite different world, a sort of underwater world far beneath it. How long he had been down there he did not know. Since the moment when they arrested him he had not seen darkness or daylight. Besides, his memories were not continuous. There had been times when consciousness, even the sort of consciousness that one has in sleep, had stopped dead and started again after a blank interval. But whether the intervals were of days or weeks or only seconds, there was no way of knowing.

With that first blow on the elbow the nightmare had started. Later he was to realise that all that then happened was merely a preliminary, a routine interrogation to which nearly all prisoners were subjected. There was a long range of crimes--espionage, sabotage, and the like--to which everyone had to confess as a matter of course. The confession was a formality, though the torture was real. How many times he had been beaten, how long the beatings had continued, he could not remember. Always there were five or six men in black uniforms at him simultaneously. Sometimes it was fists, sometimes it was truncheons, sometimes it was steel rods, sometimes it was boots. There were times when he rolled about the floor, as shameless as an animal, writhing his body this way and that in an endless, hopeless effort to dodge the kicks, and simply inviting more and yet more kicks, in his ribs, in his belly, on his elbows, on his shins, in his groin, in his testicles, on the bone at the base of his spine. There were times when it went on and on until the cruel, wicked, unforgivable thing seemed to him not that the guards continued to beat him but that he could not force himself into losing consciousness.

There were times when his nerve so forsook him that he began shouting for mercy even before the beating began, when the mere sight of a fist drawn back for a blow was enough to make him pour forth a confession of real and imaginary crimes. There were other times when he started out with the resolve of confessing nothing, when every word had to be forced out of him between gasps of pain, and there were times when he feebly tried to compromise, when he said to himself: 'I will confess, but not yet. I must hold out till the pain becomes unbearable. Three more kicks, two more kicks, and then I will tell them what they want.' Sometimes he was beaten till he could hardly stand, then flung like a sack of potatoes on to the stone floor of a cell, left to recuperate for a few hours, and then taken out and beaten again.

There were also longer periods of recovery. He remembered them dimly, because they were spent chiefly in sleep or stupor. He remembered a cell with a plank bed, a sort of shelf sticking out from the wall, and a tin wash-basin, and meals of hot soup and bread and sometimes coffee. He remembered a surly barber arriving to scrape his chin and crop his hair, and businesslike, unsympathetic men in white coats feeling his pulse, tapping his reflexes, turning up his eyelids, running harsh fingers over him in search for broken bones, and shooting needles into his arm to make him sleep.

The beatings grew less frequent, and became mainly a threat, a horror to which he could be sent back at any moment when his answers were unsatisfactory. His questioners now were not ruffians in black uniforms but Party intellectuals, little rotund men with quick movements and flashing spectacles, who worked on him in relays over periods which lasted--he thought, he could not be sure--ten or twelve hours at a stretch. These other questioners saw to it that he was in constant slight pain, but it was not chiefly pain that they relied on. They slapped his face, wrung his ears, pulled his hair, made him stand on one leg, refused him leave to urinate, shone glaring lights in his face until his eyes ran with water; but the aim of this was simply to humiliate him and destroy his power of arguing and reasoning.

Their real weapon was the merciless questioning that went on and on, hour after hour, tripping him up, laying traps for him, twisting everything that he said, convicting him at every step of lies and self-contradiction until he began weeping as much from shame as from nervous fatigue. Sometimes he would weep half a dozen times in a single session. Most of the time they screamed abuse at him and threatened at every hesitation to deliver him over to the guards again; but sometimes they would suddenly change their tune, call him comrade, appeal to him in the name of Ingsoc and Big Brother, and ask him sorrowfully whether even now he had not enough loyalty to the Party left to make him wish to undo the evil he had done.

When his nerves were in rags after hours of questioning, even this appeal could reduce him to snivelling tears. In the end the nagging voices broke him down more completely than the boots and fists of the guards. He became simply a mouth that uttered, a hand that signed, whatever was demanded of him. His sole concern was to find out what they wanted him to confess, and then confess it quickly, before the bullying started anew. He confessed to the assassination of eminent Party members, the distribution of seditious pamphlets, embezzlement of public funds, sale of military secrets, sabotage of every kind. He confessed that he had been a spy in the pay of the Eastasian government as far back as 1968. He confessed that he was a religious believer, an admirer of capitalism, and a sexual pervert.

He confessed that he had murdered his wife, although he knew, and his questioners must have known, that his wife was still alive. He confessed that for years he had been in personal touch with Goldstein and had been a member of an underground organization which had included almost every human being he had ever known. It was easier to confess everything and implicate everybody. Besides, in a sense it was all true. It was true that he had been the enemy of the Party, and in the eyes of the Party there was no distinction between the thought and the deed. There were also memories of another kind. They stood out in his mind disconnectedly, like pictures with blackness all round them. He was in a cell which might have been either dark or light, because he could see nothing except a pair of eyes. Near at hand some kind of instrument was ticking slowly and regularly. The eyes grew larger and more luminous. Suddenly he floated out of his seat, dived into the eyes, and was swallowed up.

He was strapped into a chair surrounded by dials, under dazzling lights. A man in a white coat was reading the dials. There was a tramp of heavy boots outside. The door clanged open. The waxed-faced officer marched in, followed by two guards.

'Room 101,' said the officer: The man in the white coat did not turn round. He did not look at Winston either; he was looking only at the dials.

He was rolling down a mighty corridor, a kilometre wide, full of glorious, golden light, roaring with laughter and shouting out confessions at the top of his voice. He was confessing everything, even the things he had succeeded in holding back under the torture. He was relating the entire history of his life to an audience who knew it already. With him were the guards, the other questioners, the men in white coats, O'Brien, Julia, Mr Charrington, all rolling down the corridor together and shouting with laughter. Some dreadful thing which had lain embedded in the future had somehow been skipped over and had not happened. Everything was all right, there was no more pain, the last detail of his life was laid bare, understood, forgiven.

He was starting up from the plank bed in the half-certainty that he had heard O'Brien's voice. All through his interrogation, although he had never seen him, he had had the feeling that O'Brien was at his elbow, just out of sight. It was O'Brien who was directing everything. It was he who set the guards on to Winston and who prevented them from killing him. It was he who decided when Winston should scream with pain, when he should have a respite, when he should be fed, when he should sleep, when the drugs should be pumped into his arm. It was he who asked the questions and suggested the answers. He was the tormentor, he was the protector, he was the inquisitor, he was the friend. And once--Winston could not remember whether it was in drugged sleep, or in normal sleep, or even in a moment of wakefulness--a voice murmured in his ear: 'Don't worry, Winston; you are in my keeping. For seven years I have watched over you. Now the turning-point has come. I shall save you, I shall make you perfect.' He was not sure whether it was O'Brien's voice; but it was the same voice that had said to him, 'We shall meet in the place where there is no darkness,' in that other dream, seven years ago.

He did not remember any ending to his interrogation.

There was a period of blackness and then the cell, or room, in which he now was had gradually materialized round him. He was almost flat on his back, and unable to move. His body was held down at every essential point. Even the back of his head was gripped in some manner. O'Brien was looking down at him gravely and rather sadly. His face, seen from below, looked coarse and worn, with pouches under the eyes and tired lines from nose to chin. He was older than Winston had thought him; he was perhaps forty-eight or fifty. Under his hand there was a dial with a lever on top and figures running round the face. 'I told you,' said O'Brien, 'that if we met again it would be here.'

'Yes,' said Winston: Without any warning except a slight movement of O'Brien's hand, a wave of pain flooded his body. It was a frightening pain, because he could not see what was happening, and he had the feeling that some mortal injury was being done to him. He did not know whether the thing was really happening, or whether the effect was electrically produced; but his body was being wrenched out of shape, the joints were being slowly torn apart. Although the pain had brought the sweat out on his forehead, the worst of all was the fear that his backbone was about to snap. He set his teeth and breathed hard through his nose, trying to keep silent as long as possible.

'You are afraid,' said O'Brien, watching his face, 'that in another moment something is going to break. Your especial fear is that it will be your backbone. You have a vivid mental picture of the vertebrae snapping apart and the spinal fluid dripping out of them. That is what you are thinking, is it not, Winston?'

Winston did not answer. O'Brien drew back the lever on the dial. The wave of pain receded almost as quickly as it had come.

'That was forty,' said O'Brien. 'You can see that the numbers on this dial run up to a hundred. Will you please remember, throughout our conversation, that I have it in my power to inflict pain on you at any moment and to whatever degree I choose? If you tell me any lies, or attempt to prevaricate in any way, or even fall below your usual level of intelligence, you will cry out with pain, instantly. Do you understand that?'

'Yes,' said Winston: O'Brien's manner became less severe. He resettled his spectacles thoughtfully, and took a pace or two up and down. When he spoke his voice was gentle and patient. He had the air of a doctor, a teacher, even a priest, anxious to explain and persuade rather than to punish. 'I am taking trouble with you, Winston,' he said, 'because you are worth trouble. You know perfectly well what is the matter with you. You have known it for years, though you have fought against the knowledge. You are mentally deranged. You suffer from a defective memory. You are unable to remember real events and you persuade yourself that you remember other events which never happened. Fortunately it is curable. You have never cured yourself of it, because you did not choose to. There was a small effort of the will that you were not ready to make. Even now, I am well aware, you are clinging to your disease under the impression that it is a virtue. Now we will take an example. At this moment, which power is Oceania at war with?'

'When I was arrested, Oceania was at war with Eastasia.'

'With Eastasia. Good. And Oceania has always been at war with Eastasia, has it not?'

Winston drew in his breath. He opened his mouth to speak and then did not speak. He could not take his eyes away from the dial. 'The truth, please, Winston. Your truth. Tell me what you think you remember.'

'I remember that until only a week before I was arrested, we were not at war with Eastasia at all. We were in alliance with them. The war was against Eurasia. That had lasted for four years. Before that--'

O'Brien stopped him with a movement of the hand.

'Another example,' he said. 'Some years ago you had a very serious delusion indeed. You believed that three men, three onetime Party members named Jones, Aaronson, and Rutherford men who were executed for treachery and sabotage after making the fullest possible confession--were not guilty of the crimes they were charged with. You believed that you had seen unmistakable documentary evidence proving that their confessions were false. There was a certain photograph about which you had a hallucination. You believed that you had actually held it in your hands. It was a photograph something like this.' An oblong slip of newspaper had appeared between O'Brien's fingers. For perhaps five seconds it was within the angle of Winston's vision. It was a photograph, and there was no question of its identity. It was the photograph. It was another copy of the photograph of Jones, Aaronson, and Rutherford at the party function in New York, which he had chanced upon eleven years ago and promptly destroyed. For only an instant it was before his eyes, then it was out of sight again. But he had seen it, unquestionably he had seen it! He made a desperate, agonizing effort to wrench the top half of his body free. It was impossible to move so much as a centimetre in any direction. For the moment he had even forgotten the dial. All he wanted was to hold the photograph in his fingers again, or at least to see it.

'It exists!' he cried.

'No,' said O'Brien.

He stepped across the room. There was a memory hole in the opposite wall. O'Brien lifted the grating. Unseen, the frail slip of paper was whirling away on the current of warm air; it was vanishing in a flash of flame. O'Brien turned away from the wall.

'Ashes,' he said. 'Not even identifiable ashes. Dust. It does not exist. It never existed.'

'But it did exist! It does exist! It exists in memory. I remember it. You remember it.'

'I do not remember it,' said O'Brien.

Winston's heart sank. That was doublethink. He had a feeling of deadly helplessness. If he could have been certain that O'Brien was lying, it would not have seemed to matter. But it was perfectly possible that O'Brien had really forgotten the photograph. And if so, then already he would have forgotten his denial of remembering it, and forgotten the act of forgetting. How could one be sure that it was simple trickery? Perhaps that lunatic dislocation in the mind could really happen: that was the thought that defeated him.

O'Brien was looking down at him speculatively. More than ever he had the air of a teacher taking pains with a wayward but promising child.

'There is a Party slogan dealing with the control of the past,' he said. 'Repeat it, if you please.'

'"Who controls the past controls the future: who controls the present controls the past,"' repeated Winston obediently.

'"Who controls the present controls the past,"' said O'Brien, nodding his head with slow approval. 'Is it your opinion, Winston, that the past has real existence?'

Again the feeling of helplessness descended upon Winston. His eyes flitted towards the dial. He not only did not know whether 'yes' or 'no' was the answer that would save him from pain; he did not even know which answer he believed to be the true one.

O'Brien smiled faintly. 'You are no metaphysician, Winston,' he said. 'Until this moment you had never considered what is meant by existence. I will put it more precisely. Does the past exist concretely, in space? Is there somewhere or other a place, a world of solid objects, where the past is still happening?'

'No.'

'Then where does the past exist, if at all?'

'In records. It is written down.'

'In records. And--?'

'In the mind. In human memories.'

'In memory. Very well, then. We, the Party, control all records, and we control all memories. Then we control the past, do we not?'

'But how can you stop people remembering things?' cried Winston again momentarily forgetting the dial. 'It is involuntary. It is outside oneself. How can you control memory? You have not controlled mine!'

O'Brien's manner grew stern again. He laid his hand on the dial.

'On the contrary,' he said, 'you have not controlled it. That is what has brought you here. You are here because you have failed in humility, in self-discipline. You would not make the act of submission which is the price of sanity. You preferred to be a lunatic, a minority of one. Only the disciplined mind can see reality, Winston. You believe that reality is something objective, external, existing in its own right. You also believe that the nature of reality is self-evident. When you delude yourself into thinking that you see something, you assume that everyone else sees the same thing as you. But I tell you, Winston, that reality is not external. Reality exists in the human mind, and nowhere else. Not in the individual mind, which can make mistakes, and in any case soon perishes: only in the mind of the Party, which is collective and immortal. Whatever the Party holds to be the truth, is truth. It is impossible to see reality except by looking through the eyes of the Party. That is the fact that you have got to relearn, Winston. It needs an act of self-destruction, an effort of the will. You must humble yourself before you can become sane.' He paused for a few moments, as though to allow what he had been saying to sink in.

'Do you remember,' he went on, 'writing in your diary, "Freedom is the freedom to say that two plus two make four"?'

'Yes,' said Winston.

O'Brien held up his left hand, its back towards Winston, with the thumb hidden and the four fingers extended.

'How many fingers am I holding up, Winston?'

'Four.'

'And if the party says that it is not four but five--then how many?'

'Four.'

The word ended in a gasp of pain. The needle of the dial had shot up to fifty-five. The sweat had sprung out all over Winston's body. The air tore into his lungs and issued again in deep groans which even by clenching his teeth he could not stop. O'Brien watched him, the four fingers still extended. He drew back the lever. This time the pain was only slightly eased.

'How many fingers, Winston?'

'Four.'

The needle went up to sixty.

'How many fingers, Winston?'

'Four! Four! What else can I say? Four!'

The needle must have risen again, but he did not look at it. The heavy, stern face and the four fingers filled his vision. The fingers stood up before his eyes like pillars, enormous, blurry, and seeming to vibrate, but unmistakably four.

'How many fingers, Winston?'

'Four! Stop it, stop it! How can you go on? Four! Four!'

'How many fingers, Winston?'

'Five! Five! Five!'

'No, Winston, that is no use. You are lying. You still think there are four. How many fingers, please?'

'Four! five! Four! Anything you like. Only stop it, stop the pain!'

Abruptly he was sitting up with O'Brien's arm round his shoulders. He had perhaps lost consciousness for a few seconds. The bonds that had held his body down were loosened. He felt very cold, he was shaking uncontrollably, his teeth were chattering, the tears were rolling down his cheeks. For a moment he clung to O'Brien like a baby, curiously comforted by the heavy arm round his shoulders. He had the feeling that O'Brien was his protector, that the pain was something that came from outside, from some other source, and that it was O'Brien who would save him from it.

'You are a slow learner, Winston,' said O'Brien gently.

'How can I help it?' he blubbered. 'How can I help seeing what is in front of my eyes? Two and two are four.'

'Sometimes, Winston. Sometimes they are five. Sometimes they are three. Sometimes they are all of them at once. You must try harder. It is not easy to become sane.'

He laid Winston down on the bed. The grip of his limbs tightened again, but the pain had ebbed away and the trembling had stopped, leaving him merely weak and cold. O'Brien motioned with his head to the man in the white coat, who had stood immobile throughout the proceedings. The man in the white coat bent down and looked closely into Winston's eyes, felt his pulse, laid an ear against his chest, tapped here and there, then he nodded to O'Brien.

'Again,' said O'Brien: The pain flowed into Winston's body. The needle must be at seventy, seventy-five. He had shut his eyes this time. He knew that the fingers were still there, and still four. All that mattered was somehow to stay alive until the spasm was over. He had ceased to notice whether he was crying out or not. The pain lessened again. He opened his eyes. O'Brien had drawn back the lever.

'How many fingers, Winston?'

'Four. I suppose there are four. I would see five if I could. I am trying to see five.'

'Which do you wish: to persuade me that you see five, or really to see them?'

'Really to see them.'

'Again,' said O'Brien.

Perhaps the needle was eighty--ninety. Winston could not intermittently remember why the pain was happening. Behind his screwed-up eyelids a forest of fingers seemed to be moving in a sort of dance, weaving in and out, disappearing behind one another and reappearing again. He was trying to count them, he could not remember why. He knew only that it was impossible to count them, and that this was somehow due to the mysterious identity between five and four. The pain died down again.

When he opened his eyes it was to find that he was still seeing the same thing. Innumerable fingers, like moving trees, were still streaming past in either direction, crossing and recrossing. He shut his eyes again.

'How many fingers am I holding up, Winston?'

'I don't know. I don't know. You will kill me if you do that again. Four, five, six--in all honesty I don't know.'

'Better,' said O'Brien.

A needle slid into Winston's arm. Almost in the same instant a blissful, healing warmth spread all through his body. The pain was already half-forgotten. He opened his eyes and looked up gratefully at O'Brien. At sight of the heavy, lined face, so ugly and so intelligent, his heart seemed to turn over. If he could have moved he would have stretched out a hand and laid it on O'Brien arm. He had never loved him so deeply as at this moment, and not merely because he had stopped the pain. The old feeling, that it bottom it did not matter whether O'Brien was a friend or an enemy, had come back. O'Brien was a person who could be talked to.

Perhaps one did not want to be loved so much as to be understood. O'Brien had tortured him to the edge of lunacy, and in a little while, it was certain, he would send him to his death. It made no difference. In some sense that went deeper than friendship, they were intimates: somewhere or other, although the actual words might never be spoken, there was a place where they could meet and talk. O'Brien was looking down at him with an expression which suggested that the same thought might be in his own mind. When he spoke it was in an easy, conversational tone.

'Do you know where you are, Winston?' he said.

'I don't know. I can guess. In the Ministry of Love.'

'Do you know how long you have been here?'

'I don't know. Days, weeks, months--I think it is months.'

'And why do you imagine that we bring people to this place?'

'To make them confess.'

'No, that is not the reason. Try again.'

'To punish them.'

'No!' exclaimed O'Brien. His voice had changed extraordinarily, and his face had suddenly become both stern and animated. 'No! Not merely to extract your confession, not to punish you. Shall I tell you why we have brought you here? To cure you! To make you sane! Will you understand, Winston, that no one whom we bring to this place ever leaves our hands uncured? We are not interested in those stupid crimes that you have committed. The Party is not interested in the overt act: the thought is all we care about. We do not merely destroy our enemies, we change them. Do you understand what I mean by that?'

He was bending over Winston. His face looked enormous because of its nearness, and hideously ugly because it was seen from below. Moreover it was filled with a sort of exaltation, a lunatic intensity. Again Winston's heart shrank. If it had been possible he would have cowered deeper into the bed. He felt certain that O'Brien was about to twist the dial out of sheer wantonness. At this moment, however, O'Brien turned away. He took a pace or two up and down. Then he continued less vehemently:

'The first thing for you to understand is that in this place there are no martyrdoms. You have read of the religious persecutions of the past. In the Middle Ages there was the Inquisition. It was a failure. It set out to eradicate heresy, and ended by perpetuating it. For every heretic it burned at the stake, thousands of others rose up. Why was that?

Because the Inquisition killed its enemies in the open, and killed them while they were still unrepentant: in fact, it killed them because they were unrepentant. Men were dying because they would not abandon their true beliefs. Naturally all the glory belonged to the victim and all the shame to the Inquisitor who burned him. Later, in the twentieth century, there were the totalitarians, as they were called. There were the German Nazis and the Russian Communists. The Russians persecuted heresy more cruelly than the Inquisition had done. And they imagined that they had learned from the mistakes of the past; they knew, at any rate, that one must not make martyrs. Before they exposed their victims to public trial, they deliberately set themselves to destroy their dignity.

They wore them down by torture and solitude until they were despicable, cringing wretches, confessing whatever was put into their mouths, covering themselves with abuse, accusing and sheltering behind one another, whimpering for mercy. And yet after only a few years the same thing had happened over again. The dead men had become martyrs and their degradation was forgotten. Once again, why was it? In the first place, because the confessions that they had made were obviously extorted and untrue. We do not make mistakes of that kind. All the confessions that are uttered here are true. We make them true. And above all we do not allow the dead to rise up against us. You must stop imagining that posterity will vindicate you, Winston. Posterity will never hear of you. You will be lifted clean out from the stream of history. We shall turn you into gas and pour you into the stratosphere.

Nothing will remain of you, not a name in a register, not a memory in a living brain. You will be annihilated in the past as well as in the future. You will never have existed.'

Then why bother to torture me? thought Winston, with a momentary bitterness. O'Brien checked his step as though Winston had uttered the thought aloud. His large ugly face came nearer, with the eyes a little narrowed.

'You are thinking,' he said, 'that since we intend to destroy you utterly, so that nothing that you say or do can make the smallest difference--in that case, why do we go to the trouble of interrogating you first? That is what you were thinking, was it not?' 'Yes,' said Winston.

O'Brien smiled slightly. 'You are a flaw in the pattern, Winston. You are a stain that must be wiped out. Did I not tell you just now that we are different from the persecutors of the past? We are not content with negative obedience, nor even with the most abject submission. When finally you surrender to us, it must be of your own free will. We do not destroy the heretic because he resists us: so long as he resists us we never destroy him. We convert him, we capture his inner mind, we reshape him. We burn all evil and all illusion out of him; we bring him over to our side, not in appearance, but genuinely, heart and soul. We make him one of ourselves before we kill him. It is intolerable to us that an erroneous thought should exist anywhere in the world, however secret and powerless it may be. Even in the instant of death we cannot permit any deviation. In the old days the heretic walked to the stake still a heretic, proclaiming his heresy, exulting in it.

Even the victim of the Russian purges could carry rebellion locked up in his skull as he walked down the passage waiting for the bullet. But we make the brain perfect before we blow it out. The command of the old despotisms was "Thou shalt not". The command of the totalitarians was "Thou shalt". Our command is "Thou art". No one whom we bring to this place ever stands out against us. Everyone is washed clean. Even those three miserable traitors in whose innocence you once believed--Jones, Aaronson, and Rutherford--in the end we broke them down. I took part in their interrogation myself.

I saw them gradually worn down, whimpering, grovelling, weeping--and in the end it was not with pain or fear, only with penitence. By the time we had finished with them they were only the shells of men. There was nothing left in them except sorrow for what they had done, and love of Big Brother. It was touching to see how they loved him. They begged to be shot quickly, so that they could die while their minds were still clean.' His voice had grown almost dreamy. The exaltation, the lunatic enthusiasm, was still in his face. He is not pretending, thought Winston, he is not a hypocrite, he believes every word he says. What most oppressed him was the consciousness of his own intellectual inferiority. He watched the heavy yet graceful form strolling to and fro, in and out of the range of his vision. O'Brien was a being in all ways larger than himself. There was no idea that he had ever had, or could have, that O'Brien had not long ago known, examined, and rejected. His mind contained Winston's mind. But in that case how could it be true that O'Brien was mad? It must be he, Winston, who was mad. O'Brien halted and looked down at him. His voice had grown stern again.

'Do not imagine that you will save yourself, Winston, however completely you surrender to us. No one who has once gone astray is ever spared. And even if we chose to let you live out the natural term of your life, still you would never escape from us. What happens to you here is for ever. Understand that in advance. We shall crush you down to the point from which there is no coming back. Things will happen to you from which you could not recover, if you lived a thousand years. Never again will you be capable of ordinary human feeling. Everything will be dead inside you. Never again will you be capable of love, or friendship, or joy of living, or laughter, or curiosity, or courage, or integrity. You will be hollow. We shall squeeze you empty, and then we shall fill you with ourselves.'

He paused and signed to the man in the white coat. Winston was aware of some heavy piece of apparatus being pushed into place behind his head. O'Brien had sat down beside the bed, so that his face was almost on a level with

Winston's. 'Three thousand,' he said, speaking over Winston's head to the man in the white coat.

Two soft pads, which felt slightly moist, clamped themselves against Winston's temples. He quailed. There was pain coming, a new kind of pain. O'Brien laid a hand reassuringly, almost kindly, on his. 'This time it will not hurt,' he said. 'Keep your eyes fixed on mine.'

At this moment there was a devastating explosion, or what seemed like an explosion, though it was not certain whether there was any noise. There was undoubtedly a blinding flash of light. Winston was not hurt, only prostrated. Although he had already been lying on his back when the thing happened, he had a curious feeling that he had been knocked into that position. A terrific painless blow had flattened him out. Also something had happened inside his head. As his eyes regained their focus he remembered who he was, and where he was, and recognized the face that was gazing into his own; but somewhere or other there was a large patch of emptiness, as though a piece had been taken out of his brain.

'It will not last,' said O'Brien. 'Look me in the eyes. What country is Oceania at war with?'

Winston thought. He knew what was meant by Oceania and that he himself was a citizen of Oceania. He also remembered Eurasia and Eastasia; but who was at war with whom he did not know. In fact he had not been aware that there was any war.

'I don't remember.'

'Oceania is at war with Eastasia. Do you remember that now?'

'Yes.'

'Oceania has always been at war with Eastasia. Since the beginning of your life, since the beginning of the Party, since the beginning of history, the war has continued without a break, always the same war. Do you remember that?'

'Yes.'

'Eleven years ago you created a legend about three men who had been condemned to death for treachery. You pretended that you had seen a piece of paper which proved them innocent. No such piece of paper ever existed. You invented it, and later you grew to believe in it. You remember now the very moment at which you first invented it. Do you remember that?'

'Yes.'

'Just now I held up the fingers of my hand to you. You saw five fingers. Do you remember that?'

'Yes.'

O'Brien held up the fingers of his left hand, with the thumb concealed.

'There are five fingers there. Do you see five fingers?'

'Yes.'

And he did see them, for a fleeting instant, before the scenery of his mind changed. He saw five fingers, and there was no deformity. Then everything was normal again, and the old fear, the hatred, and the bewilderment came crowding back again. But there had been a moment--he did not know how long, thirty seconds, perhaps--of luminous certainty, when each new suggestion of O'Brien's had filled up a patch of emptiness and become absolute truth, and when two and two could have been three as easily as five, if that were what was needed. It had faded but before O'Brien had dropped his hand; but though he could not recapture it, he could remember it, as one remembers a vivid experience at some period of one's life when one was in effect a different person.

'You see now,' said O'Brien, 'that it is at any rate possible.'

'Yes,' said Winston.

O'Brien stood up with a satisfied air. Over to his left Winston saw the man in the white coat break an ampoule and draw back the plunger of a syringe. O'Brien turned to Winston with a smile.

In almost the old manner he resettled his spectacles on his nose. 'Do you remember writing in your diary,' he said, 'that it did not matter whether I was a friend or an enemy, since I was at least a person who understood you and could be talked to? You were right. I enjoy talking to you. Your mind appeals to me.

It resembles my own mind except that you happen to be

insane. Before we bring the session to an end you can ask me a few questions, if you choose.'

'Any question I like?'

'Anything.' He saw that Winston's eyes were upon the dial. 'It is switched off. What is your first question?'

'What have you done with Julia?' said Winston.

O'Brien smiled again. 'She betrayed you, Winston. Immediately--unreservedly. I have seldom seen anyone come over to us so promptly. You would hardly recognize her if you saw her. All her rebelliousness, her deceit, her folly, her dirty-mindedness--everything has been burned out of her. It was a perfect conversion, a textbook case.'

'You tortured her?'

O'Brien left this unanswered. 'Next question,' he said.

'Does Big Brother exist?'

'Of course he exists. The Party exists. Big Brother is the embodiment of the Party.'

'Does he exist in the same way as I exist?'

'You do not exist,' said O'Brien.

Once again the sense of helplessness assailed him. He knew, or he could imagine, the arguments which proved his own nonexistence; but they were nonsense, they were only a play on words. Did not the statement, 'You do not exist', contain a logical absurdity? But what use was it to say so? His mind shrivelled as he thought of the unanswerable, mad arguments with which O'Brien would demolish him.

'I think I exist,' he said wearily. 'I am conscious of my own identity. I was born and I shall die. I have arms and legs. I occupy a particular point in space. No other solid object can occupy the same point simultaneously. In that sense, does Big Brother exist?'

'It is of no importance. He exists.'

'Will Big Brother ever die?'

'Of course not. How could he die? Next question.'

'Does the Brotherhood exist?'

'That, Winston, you will never know. If we choose to set you free when we have finished with you, and if you live to be ninety years old, still you will never learn whether the answer to that question is Yes or No. As long as you live it will be an unsolved riddle in your mind.'

Winston lay silent. His breast rose and fell a little faster. He still had not asked the question that had come into his mind the first. He had got to ask it, and yet it was as though his tongue would not utter it. There was a trace of amusement in O'Brien's face. Even his spectacles seemed to wear an ironical gleam. He knows, thought Winston suddenly, he knows what I am going to ask! At the thought the words burst out of him:

'What is in Room 101?'

The expression on O'Brien's face did not change. He answered drily: 'You know what is in Room 101, Winston. Everyone knows what is in Room 101.'

He raised a finger to the man in the white coat. Evidently the session was at an end. A needle jerked into Winston's arm. He sank almost instantly into deep sleep.

Part 3 Chapter 5

At each stage of his imprisonment he had known, or seemed to know, whereabouts he was in the windowless building. Possibly there were slight differences in the air pressure. The cells where the guards had beaten him were below ground level. The room where he had been interrogated by O'Brien was high up near the roof. This place was many metres underground, as deep down as it was possible to go.

It was bigger than most of the cells he had been in. But he hardly noticed his surroundings. All he noticed was that there were two small tables straight in front of him, each covered with green baize. One was only a metre or two from him, the other was further away, near the door. He was strapped upright in a chair, so tightly that he could move nothing, not even his head. A sort of pad gripped his head from behind, forcing him to look straight in front of him.

For a moment he was alone, then the door opened and O'Brien came in.

'You asked me once,' said O'Brien, 'what was in Room 101. I told you that you knew the answer already. Everyone knows it. The thing that is in Room 101 is the worst thing in the world.'

The door opened again. A guard came in, carrying something made of wire, a box or basket of some kind. He set it down on the further table. Because of the position in which O'Brien was standing. Winston could not see what the thing was.

'The worst thing in the world,' said O'Brien, 'varies from individual to individual. It may be burial alive, or death by fire, or by drowning, or by impalement, or fifty other deaths. There are cases where it is some quite trivial thing, not even fatal.'

He had moved a little to one side, so that Winston had a better view of the thing on the table. It was an oblong wire cage with a handle on top for carrying it by. Fixed to the front of it was something that looked like a fencing mask, with the concave side outwards. Although it was three or four metres away from him, he could see that the cage was divided lengthways into two compartments, and that there was some kind of creature in each. They were rats.

'In your case,' said O'Brien, 'the worst thing in the world happens to be rats.'

A sort of premonitory tremor, a fear of he was not certain what, had passed through Winston as soon as he caught his first glimpse of the cage. But at this moment the meaning of the mask-like attachment in front of it suddenly sank into him. His bowels seemed to turn to water.

'You can't do that!' he cried out in a high cracked voice. 'You couldn't, you couldn't! It's impossible.'

'Do you remember,' said O'Brien, 'the moment of panic that used to occur in your dreams? There was a wall of blackness in front of you, and a roaring sound in your ears. There was something terrible on the other side of the wall. You knew that you knew what it was, but you dared not drag it into the open. It was the rats that were on the other side of the wall.'

'O'Brien!' said Winston, making an effort to control his voice. 'You know this is not necessary. What is it that you want me to do?'

O'Brien made no direct answer. When he spoke it was in the schoolmasterish manner that he sometimes affected. He looked thoughtfully into the distance, as though he were addressing an audience somewhere behind Winston's back.

'By itself,' he said, 'pain is not always enough. There are occasions when a human being will stand out against pain, even to the point of death. But for everyone there is something unendurable--something that cannot be contemplated. Courage and cowardice are not involved. If you are falling from a height it is not cowardly to clutch at a rope. If you have come up from deep water it is not cowardly to fill your lungs with air. It is merely an instinct which cannot be destroyed. It is the same with the rats. For you, they are unendurable. They are a form of pressure that you cannot withstand, even if you wished to. You will do what is required of you.

'But what is it, what is it? How can I do it if I don't know what it is?'

O'Brien picked up the cage and brought it across to the nearer table. He set it down carefully on the baize cloth. Winston could hear the blood singing in his ears. He had the feeling of sitting in utter loneliness. He was in the middle of a great empty plain, a flat desert drenched with sunlight, across which all sounds came to him out of immense distances. Yet the cage with the rats was not two metres away from him. They were enormous rats. They were at the age when a rat's muzzle grows blunt and fierce and his fur brown instead of grey.

'The rat,' said O'Brien, still addressing his invisible audience, 'although a rodent, is carnivorous. You are aware of that. You will have heard of the things that happen in the poor quarters of this town. In some streets a woman dare not leave her baby alone in the house, even for five minutes. The rats are certain to attack it. Within quite a small time they will strip it to the bones. They also attack sick or dying people. They show astonishing intelligence in knowing when a human being is helpless.'

There was an outburst of squeals from the cage. It seemed to reach Winston from far away. The rats were fighting; they were trying to get at each other through the partition. He heard also a deep groan of despair. That, too, seemed to come from outside himself.

O'Brien picked up the cage, and, as he did so, pressed something in it. There was a sharp click. Winston made a frantic effort to tear himself loose from the chair. It was hopeless; every part of him, even his head, was held immovably. O'Brien moved the cage nearer. It was less than a metre from Winston's face.

'I have pressed the first lever,' said O'Brien. 'You understand the construction of this cage. The mask will fit over your head, leaving no exit. When I press this other lever, the door of the cage will slide up. These starving brutes will shoot out of it like bullets. Have you ever seen a rat leap through the air? They will leap on to your face and bore straight into it. Sometimes they attack the eyes first. Sometimes they burrow through the cheeks and devour the tongue.'

The cage was nearer; it was closing in. Winston heard a succession of shrill cries which appeared to be occurring in the air above his head. But he fought furiously against his panic. To think, to think, even with a split second left--to think was the only hope. Suddenly the foul musty odour of the brutes struck his nostrils. There was a violent convulsion of nausea inside him, and he almost lost consciousness. Everything had gone black. For an instant he was insane, a screaming animal. Yet he came out of the blackness clutching an idea. There was one and only one way to save himself. He must interpose another human being, the body of another human being, between himself and the rats.

The circle of the mask was large enough now to shut out the vision of anything else. The wire door was a couple of hand-spans from his face. The rats knew what was coming now. One of them was leaping up and down, the other, an old scaly grandfather of the sewers, stood up, with his pink hands against the bars, and fiercely sniffed the air. Winston could see the whiskers and the yellow teeth. Again the black panic took hold of him. He was blind, helpless, mindless.

'It was a common punishment in Imperial China,' said O'Brien as didactically as ever.

The mask was closing on his face. The wire brushed his cheek. And then--no, it was not relief, only hope, a tiny fragment of hope. Too late, perhaps too late. But he had suddenly understood that in the whole world there was just one person to whom he could transfer his punishment--one body that he could thrust between himself and the rats. And he was shouting frantically, over and over.

'Do it to Julia! Do it to Julia! Not me! Julia! I don't care what you do to her. Tear her face off, strip her to the bones. Not me! Julia! Not me!'

He was falling backwards, into enormous depths, away from the rats. He was still strapped in the chair, but he had fallen through the floor, through the walls of the building, through the earth, through the oceans, through the atmosphere, into outer space, into the gulfs between the stars--always away, away, away from the rats. He was light years distant, but O'Brien was still standing at his side. There was still the cold touch of wire against his cheek. But through the darkness that enveloped him he heard another metallic click, and knew that the cage door had clicked shut and not open.

Part 3 Chapter 6

The Chestnut Tree was almost empty. A ray of sunlight slanting through a window fell on dusty table-tops. It was the lonely hour of fifteen. A tinny music trickled from the telescreens.

Winston sat in his usual corner, gazing into an empty glass. Now and again he glanced up at a vast face which eyed him from the opposite wall. BIG BROTHER IS WATCHING YOU, the caption said. Unbidden, a waiter came and filled his glass up with Victory Gin, shaking into it a few drops from another bottle with a quill through the cork. It was saccharine flavoured with cloves, the speciality of the cafe.

Winston was listening to the telescreen. At present only music was coming out of it, but there was a possibility that at any moment there might be a special bulletin from the Ministry of Peace. The news from the African front was disquieting in the extreme. On and off he had been worrying about it all day. A Eurasian army (Oceania was at war with Eurasia: Oceania had always been at war with Eurasia) was moving southward at terrifying speed. The mid-day bulletin had not mentioned any definite area, but it was probable that already the mouth of the Congo was a battlefield. Brazzaville and Leopoldville were in danger. One did not have to look at the map to see what it meant. It was not merely a question of losing Central Africa: for the first time in the whole war, the territory of Oceania itself was menaced.

A violent emotion, not fear exactly but a sort of undifferentiated excitement, flared up in him, then faded again. He stopped thinking about the war. In these days he could never fix his mind on any one subject for more than a few moments at a time. He picked up his glass and drained it at a gulp. As always, the gin made him shudder and even retch slightly. The stuff was horrible. The cloves and saccharine, themselves disgusting enough in their sickly way, could not disguise the flat oily smell; and what was worst of all was that the smell of gin, which dwelt with him night and day, was inextricably mixed up in his mind with the smell of those--

He never named them, even in his thoughts, and so far as it was possible he never visualized them. They were something that he was half-aware of, hovering close to his face, a smell that clung to his nostrils. As the gin rose in him he belched through purple lips. He had grown fatter since they released him, and had regained his old colour--indeed, more than regained it. His features had thickened, the skin on nose and cheekbones was coarsely red, even the bald scalp was too deep a pink. A waiter, again unbidden, brought the chessboard and the current issue of the Times, with the page turned down at the chess problem. Then, seeing that Winston's glass was empty, he brought the gin bottle and filled it. There was no need to give orders. They knew his habits. The chessboard was always waiting for him, his corner table was always reserved; even when the place was full he had it to himself, since nobody cared to be seen sitting too close to him. He never even bothered to count his drinks. At irregular intervals they presented him with a dirty slip of paper which they said was the bill, but he had the impression that they always undercharged him. It would have made no difference if it had been the other way about. He had always plenty of money nowadays. He even had a job, a sinecure, more highly-paid than his old job had been.

The music from the telescreen stopped and a voice took over. Winston raised his head to listen. No bulletins from the front, however. It was merely a brief announcement from the Ministry of Plenty. In the preceding quarter, it appeared, the Tenth Three-Year Plan's quota for bootlaces had been over-fulfilled by 98 per cent.

He examined the chess problem and set out the pieces. It was a tricky ending, involving a couple of knights. 'White to play and mate in two moves.' Winston looked up at the portrait of Big Brother. White always mates, he thought with a sort of cloudy mysticism. Always, without exception, it is so arranged. In no chess problem since the beginning of the world has black ever won. Did it not symbolize the eternal, unvarying triumph of Good over Evil? The huge face gazed back at him, full of calm power. White always mates.

The voice from the telescreen paused and added in a different and much graver tone: 'You are warned to stand by for an important announcement at fifteen-thirty. Fifteen-thirty! This is news of the highest importance. Take care not to miss it. Fifteen-thirty!' The tinking music struck up again.

Winston's heart stirred. That was the bulletin from the front; instinct told him that it was bad news that was coming. All day, with little spurts of excitement, the thought of a smashing defeat in Africa had been in and out of his mind. He seemed actually to see the Eurasian army swarming across the never-broken frontier and pouring down into the tip of Africa like a column of ants. Why had it not been possible to outflank them in some way? The outline of the West African coast stood out vividly in his mind. He picked up the white knight and moved it across the board. There was the proper spot. Even while he saw the black horde racing southward he saw another force, mysteriously assembled, suddenly planted in their rear, cutting their comunications by land and sea. He felt that by willing it he was bringing that other force into existence. But it was necessary to act quickly. If they could get control of the whole of Africa, it they had airfields and submarine bases at the Cape, it would cut Oceania in two. It might mean anything: defeat, breakdown, the redivision of the world, the destruction of the Party! He drew a deep breath. An extraordinary medley of feeling--but it was not a medley, exactly; rather it was successive layers of feeling, in which one could not say which layer was undermost--struggled inside him.

The spasm passed. He put the white knight back in its place, but for the moment he could not settle down to serious study of the chess problem. His thoughts wandered again. Almost unconsciously he traced with his finger in the dust on the table: 2 + 2.

'They can't get inside you,' she had said. But they could get inside you. 'What happens to you here is for ever,' O'Brien had said. That was a true word. There were things, your own acts, from which you could never recover. Something was killed in your breast: burnt out, cauterized out.

He had seen her; he had even spoken to her. There was no danger in it. He knew as though instinctively that they now took almost no interest in his doings. He could have arranged to meet her a second time if either of them had wanted to. Actually it was by chance that they had met. It was in the Park, on a vile, biting day in March, when the earth was like iron and all the grass seemed dead and there was not a bud anywhere except a few crocuses which had pushed themselves up to be dismembered by the wind. He was hurrying along with frozen hands and watering eyes when he saw her not ten metres away from him. It struck him at once that she had changed in some ill-defined way. They almost passed one another without a sign, then he turned and followed her, not very eagerly. He knew that there was no danger, nobody would take any interest in him. She did not speak. She walked obliquely away across the grass as though trying to get rid of him, then seemed to resign herself to having him at her side. Presently they were in among a clump of ragged leafless shrubs, useless either for concealment or as protection from the wind. They halted. It was vilely cold. The wind whistled through the twigs and fretted the occasional, dirty-looking crocuses. He put his arm round her waist.

There was no telescreen, but there must be hidden microphones: besides, they could be seen. It did not matter, nothing mattered. They could have lain down on the ground and done that if they had wanted to. His flesh froze with horror at the thought of it. She made no response whatever to the clasp of his arm; she did not even try to disengage herself. He knew now what had changed in her. Her face was sallower, and there was a long scar, partly hidden by the hair, across her forehead and temple; but that was not the change. It was that her waist had grown thicker, and, in a surprising way, had stiffened. He remembered how once, after the explosion of a rocket bomb, he had helped to drag a corpse out of some ruins, and had been astonished not only by the incredible weight of the thing, but by its rigidity and awkwardness to handle, which made it seem more like stone than flesh. Her body felt like that. It occurred to him that the texture of her skin would be quite different from what it had once been.

He did not attempt to kiss her, nor did they speak. As they walked back across the grass, she looked directly at him for the first time. It was only a momentary glance, full of contempt and dislike. He wondered whether it was a dislike that came purely out of the past or whether it was inspired also by his bloated face and the water that the wind kept squeezing from his eyes. They sat down on two iron chairs, side by side but not too close together. He saw that she was about to speak. She moved her clumsy shoe a few centimetres and deliberately crushed a twig. Her feet seemed to have grown broader, he noticed.

'I betrayed you,' she said baldly.

'I betrayed you,' he said.

She gave him another quick look of dislike.

'Sometimes,' she said, 'they threaten you with something--something you can't stand up to, can't even think about. And then you say, "Don't do it to me, do it to somebody else, do it to So-and-so." And perhaps you might pretend, afterwards, that it was only a trick and that you just said it to make them stop and didn't really mean it. But that isn't true. At the time when it happens you do mean it. You think there's no other way of saving yourself, and you're quite ready to save yourself that way. You want it to happen to the other person. You don't give a damn what they suffer. All you care about is yourself.'

'All you care about is yourself,' he echoed.

'And after that, you don't feel the same towards the other person any longer.'

'No,' he said, 'you don't feel the same.'

There did not seem to be anything more to say. The wind plastered their thin overalls against their bodies. Almost at once it became embarrassing to sit there in silence: besides, it was too cold to keep still. She said something about catching her Tube and stood up to go.

'We must meet again,' he said.

'Yes,' she said, 'we must meet again.'

He followed irresolutely for a little distance, half a pace behind her. They did not speak again. She did not actually try to shake him off, but walked at just such a speed as to prevent his keeping abreast of her. He had made up his mind that he would accompany her as far as the Tube station, but suddenly this process of trailing along in the cold seemed pointless and unbearable. He was overwhelmed by a desire not so much to get away from Julia as to get back to the Chestnut Tree Cafe, which had never seemed so attractive as at this moment. He had a nostalgic vision of his corner table, with the newspaper and the chessboard and the everflowing gin. Above all, it would be warm in there. The next moment, not altogether by accident, he allowed himself to become separated from her by a small knot of people. He made a half-hearted attempt to catch up, then slowed down, turned, and made off in the opposite direction. When he had gone fifty metres he looked back. The street was not crowded, but already he could not distinguish her. Any one of a dozen hurrying figures might have been hers. Perhaps her thickened, stiffened body was no longer recognizable from behind.

'At the time when it happens,' she had said, 'you do mean it.' He had meant it. He had not merely said it, he had wished it. He had wished that she and not he should be delivered over to the--

Something changed in the music that trickled from the telescreen. A cracked and jeering note, a yellow note, came into it. And then--perhaps it was not happening, perhaps it was only a memory taking on the semblance of sound--a voice was singing:

'Under the spreading chestnut tree
I sold you and you sold me--'

The tears welled up in his eyes. A passing waiter noticed that his glass was empty and came back with the gin bottle.

He took up his glass and sniffed at it. The stuff grew not less but more horrible with every mouthful he drank. But it had become the element he swam in. It was his life, his death, and his resurrection. It was gin that sank him into stupor every night, and gin that revived him every morning. When he woke, seldom before eleven hundred, with gummed-up eyelids and fiery mouth and a back that seemed to be broken, it would have been impossible even to rise from the horizontal if it had not been for the bottle and teacup placed beside the bed overnight. Through the midday hours he sat with glazed face, the bottle handy, listening to the telescreen. From fifteen to closing-time he was a fixture in the Chestnut Tree. No one cared what he did any longer, no whistle woke him, no telescreen admonished him. Occasionally, perhaps twice a week, he went to a dusty, forgotten-looking office in the Ministry of Truth and did a little work, or what was called work. He had been appointed to a sub-committee of a sub-committee which had sprouted from one of the innumerable committees dealing with minor difficulties that arose in the compilation of the Eleventh Edition of the Newspeak Dictionary. They were engaged in producing something called an Interim Report, but what it was that they were reporting on he had never definitely found out. It was something to do with the question of whether commas should be placed inside brackets, or outside. There were four others on the committee, all of them persons similar to himself. There were days when they assembled and then promptly dispersed again, frankly admitting to one another that there was not really anything to be done. But there were other days when they settled down to their work almost eagerly, making a tremendous show of entering up their minutes and drafting long memoranda which were never finished--when the argument as to what they were supposedly arguing about grew extraordinarily involved and abstruse, with subtle haggling over definitions, enormous digressions, quarrels, threats, even, to appeal to higher authority. And then suddenly the life would go out of them and they would sit round the table looking at one another with extinct eyes, like ghosts fading at cock-crow.

The telescreen was silent for a moment. Winston raised his head again. The bulletin! But no, they were merely changing the music. He had the map of Africa behind his eyelids. The movement of the armies was a diagram: a black arrow tearing vertically southward, and a white arrow horizontally eastward, across the tail of the first. As though for reassurance he looked up at the imperturbable face in the portrait. Was it conceivable that the second arrow did not even exist?

His interest flagged again. He drank another mouthful of gin, picked up the white knight and made a tentative move. Check. But it was evidently not the right move, because--

Uncalled, a memory floated into his mind. He saw a candle-lit room with a vast white-counterpaned bed, and himself, a boy of nine or ten, sitting on the floor, shaking a dice-box, and laughing excitedly. His mother was sitting opposite him and also laughing.

It must have been about a month before she disappeared. It was a moment of reconciliation, when the nagging hunger in his belly was forgotten and his earlier affection for her had temporarily revived. He remembered the day well, a pelting, drenching day when the water streamed down the window-pane and the light indoors was too dull to read by. The boredom of the two children in the dark, cramped bedroom became unbearable. Winston whined and grizzled, made futile demands for food, fretted about the room pulling everything out of place and kicking the wainscoting until the neighbours banged on the wall, while the younger child wailed intermittently. In the end his mother said, 'Now be good, and I'll buy you a toy. A lovely toy--you'll love it'; and then she had gone out in the rain, to a little general shop which was still sporadically open nearby, and came back with a cardboard box containing an outfit of Snakes and Ladders. He could still remember the smell of the damp cardboard. It was a miserable outfit. The board was cracked and the tiny wooden dice were so ill-cut that they would hardly lie on their sides. Winston looked at the thing sulkily and without interest. But then his mother lit a piece of candle and they sat down on the floor to play. Soon he was wildly excited and shouting with laughter as the tiddly-winks climbed hopefully up the ladders and then came slithering down the snakes again, almost to the starting-point. They played eight games, winning four each. His tiny sister, too young to understand what the game was about, had sat propped up against a bolster, laughing because the others were laughing. For a whole afternoon they had all been happy together, as in his earlier childhood.

He pushed the picture out of his mind. It was a false memory. He was troubled by false memories occasionally. They did not matter so long as one knew them for what they were. Some things had happened, others had not happened. He turned back to the chessboard and picked up the white knight again. Almost in the same instant it dropped on to the board with a clatter. He had started as though a pin had run into him. A shrill trumpet-call had pierced the air. It was the bulletin! Victory! It always meant victory when a trumpet-call preceded the news. A sort of electric drill ran through the cafe. Even the waiters had started and pricked up their ears.

The trumpet-call had let loose an enormous volume of noise. Already an excited voice was gabbling from the telescreen, but even as it started it was almost drowned by a roar of cheering from outside. The news had run round the streets like magic. He could hear just enough of what was issuing from the telescreen to realise that it had all happened, as he had foreseen; a vast seaborne armada had secretly assembled a sudden blow in the enemy's rear, the white arrow tearing across the tail of the black. Fragments of triumphant phrases pushed themselves through the din: 'Vast strategic manoeuvre--perfect co-ordination--utter rout--half a million prisoners--complete demoralization--control of the whole of Africa--bring the war within measurable distance of its end victory--greatest victory in human history--victory, victory, victory!' Under the table Winston's feet made convulsive movements. He had not stirred from his seat, but in his mind he was running, swiftly running, he was with the crowds outside, cheering himself deaf. He looked up again at the portrait of Big Brother. The colossus that bestrode the world! The rock against which the hordes of Asia dashed themselves in vain! He thought how ten minutes ago--yes, only ten minutes--there had still been equivocation in his heart as he wondered whether the news from the front would be of victory or defeat. Ah, it was more than a Eurasian army that had perished! Much had changed in him since that first day in the Ministry of Love, but the final, indispensable, healing change had never happened, until this moment.

The voice from the telescreen was still pouring forth its tale of prisoners and booty and slaughter, but the shouting outside had died down a little. The waiters were turning back to their work. One of them approached with the gin bottle. Winston, sitting in a blissful dream, paid no attention as his glass was filled up. He was not running or cheering any longer. He was back in the Ministry of Love, with everything forgiven, his soul white as snow. He was in the public dock, confessing everything, implicating everybody. He was walking down the white-tiled corridor, with the feeling of walking in sunlight, and an armed guard at his back. The longhoped-for bullet was entering his brain.

He gazed up at the enormous face. Forty years it had taken him to learn what kind of smile was hidden beneath the dark moustache. O cruel, needless misunderstanding! O stubborn, self-willed exile from the loving breast! Two gin-scented tears trickled down the sides of his nose. But it was all right, everything was all right, the struggle was finished. He had won the victory over himself. He loved Big Brother.

Chapter 11

Glossary of Terms

"The book": Titled "Theory and Practice of Oligarchical Collectivism" and supposedly written by Goldstein, it contains the story of humankind and the Revolution, arguing that there is hope for a stronger future without the dishonesty and manipulation of the Party.

Airstrip One: Part of Oceania, once known as Britain.

Artsem: Newspeak for artificial insemination.

Black Market: Illegal trade resource for all "good quality" materials, such as real coffee, sugar, razors, etc.

Doublethink: Newspeak word with two mutually contradictory meanings. The first is used to refer to an opponent, and can be defined as habitually contradicting plain facts. The second is used to refer to a Party member, and can be defined as a loyal willingness to believe contradictory statements when the Party demands it, which allows for continual alteration of the past.

Floating Fortress: Part of Oceania's offensive/defensive armaments. Literally an unsinkable fortress floating on the ocean.

Hate Week: A week of hate mongering against enemies of war. Supported by massive rallies and organized through the Ministry of Truth, Hate Week rallies Party members around Oceania and Big Brother.

House of the Lords: Part of the British government in the capitalist days. Referred to by an old man Winston meets at a pub, although Winston does not understand the reference or the man's meaning.

Ingsoc: Newspeak for English Socialism.

Junior Anti-Sex League: A youth organization advocating complete celibacy for both sexes and encouraging artsem. Julia is a member and wears the organization's symbolic scarlet sash.

Jus primae noctis: A supposed capitalist law that allowed any capitalist the right to sleep with any woman working in one of his factories. A "fact" the party cites about capitalist history.

Ministry of Love (Miniluv): Maintains law and order. Protected with great force. Only those arrested for Thought Crime or who are on official Party business can enter. Referred to within the novel as "the place with no darkness" because the lights are always on. Dissidents are taken here to be tortured, reformed, or killed.

Ministry of Peace: Responsible for the Party's management of issues surrounding war.

Ministry of Plenty: Responsible for the Party's economic affairs.

Ministry of Truth: Responsible for all Party news, entertainment, education and fine arts. The Party's propaganda machine.

Newspeak: The official language of Oceania and the new language of the Party, devised to meet the ideological needs of Ingsoc. The goal of Newspeak is to reduce the English language to the fewest words possible and supercede Oldspeak by 2050. Removing words removes ways to define anti-Party feelings and the ability to disagree. For example, the word "speedful" can be used in place of the word "rapid."

Party Slogans: Examples include: "War is Peace"; "Freedom is Slavery"; "Ignorance is Strength."

Pornosec: The area of the Fiction Department in the Ministry of Truth devoted to creating written pornographic material for the proles. Dominated by women because the Party believes women are less likely to be corrupted by the material.

Prole: One of the 85% of the Oceania population that are not Party members and live in poverty. Regulated loosely to weed out the overly intellectual and protect the Party.

Reclamation Centers: Colonies for homeless children.

Saccharine: A chemical sweetener or sugar substitute; excessively sweet.

Spanner: Wrench.

Speakwrite: A party tool used to translate spoken word into written word.

Spies and Youth League: A Party youth organization that encourages children to spy on and report elders, including parents, to the Thought Police. Indoctrinates children into the Party.

St. Clement's Dane: A building bombed many years ago that once stood by the Law Courts in London. A rendering of the building hangs on the wall in Mr. Charrington's rented room and turns out to be a hidden telescreen.

Telescreen: An oblong metal plaque that looks like a dulled mirror and acts like a television, a camera, and a listening device for the Inner Party and Thought Police. There is no way to shut it off completely, and it keeps tabs on all Party members.

The Physical Jerks: Daily morning exercises all Party members must take part in. Dictated via the telescreen.

The Revolution: The rise of new socialism (versus democracy and capitalism) that resulted in Ingsoc in Oceania, Neo-Bolshevism in Eurasia, and Death Worship in Eastasia. Each regime has the conscious aim of perpetuating unfreedom and inequality, arresting progress, freezing history in a chosen moment, and perpetuating war.

The Times: A Party-sponsored news publication for which Winston works.

Thought Police: The arm of the Inner Party that seeks out those against the Party, searching out anyone with even the smallest thoughts against the Party or Big Brother. Their powers of observation force everyone to live as though they are always being watched or listened to. Mr. Charrington is a member.

Thoughtcrime Thinking against the Party, having misgivings about the Party, doubting Big Brother, or questioning any Party action or "fact."

Tube: Subway system.

Two Minutes Hate: Daily requirement for all Party members. Organized group of members watches Party presentations on a telescreen denouncing Goldstein and war enemies (either Eastasia or Eurasia), and celebrating Big Brother. Causes great outbursts of hatred such as directed screaming and violence at screen representations of the enemy.

Vaporized: The fate of those who commit Thoughtcrimes. Those who are vaporized are removed from society in that they are killed and all evidence of their existence is removed.

Victory products: Party-made products, such as gin, cigarettes, clothing, food, and even housing. All of poor quality.

Chapter 12

Important Questions

Q. Analyse the of Major Characters of the novel.

Orwell's primary goal in 1984 is to demonstrate the terrifying possibilities of totalitarianism. The reader experiences the nightmarish world that Orwell envisions through the eyes of the protagonist, Winston. His personal tendency to resist the stifling of his individuality, and his intellectual ability to reason about his resistance, enables the reader to observe and understand the harsh oppression that the Party, Big Brother, and the Thought Police institute. Whereas Julia is untroubled and somewhat selfish, interested in rebelling only for the pleasures to be gained, Winston is extremely pensive and curious, desperate to understand how and why the Party exercises such absolute power in Oceania. Winston's long reflections give Orwell a chance to explore the novel's important themes, including language as mind control, psychological and physical intimidation and manipulation, and the importance of knowledge of the past.

Apart from his thoughtful nature, Winston's main attributes are his rebelliousness and his fatalism. Winston hates the Party passionately and wants to test the limits of its power; he commits innumerable crimes throughout the novel, ranging from writing "DOWN WITH BIG BROTHER" in his diary, to having an illegal love affair with Julia, to getting himself secretly indoctrinated into the anti-Party Brotherhood. The effort Winston puts into his attempt to achieve freedom and independence ultimately underscores the Party's devastating power. By the end of the novel, Winston's rebellion is revealed as playing into O'Brien's campaign of physical and psychological torture, transforming Winston into a loyal subject of Big Brother.

One reason for Winston's rebellion, and eventual downfall, is his sense of fatalism-his intense (though entirely justified) paranoia about the Party and his overriding belief that the Party will eventually catch and punish him. As soon as he writes "DOWN WITH BIG BROTHER" in his diary, Winston is positive that the Thought Police will quickly capture him for committing a thoughtcrime. Thinking that he is helpless to evade his doom, Winston allows himself to take unnecessary risks, such as trusting O'Brien and renting the room above Mr. Charrington's shop. Deep down, he knows that these risks will increase his chances of being caught by the Party; he even admits this to O'Brien while in prison. But because he believes that he will be caught no matter what he does, he convinces himself that he must continue to rebel. Winston lives in a world in which legitimate optimism is an impossibility; lacking any real hope, he gives himself false hope, fully aware that he is doing so.

Julia: Julia is Winston's lover and the only other person who Winston can be sure hates the Party and wishes to rebel against it as he does. Whereas Winston is restless, fatalistic, and concerned about large-scale social issues, Julia is sensual, pragmatic, and generally content to live in the moment and make the best of her life. Winston longs to join the Brotherhood and read Emmanuel Goldstein's abstract manifesto; Julia is more concerned with enjoying sex and making practical plans to avoid getting caught by the Party. Winston essentially sees their affair as temporary; his fatalistic attitude makes him unable to imagine his relationship with Julia lasting very long. Julia, on the other hand, is well adapted to her chosen forms of small-scale rebellion. She claims to have had affairs with various Party members, and has no intention of terminating her pleasure seeking, or of being caught (her involvement with Winston is what leads to her capture). Julia is a striking contrast with Winston: apart from their mutual sexual desire and hatred of the Party, most of their traits are dissimilar, if not contradictory.

O'Brien: One of the most fascinating aspects of 1984 is the manner in which Orwell shrouds an explicit portrayal of a totalitarian world in an enigmatic aura. While Orwell gives the reader a close look into the personal life of Winston Smith, the reader's only glimpses of Party life are those that Winston himself catches. As a result, many of the Party's inner workings remain unexplained, as do its origins, and the identities and motivations of its leaders.

This sense of mystery is centralized in the character of O'Brien, a powerful member of the Inner Party who tricks Winston into believing that he is a member of the revolutionary group called the Brotherhood. O'Brien inducts Winston into the Brotherhood.

Later, though, he appears at Winston's jail cell to abuse and brainwash him in the name of the Party. During the process of this punishment, and perhaps as an act of psychological torture, O'Brien admits that he pretended to be connected to the Brotherhood merely to trap Winston in an act of open disloyalty to the Party.

This revelation raises more questions about O'Brien than it answers. Rather than developing as a character throughout the novel, O'Brien actually seems to un-develop: by the end of the book, the reader knows far less about him than they previously had thought. When Winston asks O'Brien if he too has been captured by the Party, O'Brien replies, "They got me long ago." This reply could signify that O'Brien himself was once rebellious, only to be tortured into passive acceptance of the Party.

One can also argue that O'Brien pretends to sympathize with Winston merely to gain his trust. Similarly, one cannot be sure whether the Brotherhood actually exists, or if it is simply a Party invention used to trap the disloyal and give the rest of the populace a common enemy. The novel does not answer these questions, but rather leaves O'Brien as a shadowy, symbolic enigma on the fringes of the even more obscure Inner Party.

Q. Discuss the major Themes, Motifs & Symbols in the novel.

Themes: Themes are the fundamental and often universal ideas explored in a literary work. The major themes in the novel are

The Dangers of Totalitarianism

1984 is a political novel written with the purpose of warning readers in the West of the dangers of totalitarian government. Having witnessed firsthand the horrific lengths to which totalitarian governments in Spain and Russia would go in order to sustain and increase their power, Orwell designed 1984 to sound the alarm in Western nations still unsure about how to approach the rise of communism. In 1949, the Cold War had not yet escalated, many American intellectuals supported communism, and the state of diplomacy between democratic and communist nations was highly ambiguous.

In the American press, the Soviet Union was often portrayed as a great moral experiment. Orwell, however, was deeply disturbed by the widespread cruelties and oppressions he observed in communist countries, and seems to have been particularly concerned by the role of technology in enabling oppressive governments to monitor and control their citizens.

In 1984, Orwell portrays the perfect totalitarian society, the most extreme realization imaginable of a modern-day government with absolute power. The title of the novel was meant to indicate to its readers in 1949 that the story represented a real possibility for the near future: if totalitarianism were not opposed, the title suggested, some variation of the world described in the novel could become a reality in only thirty-five years. Orwell portrays a state in which government monitors and controls every aspect of human life to the extent that even having a disloyal thought is against the law.

As the novel progresses, the timidly rebellious Winston Smith sets out to challenge the limits of the Party's power, only to discover that its ability to control and enslave its subjects dwarfs even his most paranoid conceptions of its reach. As the reader comes to understand through Winston's eyes, The

Party uses a number of techniques to control its citizens, each of which is an important theme of its own in the novel. These include:

Psychological Manipulation: The Party barrages its subjects with psychological stimuli designed to overwhelm the mind's capacity for independent thought. The giant telescreen in every citizen's room blasts a constant stream of propaganda designed to make the failures and shortcomings of the Party appear to be triumphant successes. The telescreens also monitor behaviour-everywhere they go, citizens are continuously reminded, especially by means of the omnipresent signs reading "BIG BROTHER IS WATCHING YOU," that the authorities are scrutinizing them. The Party undermines family structure by inducting children into an organization called the Junior Spies, which brainwashes and encourages them to spy on their parents and report any instance of disloyalty to the Party. The Party also forces individuals to suppress their sexual desires, treating sex as merely a procreative duty whose end is the creation of new Party members. The Party then channels people's pent-up frustration and emotion into intense, ferocious displays of hatred against the Party's political enemies. Many of these enemies have been invented by the Party expressly for this purpose.

Physical Control: In addition to manipulating their minds, the Party also controls the bodies of its subjects. The Party constantly watches for any sign of disloyalty, to the point that, as Winston observes, even a tiny facial twitch could lead to an arrest. A person's own nervous system becomes his greatest enemy. The Party forces its members to undergo mass morning-exercises called the Physical Jerks, and then to work long, grueling days at government agencies, keeping people in a general state of exhaustion. Anyone who does manage to defy the Party is punished and "reeducated" through systematic and brutal torture. After being subjected to weeks of this intense treatment, Winston himself comes to the conclusion that nothing is more powerful than physical pain-no emotional loyalty or moral conviction can overcome it. By conditioning the minds of their victims with physical torture, the Party is able to control reality, convincing its subjects that 2 + 2 = 5.

Control of Information and History: The Party controls every source of information, managing and rewriting the content of all newspapers and histories for its own ends. The Party does not allow individuals to keep records of their past, such as photographs or documents. As a result, memories become fuzzy and unreliable, and citizens become perfectly willing to believe whatever the Party tells them. By controlling the present, the Party is able to manipulate the past. And in controlling the past, the Party can justify all of its actions in the present.

Technology: By means of telescreens and hidden microphones across the city, the Party is able to monitor its members almost all of the time. Additionally, the Party employs complicated mechanisms (1984 was written in the era before computers) to exert large-scale control on economic production and sources of information, and fearsome machinery to inflict torture upon those it deems enemies. 1984 reveals that technology, which is generally perceived as working toward moral good, can also facilitate the most diabolical evil.

Language as Mind Control: One of Orwell's most important messages in 1984 is that language is of central importance to human thought because it structures and limits the ideas that individuals are capable of formulating and expressing. If control of language were centralized in a political agency, Orwell proposes, such an agency could possibly alter the very structure of language to make it impossible to even conceive of disobedient or rebellious thoughts, because there would be no words with which to think them. This idea manifests itself in the language of Newspeak, which the Party has introduced to replace English. The Party is constantly refining and perfecting Newspeak, with the ultimate goal that no one will be capable of conceptualizing anything that might question the Party's absolute power.

Interestingly, many of Orwell's ideas about language as a controlling force have been modified by writers and critics seeking to deal with the legacy of colonialism. During colonial times, foreign powers took political and military control of distant regions and, as a part of their occupation, instituted their own language as the language of government and business. Postcolonial writers often analyse or redress the damage done to local populations by the loss of language and the attendant loss of culture and historical connection.

Motifs: Motifs are recurring structures, contrasts, or literary devices that can help to develop and inform the text's major themes.The major motifs in the novel are as follows.

Doublethink: The idea of "doublethink" emerges as an important consequence of the Party's massive campaign of large-scale psychological manipulation. Simply put, doublethink is the ability to hold two contradictory ideas in one's mind at the same time. As the Party's mind-control techniques break down an individual's capacity for independent thought, it becomes possible for that individual to believe anything that the Party tells them, even while possessing information that runs counter to what they are being told. At the Hate Week rally, for instance, the Party shifts its diplomatic allegiance, so the nation it has been at war with suddenly becomes its ally, and its former ally becomes its new enemy. When the Party speaker suddenly changes the nation he refers to as an enemy in the middle of his speech, the crowd accepts his words immediately, and is ashamed to find that it has made the wrong signs for the event. In the same way, people are able to accept the Party ministries' names, though they contradict their functions: the Ministry of Plenty oversees economic shortages, the Ministry of Peace wages war, the Ministry of Truth conducts propaganda and historical revisionism, and the Ministry of Love is the centre of the Party's operations of torture and punishment.

Urban Decay: Urban decay proves a pervasive motif in 1984. The London that Winston Smith calls home is a dilapidated, rundown city in which buildings are crumbling, conveniences such as elevators never work, and necessities such as electricity and plumbing are extremely unreliable. Though Orwell never discusses the theme openly, it is clear that the shoddy disintegration of London, just like the widespread hunger and poverty of its inhabitants, is due to the Party's mismanagement and incompetence. One of the themes of 1984, inspired by the history of twentieth-century communism, is that totalitarian regimes are viciously effective at enhancing their own power and miserably incompetent at providing for their citizens. The grimy urban decay in London is an important visual reminder of this idea, and offers insight into the Party's priorities through its contrast to the immense technology the Party develops to spy on its citizens.

Symbols: Symbols are objects, characters, figures, or colors used to represent abstract ideas or concepts. The major symbols in the novel are discussed below.

Big Brother: Throughout London, Winston sees posters showing a man gazing down over the words "BIG BROTHER IS WATCHING YOU" everywhere he goes. Big Brother is the face of the Party. The citizens are told that he is the leader of the nation and the head of the Party, but Winston can never determine whether or not he actually exists. In any case, the face of Big Brother symbolizes the Party in its public manifestation; he is a reassurance to most people (the warmth of his name suggests his ability to protect), but he is also an open threat (one cannot escape his gaze). Big Brother also symbolizes the vagueness with which the higher ranks of the Party present themselves-it is impossible to know who really rules Oceania, what life is like for the rulers, or why they act as they do. Winston thinks he remembers that Big Brother emerged around 1960, but the Party's official records date Big Brother's existence back to 1930, before Winston was even born.

The Glass Paperweight and St. Clement's Church: By deliberately weakening people's memories and flooding their minds with propaganda, the Party is able to replace individuals' memories with its own version of the truth. It becomes nearly impossible for people to question the Party's power in the present when they accept what the Party tells them about the past-that the Party arose to protect them from bloated, oppressive capitalists, and that the world was far uglier and harsher before the Party came to power. Winston vaguely understands this principle. He struggles to recover his own memories and formulate a larger picture of what has happened to the world. Winston buys a paperweight in an antique store in the prole district that comes to symbolize his attempt to reconnect with the past. Symbolically, when the Thought Police arrest Winston at last, the paperweight shatters on the floor.

The old picture of St. Clement's Church in the room that Winston rents above Mr. Charrington's shop is another representation of the lost past. Winston associates a song with the picture that ends with the words "Here comes the chopper to chop off your head!" This is an important foreshadow, as it is the telescreen hidden behind the picture that ultimately leads the Thought Police to Winston, symbolizing the Party's corrupt control of the past.

The Place Where There Is No Darkness: Throughout the novel Winston imagines meeting O'Brien in "the place where there is no darkness." The words first come to him in a dream, and he ponders them for the rest of the novel. Eventually, Winston does meet O'Brien in the place where there is no darkness; instead of being the paradise Winston imagined, it is merely a prison cell in which the light is never turned off. The idea of "the place where there is no darkness" symbolizes Winston's approach to the future: possibly because of his intense fatalism (he believes that he is doomed no matter what he does), he unwisely allows himself to trust O'Brien, even though inwardly he senses that O'Brien might be a Party operative.

The Telescreens: The omnipresent telescreens are the book's most visible symbol of the Party's constant monitoring of its subjects. In their dual capability to blare constant propaganda and observe citizens, the telescreens also symbolize how totalitarian government abuses technology for its own ends instead of exploiting its knowledge to improve civilization.

The Red-Armed Prole Woman: The red-armed prole woman that Winston hears singing through the window represents Winston's one legitimate hope for the long-term future: the possibility that the proles will eventually come to recognize their plight and rebel against the Party. Winston sees the prole woman as a prime example of reproductive virility; he often imagines her giving birth to the future generations that will finally challenge the Party's authority.

Q.Explain the given lines
"war is peace
freedom is slavery
ignorance is strength"

These words are the official slogans of the Party, and are inscribed in massive letters on the white pyramid of the Ministry of Truth, as Winston observes in Book One, Chapter I. Because it is introduced so early in the novel, this creed serves as the reader's first introduction to the idea of doublethink. By weakening the independence and strength of individuals' minds and forcing them to live in a constant state of propaganda-induced fear, the Party is able to force its subjects to accept anything it decrees, even if it is entirely illogical-for instance, the Ministry of Peace is in charge of waging war, the Ministry of Love is in charge of political torture, and the Ministry of Truth is in charge of doctoring history books to reflect the Party's ideology.

That the national slogan of Oceania is equally contradictory is an important testament to the power of the Party's mass campaign of psychological control. In theory, the Party is able to maintain that "War Is Peace" because having a common enemy keeps the people of Oceania united. "Freedom Is Slavery" because, according to the Party, the man who is independent is doomed to fail. By the same token, "Slavery Is Freedom," because the man subjected to the collective will is free from danger and want. "Ignorance Is Strength" because the inability of the people to recognize these contradictions cements the power of the authoritarian regime.

Q. Explain the given lines "Who controls the past controls the future. Who controls the present controls the past."

This Party slogan appears twice in the novel, once in Book One, Chapter III, when Winston is thinking about the Party's control of history and memory, and once in Book Three, Chapter II, when Winston, now a prisoner in the Ministry of

Love, talks to O'Brien about the nature of the past. The slogan is an important example of the Party's technique of using false history to break down the psychological independence of its subjects. Control of the past ensures control of the future, because the past can be treated essentially as a set of conditions that justify or encourage future goals: if the past was idyllic, then people will act to re-create it; if the past was nightmarish, then people will act to prevent such circumstances from recurring. The Party creates a past that was a time of misery and slavery from which it claims to have liberated the human race, thus compelling people to work toward the Party's goals.

The Party has complete political power in the present, enabling it to control the way in which its subjects think about and interpret the past: every history book reflects Party ideology, and individuals are forbidden from keeping mementos of their own pasts, such as photographs and documents. As a result, the citizens of Oceania have a very short, fuzzy memory, and are willing to believe anything that the Party tells them. In the second appearance of this quote, O'Brien tells Winston that the past has no concrete existence and that it is real only in the minds of human beings. O'Brien is essentially arguing that because the Party's version of the past is what people believe, that past, though it has no basis in real events, has become the truth.

Q. Explain the given lines "In the end the Party would announce that two and two made five, and you would have to believe it. It was inevitable that they should make that claim sooner or later: the logic of their position demanded it. Not merely the validity of experience, but the very existence of external reality was tacitly denied by their philosophy."

This quote occurs in Book One, Chapter VII, as Winston looks at a children's history book and marvels at the Party's control of the human mind. These lines play into the theme of psychological manipulation. In this case, Winston considers the Party's exploitation of its fearful subjects as a means to suppress the intellectual notion of objective reality. If the universe exists only in the mind, and the Party controls the mind, then the Party controls the universe. As Winston thinks, "For, after all, how do we know that two and two make four? Or that the force of gravity works? Or that the past is unchangeable? If both the past and the external world exist only in the mind, and if the mind itself is controllable-what then?" The mathematical sentence 2 + 2 = 5 thus becomes a motif linked to the theme of psychological independence. Early in the novel, Winston writes that "Freedom is the freedom to say that two plus two make four." The motif comes full circle at the end of the novel after the torture Winston suffers in the Ministry of Love breaks his soul; he sits at the Chestnut Tree Café and traces "2 + 2 = 5" in the dust on his table.

Q. Explain the given lines "And when memory failed and written records were falsified-when that happened, the claim of the Party to have improved the conditions of human life had got to be accepted, because there did not exist, and never again could exist, any standard against which it could be tested."

This quote from Book One, Chapter VIII, emphasizes how one's understanding of the past affects one's attitude about the present. Winston has just had a frustrating conversation with an old man about life before the Revolution, and he realizes that the Party has deliberately set out to weaken people's memories in order to render them unable to challenge what the Party claims about the present. If no one remembers life before the Revolution, then no one can say that the Party has failed mankind by forcing people to live in conditions of poverty, filth, ignorance, and hunger. Rather, the Party uses rewritten history books and falsified records to prove its good deeds.

Q. Explain the given lines "And perhaps you might pretend, afterwards, that it was only a trick and that you just said it to make them stop and didn't really mean it. But that isn't true. At the time when it happens you do mean it. You think there's no other way of saving yourself and you're quite ready to save yourself that way. You want it to happen to the other person. You don't give a damn what they suffer. All you care about is yourself."

Julia speaks these lines to Winston in Book Three, Chapter VI, as they discuss what happened to them in Room 101. She tells him that she wanted her torture to be shifted to him, and he responds that he felt exactly the same way. These acts of mutual betrayal represent the Party's final psychological victory. Soon after their respective experiences in Room 101, Winston and Julia are set free as they no longer pose a threat to the Party. Here, Julia says that despite her efforts to make herself feel better, she knows that in order to save herself she really did want the Party to torture Winston. In the end, the Party proves to Winston and Julia that no moral conviction or emotional loyalty is strong enough to withstand torture. Physical pain and fear will always cause people to betray their convictions if doing so will end their suffering.

Winston comes to a similar conclusion during his own stint at the Ministry of Love, bringing to its culmination the novel's theme of physical control: control over the body ultimately grants the Party control over the mind. As with most of the Party's techniques, there is an extremely ironic strain of doublethink running underneath: self-love and self-preservation, the underlying components of individualism and independence, lead one to fear pain and suffering, ultimately causing one to accept the principles of anti-individualist collectivism that allows the Party to thrive.

Q. 1984 is full of images and ideas that do not directly affect the plot, but nevertheless attain thematic importance. What are some of these symbols and motifs, and how does Orwell use them?

Some of the most important symbols and motifs in 1984 include Winston's paperweight, the St. Clement's Church picture and the rhyme associated with it, the prole woman singing outside the window, and the phrase "the place where there is no darkness." In addition to unifying the novel, these symbols and motifs represent Winston's attempts to escape or undermine the oppressive rule of the Party. Winston conceives of the singing prole woman as an incubator for future rebels; she symbolizes for him the eventual overthrow of the Party by the working class. The St. Clement's Church picture is a double symbol. For Winston it symbolizes a stolen past, but it also symbolizes the Party's complete power and betrayal of humanity, since the picture hides the telescreen by which the Party monitors Winston when he believes himself to be safe. The St. Clement's song is a mysterious, ominous, and enigmatic relic of the past for Winston and Julia. Its ending-"Here comes the chopper to chop off your head!"-foreshadows their eventual capture and torture.

Winston's paperweight is another symbol of the past, but it also comes to represent a kind of temporal stasis in which Winston can dream without fear, imagining himself floating inside the glass walls of the paperweight with his mother. The phrase "the place where there is no darkness" works as another symbol of escapist hope throughout the novel, as Winston recalls the dream in which O'Brien tells him about this place and says that they will meet there one day. The phrase therefore orients Winston toward the end of the novel, when the phrase becomes bitterly ironic: the place where there is no darkness is the Ministry of Love, where the lights remain on in the prisons all day and all night.

Q. Discuss the idea of doublethink. How important is doublethink to the Party's control of Oceania? How important is it to Winston's brainwashing?

One of the most compelling aspects of 1984 is Orwell's understanding of the roles that thought and language play in rebellion and control. In Newspeak, Orwell invents a language that will make rebellion impossible, because the words to conceive of such an action cease to exist. Doublethink, the ability to maintain two contradictory ideas in one's head simultaneously and believe them both to be true, functions as a psychological mechanism that explains people's willingness to accept control over their memories and their past. Doublethink is crucial to the Party's control of Oceania, because it enables the Party to alter historical records and pass off these distorted accounts as authentic. The brainwashed populace no longer recognizes contradictions. Instead, it accepts the Party's version of the past as accurate, even though that representation may change from minute to minute.

Emmanuel Goldstein's manifesto even suggests that doublethink is strongest among the powerful Inner Party members who convince themselves that they act for Big Brother, even though they know that Big Brother is a myth. Doublethink is equally crucial to Winston's gradual conversion to loving Big Brother because it enables him to accept his torturers' words as true, even though his own fading memories-of the photograph of the three Party traitors, for instance-contradict them.

Q. Describe Julia's character as it relates to Winston. How is she different from him? How is she similar to him? How does Julia's age make her attitude toward the Party very different from Winston's?

Winston is thirty-nine, Julia is twenty-six. His childhood took place largely before the Party came to power around 1960. Julia, on the other hand, is a child of the Party era. Many of the regime's elements that seem most frightening and evil to Winston fail to upset or even faze Julia. Like Winston, she hates the Party and sees through many of its techniques. She understands, for instance, that it uses sexual repression to control the populace. She even has a better intuitive grasp of the Party's methods than Winston does, planning their affair and often explaining aspects of the Party to him. However, the Party's large-scale control of history does not interest or trouble her as it does Winston, because she does not remember a time when the Party was not in control.

In stark defiance of Party doctrine, Julia enjoys sex and rebels against the Party in small ways. But growing up under the Party regime has made her apathetic to the difference between truth and falsehood. She has no patience for Winston's desire for a categorical, abstract rejection of Party doctrine. Rather, she falls asleep when Winston reads to her from Emmanuel Goldstein's book, epitomizing her simple, self-centered, pleasure-seeking approach to life.

Q. Discuss George Orwell 's 1984 as a novel where no personal freedom exists.

1984 is about life in a world where no personal freedoms exist. Winston the main character is a man of 39 whom is not extraordinary in either intelligence or character, but is disgusted with the world he lives in. He works in the Ministry of Truth, a place where history and the truth is rewritten to fit the party's beliefs. Winston is aware of the untruths, because he makes them true. This makes him very upset with the government of Oceania, where Big Brother, a larger than life figure, controls the people. His dissatisfaction increases to a point where he rebels against the government in small ways. Winston's first act of rebellion is buying and writing in a diary. This act is known as a thought crime and is punishable by death. A thought crime is any bad thought against the government of Oceania. Winston commits many thought crimes and becomes paranoid about being caught, which he knows is inevitable. He becomes paranoid because a young woman who is actively involved in many community groups follows him. Winston is obsessed with the past, a time before Oceania was under strict dictatorship. He goes into an antique shop and buys a shell covered in glass, which is another crime punishable by death. He sees the same woman following him. Many thoughts race through his mind "I wanted to rape you and then murder you afterwards. Two weeks ago I thought seriously of smashing your head in with a cobblestone. If you really want to know, I imagined that you had something to do with the Thought Police". The girl who was following him slipped him a note while at work. The note said, "I love you". They make plans to meet each other and carry on an illegal love affair. This love affair is another rebellion against the government. It goes on for some time. Winston rents a room where he and Julia can be secluded from the outside world. They meet a man named O'Brien who indicates that he is another revolutionary. Winston and Julia go to his house to meet with him. O'Brien gives than a seditious book to read. Soon after that, they are caught by the Thought Police and never see each other again. O'Brien, becomes Winston's rehabilitator and torturer for the next 9 months. O'Brien tortures Winston in stages.

The first two stages are to force the party's beliefs on him then learn and understand what is expected of him. In the third stage, Winston is made to face what he secretly fears most, rats eating his face. After being completely rehabilitated by O'Brien, Winston now loves the establishment and the government. He is set free. Big Brother is the figurehead of a government that has total control. The Big Brother regime uses propaganda and puts fear in its citizens to keep the general population in line. "Big Brother is watching you" is just one example of many party slogans that puts fear in its citizens. Big Brother uses various ways to catch people guilty of bad thoughts "In the world of 1984 the tyrant Big Brother does employ a vast army of informers called thought police, who watch every citizen at all times for the least signs of criminal deviation which may consist simply of unorthodox thoughts". Winston Smith represents Orwell's view on totalitarianism. Winston rebels against the government of Oceania by starting a diary and constantly having bad thoughts against the government. "Winston knows that he is doomed from the moment he has his first heretical thought. The tensions of the novel concerns how long he can stay alive and whether it is possible for Winston to die without mentally betraying his rebellion". Winston starts writing in a diary for two reasons. The first is that he wants to be able to remember the daily occurrences in the world. In 1984, the memory of individuals, is effectively manipulated, programmed, and controlled from the outside by the party. People don't know what they are consciously remembering and what is told to them. "The party had invented airplanes" is just one example of the party's propaganda and false statements that change every day. The other reason for the diary is so that people in the future will be able to read what went on during Winston's time and to tell them about his daily reflections on his feelings about the party. These are the same reasons why Orwell wrote 1984. He wanted to expose a communist country.

The specific political purpose that had used Orwell's sense of urgency was his desire to explode the myth of the Soviet Union as the paradigm of the socialist state. He also wanted to expose the dangers of totalitarianism, which the devaluation of objective truth, and the systematic manipulation of the common people through propaganda. O'Brien is an informant to Big Brother. He is not who he seems to be. He appears to Winston as a fellow conspirator, but actually becomes Winston's torturer and rehabilitator. O'Brien and the party can't tolerate Winston's betrayal of the government. O'Brien tells his victim: You are a flaw in the pattern, Winston. You are a stain that must be wiped out...It is intolerable that an erroneous thought should exist anywhere in the world, however secret and powerless it may be. In fact, the party can't comprehend his disbelief and must change his thoughts through torture and brainwash. "You will be hollow. We shall squeeze you empty and then we shall fill you with ourselves". O'Brien represents the core of communist or totalitarian rule, making the victims suffer by using brainwashing to control them. O'Brien also tells Winston what he should feel about Big Brother when Winston is at his lowest point mentally and physically. O'Brien's speeches to the broken Winston Smith in the Thought Polices' torture chamber represents for Orwell the core of our century's political hideousness. Although O'Brien says that power seeks power and needs no ideological excuse. He does in fact explain to his victim what this power is. Julia is considered a sexual deviant in the oppressed world of 1984.

In a normal world sex is free, in 1984 it's a forbidden act only allowed for reproduction purposes to keep the party's numbers constant. Julia has been sexually active since her teenage years. "She had had her first love affair when she was sixteen, with a party member of sixty". Love and sex is not allowed in this totalitarian state so Julia has to look as pure as possible so that she does not show any guilt. "You thought I was a good party member, pure in word and deed. Banners, processions, slogans, games, and community hikes all that stuff. And you thought that if I had a quarter of a chance I'd denounce you as a thought criminal and get you killed off ". The owner of the antique shop is another example of someone appearing to be what he is not. Orwell uses the shop owner to illustrate a point. Orwell shows that no one can be trusted in a totalitarian country.

Someone who appears to be your friend will actually turn

you in and have you killed. The shop owner appears to be an old widower who enjoys having conversations with Winston Smith. Throughout the book it can be seen that looks can be deceiving. He is actually a member of the Thought Police and gets a good laugh when Winston and Julia getting caught. Now all he can do is wait for his next victim to enter his store. The Ministry of Truth is a place where history and facts--significant and insignificant are rewritten to reflect the party's utopian beliefs. They thoroughly destroy the records of the past; they print up new, up to-date editions of old newspapers and books; and they know corrected versions will be replaced by another, re-corrected one. Their goal is to make people forget everything-facts, words, dead people, and the names of places. How far they succeed in obliterating the past is not fully established in Orwell's description; clearly they try hard and they score impressive results. The ideal of complete oblivion may not have been reached, yet further progress is to be expressed.

Winston and Julia are workers at the Ministry of Truth. Winston gets more mentally involved in his work than Julia. "Winston Smith and his fellows at the Ministry of Truth spend their days rewriting the past: Most of the material you were dealing with had no connection with anything in the real world, not even the kind of connection that is contained in a direct lie'". Winston is not as strong mentally as Julia is. His work affects him more. The Ministry of Truth is like a totalitarian country, because it has ways to scare its citizens. People guilty of crimes are erased from having ever existed. "Your name was removed from the registers, every record of your existence was denied and then forgotten". Again people were taken away without any rights. "...There was no trial no report of arrest". The actual purpose of the Ministry of Truth is to spread lies and to have control over its citizens using memory-erasing techniques. "...The distinction between true and false in their usual meaning has disappeared. This is the great cognitive triumph of totalitarianism: it cannot be accused of lying any longer since it has succeeded in abrogating the very idea of truth. These same control techniques are used by totalitarian nations that seek control over there citizens. The Ministry of Truth is a complete contradiction of itself. A Ministry of Truth should not change past occurrences or say people never existed. It should exemplify the truth and not erase records of the existence of people. The Ministry of Love is where all criminals are tortured, rehabilitated, then set free or killed. As soon as Winston is captured he knows he is going to the Ministry of Love. The Ministry of Love was the really frightening one. There were no windows in it at all. Winston had never been inside the Ministry of Love, nor within half a kilometre of it. It was a place impossible to enter except on official business, and then only by penetrating through a maze of barbed-wire entanglements, steel doors, and hidden machine-gun nests. Even the streets leading up to its outer barriers were roamed by gorilla-faced guards in black uniforms, armed with jointed truncheons.

In a totalitarian state something resembling a Ministry of Love is common place. It's a place where the government can inflict pain on its subjects for crimes big and small. That is how totalitarian nations keep, power over their citizens--by fear of pain. The name Ministry of Love is a contradiction of itself. Its name shows a feeling of love and warmth, but in actuality it's the complete opposite. It's a place of hate and pain and is cold and dark. A better name for it would be the Ministry of Hate. George Orwell lived during a time when Europe was in a period of rebuilding after World War II. During that time Soviets gained six nations as satellites. England was helpless and had to worry about their own problems and had to watch the Soviet Union take control of half of Germany.

The leader of the Soviet Union, Stalin, closely resembles Big Brother. They were both larger than life figures in their respective countries. In the Soviet Union you could easily have found large posters with Stalin's face on them. The same holds true in 1984; Big Brother's face is everywhere. A famous quote from 1984 is "Big Brother is watching you". Meaning if his Thought Police don't catch you, his telescreens and hidden microphones would. In the Soviet Union, Stalin's KGB sought criminals who plotted against the government. In Stalin's regime over 10 million people were killed. In 1984 hundreds of criminals were killed daily. Another aspect of the 1940's was the new broadcast TVs and mainframe computers. The new technologies could be used for means of control. Orwell saw communist countries using these technologies for control. This is where Orwell's idea of telescreens and hidden microphones came from. Before World War II, Orwell had his worst encounter with communists.

While Orwell was in the Spanish Civil War, he was running away from Soviet communists who were trying to kill him. After that experience he got out of the army and became a writer full time. "Another shock to Orwell was when the Nazi-Soviet pact signaled the breakdown and the beginning of the mental and emotional state out of which grew Animal Farm and 1984". Orwell may of have extracted what he saw in his world while writing but it was done to get people's attention of problems in the existing world.

"Orwell's primary purpose is to distort disturbing conditions tendencies and habits of thought that he saw existing in the world". Orwell saw, the whole world steadily moving toward a vast ruthless tyranny. He felt nothing could stop its monstrous progress. 1984, in spite of its setting in the future, is not primarily a utopian fantasy prophesying what the world will be like in thirty or forty years but a novel about what the world is like now. Orwell always relates characters in his books to points of view and real people. In Animal Farm every farm animal represents a person in the Soviet Union. In 1984, Orwell represents his point of view in Winston. He shows a totalitarian leader, in O'Brien and Big Brother, while Julia is the desire and lust in every human being.

George Orwell had deep resentment against totalitarianism and what it stood for. He saw the problem of totalitarianism in his existing world. He also understood how the problem could fester and become larger due to instability in Europe's economy after World War II. He purposely makes the story, 1984, unrealistic and blown out of proportion to capture people's attention and make them think maybe it wouldn't be unrealistic in the near future. With his deep resentment toward totalitarianism it became the focal point of his novels. George Orwell's, novels were directed toward against totalitarianism and for Socialism and what it stood for.

Q. Discuss Satire in 1984

1984 is a political parable. George Orwell wrote the novel to show society what it could become if things kept getting worse. The first paragraph of the book tells the reader of the "swirl of gritty dust....The hallway smelt of boiled cabbage and old rag mats." Just from these few lines Orwell makes it clear that there was absolutely nothing victorious abuot Victory Mansions. Every image the reader recieves from Winston Smith is pessimistic. Hate week, for example, is a big event in Oceania. The citizens prepare for it like Christmas. Instead of jolly songs with family and friends over punch, Hate week is celebrated with fists in the air while chanting about death, Goldstien, and whatever the party wanted the citizens to disgust.

Winston hates the party and Big Brother. He hates the "pure" ones, also. Everthing about Winston's life drives him closer and closer to a suicidal point each day. What makes things worse, hte Party makes Winston think that he is crazy for wanting to be free to think and for wanting to remember. These simple things are taken for granted today. George Orwell devilishly illustrates the brutality that man can be capabel of when he is given such power. The people of Oceania are forced to love Big Brother. There is possibly no one that loves Bill Clinton, besides his family. there are several that love to makes fun of him, but on the political mainstream love is not involved as it is in Oceania. The setting in itself is an extremely important part of the novel. Winston lived in a "dark, gray drab jungle." Posters of Big Brothr were everywhere. The telescreen could see and hear asmost everything that Winston did. However, Winston could hide from it long enough to write in his diary even though he knew he would get caught eventually. Winston was alienated before Julia. He didn't have much contact with other people; he was constantly hungry both physically and emotionally. However, it is ironic that Winston enjoys the work he does but he hates the falsification. 1984 is a satire of the upper class. The members of the Upper class believe that they have supeiority over the common people. They are always wanting more than what is given to them. Very much like O'Brien telling Winston in hte Ministry of Love that it wasn't good enough just for him to say that 2+2=5; he had to believe it with his entire being, to know that 2+2=5 or 3 or whatever the party said.

Bibliography

George Orwell by L. Brander (1954);

The Crystal Spirit by G. Woodcock (1966);

Orwell by Raymond Williams (1971);

The Unknown Orwell by Peter Stansky (1972);

Road to Miniluv by C. Small (1975);

George Orwell: The Critical Heritage, ed. by Jeffrey Meyers (1975);

A Reader's Guide to George Orwell, ed. by Jeffrey Meyers (19757);

George Orwell: A Life by B. Crick (1981);

A George Orwell Companion by J.R. Hammond (1982);

The Language of 1984 by W.F. Bolton (1984);

George Orwell, ed. by Courtney T. Wemyss and Alexej Ugrinsky (1987);

Orwell by Michel Shelden (1991); Orwell:

Wintry Conscience of a Generation by Jeffrey Meyers (2000);

Orwell's Victory by Christopher Hitchens (2002);

George Orwell and the Betrayal of Dissent by Scott Lucas (2003);

George Orwell by Gordon Bowker (2003);

Orwell: The Life by D.J. Taylor (2003)-For further information: Charles' George Orwell.